THE POWER
OF POSITIVE
REINFORCEMENT

THE POWER
OF POSITIVE
REINFORCEMENT

A Handbook of Behavior Modification

By

JUDITH ELBERT FAVELL, Ph.D.

Research Scientist
Western Carolina Center
Morganton, North Carolina

CHARLES C THOMAS • PUBLISHER
Springfield • Illinois • U.S.A.

Published and Distributed Throughout the World by
CHARLES C THOMAS ● **PUBLISHER**
Bannerstone House
301-327 East Lawrence Avenue, Springfield, Illinois, U.S.A.

© *1977, by* CHARLES C THOMAS ● PUBLISHER
ISBN 0-398-03620-9
Library of Congress Catalog Card Number: 76-45624

With THOMAS BOOKS *careful attention is given to all details of
manufacturing and design. It is the Publisher's desire to present books that
are satisfactory as to their physical qualities and artistic possibilities and
appropriate for their particular use.* THOMAS BOOKS *will be true to those
laws of quality that assure a good name and good will.*

Printed in the United States of America
R-1

Library of Congress Cataloging in Publication Data
Favell, Judith E
  The power of positive reinforcement.

  Bibliography: p.
  Includes index.
  1. Behavior modification--Handbooks, manuals,
etc. I. Title.
BF637.B4F37   616.8′588′06   76-45624
ISBN 0-398-03620-9

Dedicated to my parents,
who always believed
I could write a book.

INTRODUCTION

THIS manual is about behavior modification. The teaching technology of behavior modification has been successfully applied to a wide variety of populations (for instance, retarded, emotionally disturbed, normal and delinquent individuals), behavioral areas (such as academic achievement, social adjustment, self-help, vocational skills, and self-injury), and in a broad array of situations (group and natural homes, schools, institutions, and prisons).

To be considered B.M. there are 3 facets that must be included

What Is Behavior Modification?

Behavior modification (also called applied behavior analysis, contingency management or behavior therapy) applies the logic and methods of natural science to the study of human behavior. Specifically, behavior modification includes three facets:

1. methods of measuring behavior in precise and objective ways to determine if it changes following the introduction of treatment,
2. methods of experimentation which document if treatment caused the observed improvement, and
3. therapeutic procedures which (through measurement and research) have been demonstrated effective in changing behavior.

Each of these dimensions will be described in detail in the following chapters of this book, but are summarized here.

Measurement

Behavior is measured before, during, and after treatment to

assess if it changes during the course of therapy. There are many specific techniques for recording behavior, but all are derived from a common set of basic assumptions. First, an emphasis is placed on overt *behavior*, i.e. physical, observable actions such as spelling, walking, and talking. This emphasis is not necessarily intended to deny that human beings have thoughts, feelings, and other internal dynamics. The behavioral orientation is a pragmatic necessity. It enables communication and cooperation in arriving at treatment goals, conducting therapy, and objectively evaluating the therapeutic outcome. Second, behavior is generally observed directly and in the situation in which the problem occurs. For instance, instead of relying primarily on staff or parent reports and impressions, an individual's ability to perform a self-help skill is assessed by directly observing that client in the setting in which the skill should occur. Similarly, disruptive behavior in a classroom is observed and recorded in that situation. Just as informal and subjective accounts by others are not typically used as a primary evaluation tool, behavior modification similarly does not rely heavily on standardized tests. Direct observation is considered a more valid and reliable method of assessing behavior. Finally, when conducting such observations, behavior modifiers actually count the occurrence of the behavior, record its duration, or otherwise describe responding in precise, numerical terms. Statements such as "Tantrums have been reduced from an average of fourteen per day to one or two per week" avoid the difficulties of interpreting claims such as "His tantrums are a lot better." In general, numerical (quantitative) descriptions of behavior enhance the clarity and precision with which a problem is described and improvement evaluated.

Experimentation

Measurement can reveal if a behavior changes during treatment and the magnitude of that change. However, measurement alone cannot indicate what *caused* improvement. Experimentation can document if treatment was responsible for the observed alteration in behavior. Research in behavior modification typically has an "applied" orientation: the effects of a practical therapeutic procedure are evaluated on individuals with real problems. In short, it is a combination of therapy and research. By systematically conducting therapy with one or more clients and experimentally verifying that the treatment procedure caused remediation of their problems, methods are discovered which may be therapeutic with other persons, other types of problems and in other situations. With each successful application of the technique, scientific confidence in its effectiveness is increased. In this way, behavior modification accumulates a set of treatment procedures which have been documented effective in a wide variety of cases. Conversely, ineffective techniques can be identified and discarded. The development of treatment procedures by the use of the scientific method represents a departure from the traditional evolution of therapeutic approaches. Many of the practices of psychology and education have been based on theory, intuition, and guesses. The proponents of a particular approach typically supported their position with subjective accounts of their technique's success. In contrast, behavior modification subjects a potential treatment method to rigorous experimentation and empirically documents its effects in each case.

Therapeutic Technology

Finally, behavior modification consists of an extensive array of procedures which measurement and research have demonstrated to be effective in altering behavior. Much of this book is concerned with a description of these specific treatment techniques. Therapeutic procedures in behavior modification concentrate on changing behavior by altering physical and social events in an individual's environment. Often these treatment techniques involve arranging consequences for behavior, for instance rewarding a desirable response such as social interaction with praise, tokens, or a favorite food. However, applied behavior analysis is *also* concerned with other environmental dimensions which affect individuals. Research in areas such as architectural arrangements of classrooms and cottages, curriculum design and programmed instruction, self-management, and many others have greatly expanded the scope of therapeutic procedures which have been demonstrated to be effective in altering human responding. In short, tokens or M&M's® are not the only tools used by the behavior modifier. Behavior therapy is primarily a way of finding out if a technique works, regardless of the procedure or the tradition from which it was derived.

The techniques which have been accumulated under the rubric of applied behavior analysis do have certain common characteristics. First, an emphasis is placed on describing all therapeutic procedures precisely, to enable others to utilize the technique. Clinical and scientific objectives necessitate that the procedure be written clearly and in sufficient detail to allow others to repeat it. In addition, there is an emphasis on developing procedures which can be utilized by a variety of practitioners, e.g. parents and paraprofessionals as well as professionals. Similarly, an attempt is made to develop practical techniques, i.e. those which do not require extensive investments in time, material and personnel. Further, treatment procedures in behavior modification are typically administered in the setting in which the problem occurs, for instance the home, classroom, or residential unit. Such an approach is in contrast to the model of treating a client in an office, clinic, or some other setting which is isolated from the situations in which his problem usually occurs. Finally, the general procedures which are incorporated into the formal technology of behavior modification are modified in individual cases to adjust the program to the client. In contrast to some traditional therapies, and to what is sometimes assumed about behavior modification, therapeutic procedures are not (or should not be) imposed on an individual without careful adjustment of that technique to the individual's unique needs, strengths, and deficits.

In summary, behavior modification includes methods of measurement and experimentation which in turn have resulted in an array of treatment procedures to alter human behavior.

Controversy About Behavior Modification

As indicated previously, behavior modification has achieved significant successes. Under these programs, individuals such as retarded and autistic children have made progress which has exceeded all expectations. Seemingly intractable behavior problems and deficits have been shown to be responsive to treatment with behavioral techniques. These positive results have been achieved in schools, institutions, homes, clinics, and other settings.

However, behavior modification has also generated criticism. Some of these concerns have arisen from a misunderstanding of what behavior modification is. For instance, applied behavior analysis has been associated with psychosurgery. Most behavior modifiers object vehemently to the association of their discipline with these methods (for a variety of reasons) and disavow their use. Other criticism has resulted from the activities of specific practitioners who have evidenced inadequate training, poor judgment, and/or questionable moral and ethical conduct. Some individuals have said that they are employing behavior modification when engaging in bizarre, abusive, inept, and/or ill-thought attempts at "treating" clients. Unfortunately, these well-publicized cases have been used to characterize the entire approach. It is also unfortunate that little public attention is paid when competent, responsible behavior modifiers express equal alarm at these "aberrations." Still other criticism has been directed at specific procedures, especially those which fall under the rubric of "aversive control" (such as punishment and negative reinforcement). The use of these procedures has raised several "patient's rights" issues, and has otherwise caused concern because of their potential (and actual) misuse, utilization for unacceptable ends, and because they sometimes do not conform to common cultural practices. Finally, some categorically oppose behavior modification on philosophical grounds. The behavioral approach requires an explicit and objective statement of goals, and the manipulation of environmental events to alter observable behavior. Much of this is in contrast to traditional therapies and certain philosophical viewpoints which object to any explicit attempt to control behavior. Proponents of this view contend that their own therapeutic efforts are, for instance, intended to "help individuals reach their fullest potentials" or "find themselves", but they rarely state their objectives in more specific (behavioral) terms, nor do they evaluate the success of their treatments by direct and objective measurement. In contrast, behavior modification's explicitly stated goals and the objective documentation of progress toward those goals appears to be more intrusive (perhaps because behavioral changes are more publicly observable) and to curtail personal freedom.

General Guidelines for the Use of Behavior Modification

These and other criticisms have continued in spite — or because of — the very conspicuous success of behavior therapy. Rather than addressing such concerns with logical or philosophical arguments, specific steps which may be taken to avoid or minimize criticism are outlined below. These guidelines are particularly intended for use in institutions, schools, prisons, and other public facilities. In addition to the suggested principles outlined below, it should be stressed that practitioners of behavior modification should abide by the legal and professional guidelines governing the conduct of *any* therapy (e.g. American Psychological Association, 1973). Several of the following suggestions are paraphrased from an article written by Philip Roos, Executive Director of the National Association for Retarded Citizens (Roos, 1974).

1. When establishing the goals of a treatment program, great care must be taken to insure that the selected objectives reflect the values of the client (rather than someone else) and are consistent with his rights. If possible, the client himself should be actively involved in these decisions. When the individual's age or disability precludes his participation, an advocate should assume this responsibility. To further avoid imposing arbitrary (or illegal) goals, as many appropriate individuals as

possible should participate in the selection of treatment objectives. Thus, parents, staff from all relevant disciplines and lay representatives should cooperate in the decision-making process. A behavior modifier may participate just as any other staff member, but it is important to stress that behavior modification's primary function is the application of behavioral principles and technology to responses which all agree should be changed for the client's well-being. In short, behavior therapy's task is not to say *what* behaviors should be altered but *how* to change the selected behaviors.

2. The treatment method employed should be the least restrictive and intrusive possible. To paraphrase Drs. Davison and Stuart (1975), therapy should expose clients to the least possible risks and mental or physical discomfort relative to the greatest possible expected benefits. In short, care must be taken that the ends justify the means. Such a consideration is particularly critical in the use of aversive control in which unpleasant or painful stimuli are used to modify behavior. For example many believe that such techniques should only be used when other, more positive methods have failed, and/or with serious and dangerous behavior problems

3. A professional and a human rights group should review the treatment method, particularly when a more controversial procedure has been selected. The professional review increases the likelihood that the procedure specified for use is designed properly, that it is well-documented in the clinical research literature, and that it represents several professionals' best judgments as to an appropriate and promising form of intervention in the case to which it will be applied.

The human rights committee is often composed of citizens, a lawyer and an advocate, and sometimes includes clients. In general, it should consist of individuals who are external to both the treatment setting and professions responsible for conducting therapy. This group should decide whether the proposed treatment conforms as closely as possible to prevailing cultural practices, whether the rights of the client are being considered and whether lay opinion concurs that the therapy seems appropriate in the present instance.

Most educational facilities which employ these types of committees have formulated guidelines as to when such reviews are necessary. For instance, the use of noncontroversial rewards such as juice or cookies for strengthening basic appropriate behaviors such as self-help skills is typically not reviewed. In contrast, the use of aversive control is usually subjected to professional and human right's review.

4. The client or his representative (e.g. advocate) should be thoroughly informed of alternative treatments, the details of the proposed treatment, possible risks (such as side effects or discomfort), as well as predicted benefits. It is typically considered most desirable (for client and therapist) if this is written, so that others might review what information the client or his representative has received.

5. In all facets of therapy, only competent, well-trained, and responsible behavior modifiers should be employed. Anyone can call himself a behavior modifier; no standardized certification process exists. However, not everyone can properly conduct behavior modification. Perhaps because of the approach's own emphasis on practical, easily communicated techniques, some have assumed that a small amount of common sense and training are sufficient preparation for employing these "simple" procedures. This is usually not the case. Extensive training by competent individuals is necessary to prepare one to utilize behavior modification. In addition, since the treatment technology is rapidly being refined and expanded it is essential that the behavior modifier continue to be exposed to recent developments in the field. Thus, to remain knowledgeable, practitioners must be expected and given the opportunity to read the literature and attend conventions and work shops.

6. In addition to being implemented by competent behavior modifiers, the treatment program should be conducted openly and the facility's administration should be fully informed and supportive of its use. All involved should be prepared to knowledgeably answer questions about the rationale for and details of the procedure. Careful attention to such issues may educate interested individuals in the theory and practice of behavior therapy, and reduce the chance that procedures may be misused

or used for unacceptable ends without the knowledge of others in that setting.

7. Finally, it is critical to systematically monitor the behavioral effects of treatment and continue to supervise the conduct of the procedure. Documenting the effects of therapy is necessary to verify its benefit to the client or justify changing the program to maximize effectiveness. Such documentation also advances science and thus increases behavior modification's ability to help other individuals.

Ongoing supervision also insures that the treatment program does not drift or degenerate into practices that are unauthorized, and which may no longer satisfy professional and humanitarian criteria. This periodic review should be conducted by professionals and the "human rights" committee, each group overseeing issues that are appropriate to their skills and function (see guideline Number 3).

Guidelines such as the seven outlines above must be translated into specific protocol and policy within each facility. Scrupulous adherence to such policy will protect both clients and therapists, and therefore increase the likelihood that adequate and humane treatment is provided.

To the Readers of This Book

This handbook attempts to describe measurement, experimental design, and treatment methods of behavior modification in sufficient detail to enable a practitioner to conduct behavioral programs in situations in which continuous access to an expert is not available. It is primarily intended as a training and resource book for college students and professionals such as teachers, nurses, and other mental health and educational personnel. With proper selection and supervision, it may also be used with paraprofessionals (such as teaching aides and cottage parents) and with parents. However, in these cases the instructor must carefully and competently select appropriate material and interpret the more technical information.

The author's attempt to provide a comprehensive and detailed account of behavior modification should not be misinterpreted. The guidelines outlined above are intended to serve as a caution that no one should be handed this handbook and "turned loose." Adequate training usually includes both reading written material (such as contained in this book) and actually practicing the techniques with supervision. Ongoing monitoring and supervision is absolutely essential for professionals and paraprofessionals.

Most of the examples in this handbook relate to training individuals with developmental disabilities, particularly the retarded. However, the principles and technology of behavior modification have been shown to be relevant to many and varied populations. Thus the manual is intended, not only for those working with the retarded, but with delinquent, normal, emotionally disturbed, psychotic, and gifted individuals. As stressed earlier, therapeutic programs must be modified to fit the special needs, strengths, and deficits of each individual. Thus, with a normal eight-year-old who is failing to acquire arithmetic skills, the procedures which rely on an ability to understand language (such as contingency contracts) might be used. In contrast, with profoundly retarded or emotionally disturbed individuals, training self-care skills may require a different complex of procedures such as *shaping, prompting*, and *chaining*. In short, a comprehensive array of techniques is presented in this handbook; experience and proper supervision is necessary to acquire an understanding of the circumstances under which each procedure is most appropriately used. (When possible, general guidelines are also presented with the description of each technique.)

REFERENCES

American Psychological Association: Casebook on Ethical Standards of Psychologists.

Davison, G. C. and Stuart, R. B.: Behavior therapy and civil liberties. *American Psychologist*, 7:775-763, 1975.

May, J. G., Risley, T. R., Twardosz, S., Friedman, P., Bijou, S., Wexler, D., et al.: Guidelines for the use of behavioral procedures in state programs for retarded persons. *MR Research Monograph*, Vol. 1, No. 1, National Association of Retarded Citizens, 1975.

Roos, P.: Human rights and behavior modification. *Mental Retardation*, 3:3-6, 1974.

ACKNOWLEDGEMENT

THE author wishes to express her deep grati-
tude to Dr. Jim Favell for his moral support and invaluable
advice concerning the content and form of this book. Many
individuals assisted in preparing the manual (and its earlier
version), but I am especially indebted to Ms. Linda McGill and
Mr. Jim McGimsey III for their perserverance and dedication.
As always, my thanks go to Dr. Iverson Riddle, Mr. Tom
Walton, Dr. Larry Larsen, and all at Western Carolina Center
who have supported this project.

J.E.F.

CONTENTS

Contents   xxi

THE POWER
OF POSITIVE
REINFORCEMENT

Chapter 1

SPECIFYING THE TARGET BEHAVIOR

CLEARLY, the first step in a program to remediate the client's problem is to identify what the problem is, i.e. to first select a desirable "target" or "terminal" behavior that is judged to be an improvement over the individual's current behavior pattern. This usually involves identifying a behavior which needs to be increased in frequency (strengthened), e.g. cooperative play, articulate speech, spoonfeeding, counting, appropriate toilet usage, dressing, correct arithmetic answering, and utilizing materials appropriately. Sometimes inappropriate behaviors are also specified as targets for change, e.g. aggression, destruction of property, tantruming, self-injury, stealing, or swearing. In this case, the objective is to decrease (weaken) the behavior.

Selecting a behavior to change is an important decision and should be done with caution. As stressed previously, the decision as to *what* behavior to modify does not technically fall within the purview of behavior modification. Although the behavior modifier must decide if he/she can ethically contribute his skills at altering a particular behavior, the decision as to what behaviors require modification should rest with many individuals. The client's guardians, the individual himself when appropriate, as well as the teaching staff must all participate in the decision as to what behaviors must be changed. In this process, every effort should be made to insure that the target behaviors selected (as well as the methods used to modify the behavior) reflect as closely as possible the values of the client as well as the community within which he will have to function. Target behaviors such as "absolute obedience" which only benefit staff convenience are usually not acceptable under such a criterion. On the other hand, appropriate manners in a restaurant may facilitate a person's return to home and his acceptance in the community, and thus be a relevant and appropriate goal. In general, the decision as to what behaviors require modification is a moral and ethical one, and should rest firmly on those behaviors which are crucial to the individual's well-being and adjustment in his normal society.

In addition, it is often useful to specify approximately *how much* the behavior must change for it to be considered improved. For instance, a parent may be satisfied if the child makes his bed four out of seven days. On the other hand, staff and parents may specify that he should *never* tantrum. Thus, not only should the target behavior(s) which require increasing or decreasing be identified, but generally it is useful to indicate how much the target behavior(s) should change in the course of treatment.

Chapter 2

DEFINING THE TARGET BEHAVIOR

As the introduction indicated, behavioral measurement is of central importance in behavior modification. There are three primary reasons why behavior is measured: (1) to assess the extent of the person's problem, e.g. to determine how frequently John slaps his sister, or how infrequently Mary plays cooperatively; (2) to evaluate the effects of treatment. A measure of the level of behavior before treatment is compared with the measure of the behavior during and subsequent to treatment. This is done to determine if the treatment is having the intended effect, i.e. if it is increasing an appropriate target behavior or decreasing an inappropriate behavior; and (3) measurement is used as a basis of communication between the student, his parents, and teachers. An individual's problems and progress cannot be discussed adequately with statements such as "Johnny is a lot better", or "Mary's tantrums are really going away." Such vague sentences lend themselves to different interpretations and misunderstandings. On the other hand, a statement such as "Johnny previously had tantrums four to six times per day, but following treatment the frequency was reduced to one tantrum per day" insures clear and precise communication. In the latter case, all concerned will be able to judge if the individual has improved, and if so, how much.

In order to measure behavior, it must be defined (described) in an observable, specific, and objective manner. First, the target behavior must be one that everyone can see (observe) and agree on whether it did or did not occur. This means that the definition must be based on the individual's physical movements, whether these are motor (such as raising an arm) *or* verbal (such as saying "Yes"). For instance, "feeling sad" is not adequate, since one cannot observe inside a person to assess how he is feeling. Instead, translate this into a definition such

5

as "sitting in the corner and crying" or "*saying* he is unhappy, lonely, or depressed." In addition, a useful definition must be very specific and objective. It must pinpoint the precise target behavior(s) in clear language so that all understand exactly what behaviors are to be treated. For instance, "sitting in a corner and not speaking" is a rather objective and specific definition, whereas "sulking" is not. The word *sulking* may mean very different things to different people. If all the staff were instructed to ignore John when he sulked, it is likely that every person would interpret *sulking* differently, and John would be ignored for a variety of behaviors, such as crying, not talking, or sitting in the corner. In some cases, this lack of clarity might not be a problem. In others, however, it is critical that the treatment only be applied to a specified behavior.

Arranging observable, objective, and specific definitions does not have to be difficult. Some examples follow:

- Tantruming: Lying on the ground while kicking legs and screaming.
- Aggression: Kicking, biting, hair-pulling, or scratching. (Each of these might need further defining, e.g. hair-pulling: grabbing a part of hair and yanking forcefully on it.)
- Instruction following: Complying with an instruction within five minutes after it is given. For instance, within five minutes after the instruction "Make your bed" is given, the bed is made. (One may then have to describe what constitutes a made bed, e.g. no sheet or covers touching the floor, etc.)
- Inappropriate use of materials (in classroom): Putting inedible materials in mouth, throwing materials, marking on anything other than coloring book or drawing pad, cutting anything other than magazines at cutting table, etc.
- Spoonfeeding: Dipping a spoonful of food and placing food in mouth with spoon (with no assistance from other hand). This must be repeated ten consecutive times.

One usually cannot guess whether the definition of the target behavior will be satisfactory or not, i.e. whether it will enable proper measurement of the behavior throughout treatment. Conducting reliability checks will indicate the accuracy of the behavioral measurement, including whether or not the definition of the target behavior is adequate. Such checks will also indicate whether measurement is affected by the observer's biases and opinions (such as a natural favoritism for a particular person which influences how accurately the observer records his behavior). In conducting such checks, the therapist first writes down the definition of the behavior and has two observers study it thoroughly so they do not have to continue referring to it during the observation. At least one of these observers should not interact with the client frequently, should not be involved in the planning or implementation of treatment and thus may be less biased. Next, he sends these two observers to the setting where the behavior occurs, and instructs them to record the behavior at the same time but independently (by one of the methods described in Chapter 3, "Selecting a Measurement Technique"). It is very important that they record independently, i.e. they should not influence each other's opinion as to when the behavior did or did not occur. For instance, they should not discuss the observation or compare records. Next, the therapist compares the behavioral records, and if these agree as to *when* the behavior occurred and *which* behavior occurred, his definition is "reliable" and will be adequate. Generally, one cannot look at the records of two observers and determine if agreement is sufficient. The therapist must calculate a score which indicates what percentage of the time the observers agreed (100 percent is perfect agreement).* Usually, a reliability score above 80 percent indicates an adequate definition. If reliability is below 80 percent, the definition may need changing, e.g. change wording to make the definition more observable, objective and specific, or the recording procedures need altering in ways described in the following section.

---

*Explanation of how to calculate such a reliability score as well as a further discussion and summary of reliability checks will be presented in the following section.

Chapter 3

SELECTING A
MEASUREMENT TECHNIQUE

AFTER a definition is arranged that the therapist thinks is observable, objective and specific, i.e. reliable, the therapist next selects a *measurement procedure with which to test reliability and to use throughout treatment*. The procedures described below involve direct observation and measurement of an individual's behavior. Generally, a behavior change is not measured by recording what staff and others say about improvement; instead the behavior is observed directly and occurrences of the target behavior are counted throughout the course of treatment. Behavior is measured directly, not because therapists and parents deliberately present an inaccurate or unrealistic account of behavior, but because everyone has biases, or different ways of reporting what they see. Casual verbal descriptions are notoriously faulty in describing progress. For instance, often upon seeing a precise record of how often an individual emits a particular behavior, one staff member will exclaim "I didn't realize he was doing it that often," while another will say "Oh, I thought he did it much more than that." To avoid misunderstandings, one directly observes and counts the client's behavior, and uses numbers to describe its frequency.

This chapter describes a variety of measurement procedures, and the circumstances under which each is most appropriately used. In general, the selection of a measurement technique should be based on two major considerations. First, the technique should reflect the target behavior accurately. It should indicate each time the behavior occurs.(or a good sample of its occurrence), and over what period of time it occurs. If a measure reveals that a target behavior occurs only once a day, and the therapist is certain that it occurs more frequently, he selects another technique or modifies the one used presently to bring about a closer correspondence between the actual occurrence of the target behavior and its record.

Second, the measurement procedure should be economically practical. Clearly, the ideal measurement involves observing at all times and in all settings in which the target behavior is likely to occur. However, rarely is there enough staff time to allow for such an investment without seriously hampering other important activities. The measurement procedure selected should provide an accurate picture of the problem without interfering with other duties of parents or staff.

In addition to selecting a specific measurement technique, a number of other decisions must also be made. First, the therapist must decide *when* and *where* the observation will be taken. If a problem occurs at specific times and places, for instance, food-throwing at mealtime, then clearly the observation should only be conducted during meals. If the problem occurs throughout the day, at no specific time or place, or if the therapist is not certain of when or where it usually occurs, then observations will have to be conducted several different times per day in a variety of situations.

Second, the therapist must decide *how frequently* per day he will record (most observations are done at least once a day). For instance, if the target behavior is food-throwing, and only occurs during meals, he must decide how many meals per day he can observe. Likewise, he determines how often he can observe a behavior that occurs throughout the day. In general, the more times per day the observation is taken, the more representative the picture of the behavior is likely to be. On the other hand, the therapist must consider the economical and efficient use of staff time.

Third, the *duration* of each observation period must be determined. With measurement techniques which consist of brief checks (such as time sampling or the PLA-Check© method described later) the therapist must decide over what period of time such checks will be made. For instance, it may be decided that a child's pants will be checked for toileting accidents once an hour (the second point, described above) for an eight-hour period each day. With other recording procedures, which require more consistent vigilance on the part of an observer, a single observation period usually lasts between fifteen minutes and one hour. The longer the observation period, the more possible it is to obtain a complete and accurate picture of the behavior. On the other hand, observers are likely to become tired (and thus less accurate) when required to record continuously for lengthy periods. Further, busy staff schedules do not typically lend themselves to long observations. If more observation is needed to accurately measure a behavior, it may be best to increase the *number* of observations, not lengthen the *duration* of each, thus providing the observer with frequent breaks.

Fourth, the therapist must decide how many different behaviors can be separately recorded. On one hand he/she must measure the problem adequately, and on the other, not require more of the observer than can be realistically observed and recorded. For instance, if an individual's aggression generally includes seven behaviors: biting, kicking, scratching, pushing, hair-pulling, slapping, and pinching, then measuring each separately provides the most detailed picture of the problem. However, it may be impossible for an observer to accurately record seven distinct behaviors. This is particularly true when the different behaviors occur simultaneously or rapidly follow one another. In general, the therapist should determine the limits of the observer by conducting several reliability checks. If the agreement between two observers is low, then the number of behaviors included in the definition may have to be reduced. On the other hand, it may *not* be that there is too much to see and record, but that each behavior is not defined adequately or that the measurement technique must be changed. However, if the therapist reduces the number of behaviors and reliability improves, he may not have to define the remaining behaviors more adequately or change the recording procedure. On the other hand, if this reduction results in a list of behaviors that is incomplete or not representative of the problem, he then modifies the definitions until high reliability can be obtained with each definition *separately*; then he sees if the observer can manage observing them all simultaneously.

Finally, it must be determined *who* will conduct the observations. It is usually considered ideal to hire personnel whose sole responsibility is evaluation, i.e. observation and recording. Such staff are less likely to be involved with or even aware of the goals or implementation of treatment, and thus may be less biased when recording a client's behavior. However, many facilities do not have the resources to support full-time observers. In this case, when beginning a program, an effort should be made to assign the task of observation to a staff member who is not directly involved with that individual's treatment. If this is not possible, it is desirable to at least have such a "disinterested party" conduct periodic reliability checks with the regular teacher/observer.

After determining which measurement technique provides the most accurate assessment of the target behavior, as well as when, where, how frequently, with what duration, how many behaviors, and by whom the observations are best conducted, these factors should remain unchanged throughout the course of baseline and treatment.

Regardless of which measurement technique and observation regime is employed, all recording should be done in such a manner so as not to alter the situation being observed. The observer should make every effort to be as inconspicuous as possible. For instance, an observer should never interact with those being observed, but should conduct himself in a quiet, unobtrusive manner.

There are eight frequently used measurement procedures by which to record the target behavior of an individual.

METHODS OF RECORDING AN INDIVIDUAL'S BEHAVIOR

Narrative Recording

Sometimes called anecdotal or continuous recording, this method consists of writing down all behavior that the client displays as well as noting the passage of time (usually in one-minute blocks). For example:

Setting: Dayroom
Client: J. E.

Start Time: 2:00
End Time: 2:02

(2:00) "He sits on floor in corner patting both hands on his knees and opening and closing his mouth without making a sound. (A cottage parent approaches.) J. E. looks up at her and smiles, gets up and lifts his arms. (2:01) (She walks away.) He jumps up and down and yells, then runs and holds her arm while yelling. (She takes his hand.) He smiles and grasps her keys, jingles them, and looks around." (2:02)

A second, more organized way of recording by this method involves writing all that is seen on two columns, one in which the client's behavior is recorded, and one in which the behavior of other people which "appears to affect" the client is written. The previous example would be written as follows:

Time	Client's behavior	Other's behavior
2:00	1. Sits on floor patting hands on knees and opening and closing mouth	2. Cottage parent approaches
2:01	3. Looks up and smiles, gets up, lifts arms	4. Cottage parent walks away
2:02	5. Jumps up and down, yells, runs, and holds arm	6. Cottage parent holds his hand
	7. Smiles, grasps, jingles keys, and looks around	

The latter method of narrative recording presents the information in a more organized form. It may better enable the therapist to see what the individual being observed is doing and how people are behaving toward him.

In either case, the narrative method has clear disadvantages. The best measurement procedures allow the observer to spend most of the time observing, and little time recording. When all behavior must be written in longhand, the observer is not likely to see all of the individual's behavior, nor write fast enough to keep up with events as they occur. Consequently, accuracy of the records will be questionable. To test these disadvantages, a reliability check can be run using this method. It is very difficult to obtain agreement between two observers on *which* behavior occurred *when*. A possible solution is to speak the narrative into a portable tape recorder and transcribe it later. However, in many situations this procedure would disrupt the ongoing situation. Another possible solution is to video-tape the client and his interactions with others, and transcribe the relevant portions later. The obvious disadvantages are : (1) the equipment is relatively expensive, and (2) the equipment is typically too cumbersome to permit inconspicuous observation.

This method may be useful when initially selecting a target behavior. After obtaining a narrative account, the therapist can examine it and determine, for example, which appropriate behaviors occur infrequently, or exactly what form the client's inappropriate behavior usually takes. He can then select one target behavior and measure it more adequately by one of the other recording techniques. Similarly, these records may provide ideas about what events in the environment (especially other people's behavior) might be modified to produce an improvement in the individual.

Event Recording

This measurement procedure involves recording each time a particular response(s) occurs and indicating over what period of time the observation is done. A common means of recording by this method is to note the time the observation begins and place the recording sheet in a location accessible to whomever is doing the observation. The observer(s) then goes about his other duties, but remains in close proximity to the client so that he may see if the target behavior occurs. When it does, he places a tally mark on the recording sheet. This observation period can continue as long as there is at least one person who can monitor the individual. When the observation period ends, the time is noted. This method can be used to record one or more behaviors which have been precisely defined. In addition to tally marks on a sheet, an observer can use a hand or golf counter on which a button is pushed each time the behavior occurs.

Event recording is typically used for a target behavior which has three characteristics: (1) It occurs relatively infrequently. This method can allow staff to perform other duties while observing a client. (2) Its occurrence is very conspicuous. For instance, one can usually be confident that a tantrum will be noticed even if one's back is turned when it starts. On the other hand, recording facial expressions, e.g. smiles, requires such close scrutiny that other jobs could not be done simultaneously. (3) Its occurrence is of relatively short duration. For instance, if the therapist is measuring an individual's running away from home, (and after he disappears he is usually gone for several hours) the event-recording method should not be used alone. This may tell him that the individual runs away once a day, and although that is true, it does not accurately reflect the extent of the client's problem, nor facilitate communication to others who are not aware of how long he remains away from home. (In this case, the duration measure described below, may be appropriate.)

When evaluating reliability with this method of recording, the total number of tally marks by the observer who recorded the *fewest* occurrences of the behavior is divided by the total number of tally marks recorded by the observer who scored the largest number of occurrences. This figure is then multiplied by 100 to convert it into a percentage. For instance, if Observer 1 recorded twenty-eight occurrences of social interaction, and Observer 2 noted fourteen, the equation would be:

$$\frac{14 \text{ social interactions}}{28 \text{ social interactions}} = .50 \ \text{X} \ 100 = 50\%$$

These observers agreed only 50 percent of the time. The problem with this method of calculating reliability is that even though the total responses recorded by the two observers may be similar, the observers may have recorded an occurrence of the target behavior at different times. For instance, if Observer 1 tallied occurrences of social interaction at 11:03, 11:15, and 11:20, and Observer 2 recorded the behavior at 11:02, 11:10, and 11:40, the totals may be identical and thus reliability would be 100 percent. However, the observers were not recording the same behavior at the same time. In this case, a high reliability score does not indicate real agreement between observers. However, this method of calculating reliability may be adequate for many clinical situations in which event recording is used.

A more precise assessment of reliability consists of defining an agreement between the two observers as the recording of a response within a similar time limit, e.g. within one minute. Thus, if Observer 1 recorded a tantrum at 11:03 and Observer 2 noted the behavior as occurring at 11:04, they would be credited with an agreement. On the other hand, if the observers differed in their time-recording by more than 1 minute, a disagreement would be scored. By defining agreement in such specific terms, the chances are increased that a high reliability score indicates that the observers are recording the same behavior at the same time, i.e. that the data are truly reliable. If agreements are defined in a specific manner, i.e. if such time limits are used, then the following reliability formula can be employed:

$$\frac{\text{total number of agreements}}{\text{total number of agreements} + \text{total number of disagreements}} \; X \; 100 \; = \% \, \text{reliability}$$

For instance, if Observer 1 records the occurrence of a behavior at 11:03, 12:15, 1:40, and 2:10, Observer 2 records the behavior at 11:04, 2:17, 1:40 and 2:15 (and if a one-minute limit is defined as an agreement), then the observers agreed two times. Thus, the equation is:

$$\frac{2}{4} \; = \; .50 \; X \; 100 = 50\%$$

In this case, the observers agreed 50 percent of the time.

Recording Products of Behavior

In certain cases, an observer need not be recording at the precise moment the response is emitted to get an indication that it occurred. Some behaviors produce products that can be observed at a later time. For instance, one need not observe an individual having a bowel movement, but will know that he did so by later observing his soiled pants. Similarly, one need not watch a student perform each arithmetic problem, but can grade the resultant answers later. Some behaviors do not have natural products, but observable traces of the behavior can be arranged. For instance, instead of following the client and recording when he sucks his thumb, one might put dye on his thumb and record if it is transferred to his mouth. (In this example, it will not be evident how many times or how long he thumbsucked, but it will indicate whether or not it occurred.)

Some products can disappear rapidly or be concealed, as, for instance, when an individual hides his soiled pants. Further, a product might not always indicate that a particular behavior occurred: for instance, dye off the thumb may reflect the fact that the individual has washed his hands, not that he has sucked his thumb. Similarly, an individual's weight may indicate medical conditions other than overeating.

When evaluating reliability with this method of recording, the score of the observer who recorded the fewest products is divided by the number of products recorded by the observer who scored the larger number of products. This number is then multiplied by 100. For instance, if Observer 1 counted fourteen toys out of place, and Observer 2 recorded twelve misplaced toys, reliability would be calculated:

$$\frac{12 \text{ toys}}{14 \text{ toys}} = .86 \ \text{X} \ \ 100 = 86\%$$

Similarly, if Observer 1 weighed one day's soiled diapers and recorded 11 pounds, and Observer 2 weighed these and noted 10 pounds, reliability would be 91 percent (90.9). The problem with this method of calculating reliability has been discussed in the section on event recording. Although a high reliability score may not accurately reflect true agreement between observers, this method is probably adequate for most applied situations in which behavioral products are recorded.

Duration Recording

In some cases, a behavior is a problem, not because it occurs too frequently or infrequently, but because of its duration, for instance when an individual requires forty-five minutes to take a shower or when a student wanders around the room for much of the class period. In these cases, duration recording may be most appropriate. This method consists of starting a stopwatch (or noting the time from a watch or clock) whenever the target behavior begins, and continuing to observe until the behavior stops. When the behavior stops, the observer stops the clock and records the time. Then, he resets the watch and waits until the behavior begins again. (It is useful to provide the observer with a stopwatch so he can immediately begin timing when the behavior begins.) Unless the behavior is occurring a great deal of the time, the observer may be able to perform other duties while waiting for the behavior to occur. However, the observer should be able to attend closely, in order to record precisely when the behavior begins and ends. As was done in event recording, the time the observation period begins and ends should be recorded to obtain a measure of total observation length.

Duration recording is most appropriate for use with behaviors which are of excessively long duration and which occur relatively infrequently. If a behavior occurs infrequently, but is of short duration, event recording is typically more appropriate. If a behavior occurs frequently, and also is of short duration, the interval method (described below) is most appropriately used.

In calculating reliability when using this method of observation, the time recorded by the observer with the smallest total duration is divided by the total time accumulated by the second observer. The quotient is then multiplied times 100. For instance, if Observer 1 recorded a total of fourteen minutes of tantrums on his stopwatch, and Observer 2 accumulated twelve minutes, the calculation is:

$$\frac{12 \text{ minutes}}{14 \text{ minutes}} = .86 \quad X \quad 100 = 86\%$$

As mentioned previously, the problem with this method of

calculating reliability is that even though the total time accumulated by the two observers may be similar (only a two-
minute discrepancy in the example above), the observers may
have recorded the occurrence of the target behavior at different
times. For instance, during one observation period, Observer 1
may record one minute of tantrums from 10:00 to 10:01; Observer 2 may also record a one minute tantrum, but from 10:12
to 10:13. Although their total times are identical (and thus
reliability is 100%), the observers were not recording the same
behavior at the same time. However, this method of calculating
reliability may be adequate for most situations in which duration recording is used.

As mentioned previously, defining an agreement between
two observers as the recording of a response within a similar
time limit will increase the accuracy of the reliability estimate.
With duration recording, this usually consists of comparing the
duration of each occurrence of a behavior and deciding whether
or not the observers have agreed as to its length. For instance, if
a two-minute discrepancy is considered the limit for an agreement, and if Observer 1 records a tantrum as occurring for three
minutes, while Observer 2 measures five minutes, they would
be scored as agreeing. In this case, reliability would be calculated as the total number of agreements divided by agreements
plus disagreements. This quotient would then be multiplied by
100 to produce a reliability percentage.

Interval Recording

This is one of the more frequently employed recording procedures. With this method, an observation period is broken down
into a number of equal time periods, for instance fifteen seconds. A recording sheet is used on which is drawn a series of
boxes, each of which represents that unit of time. A sample
recording sheet appears on the following page.

The observer places a mark in each interval in which the
target behavior(s) occurs. If, for example, aggression occurred
sometime during the first fifteen seconds of the observation,

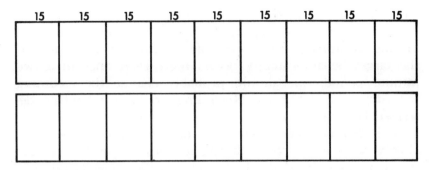

continued into the next fifteen seconds of the observation, and
then stopped, the record would look like this:

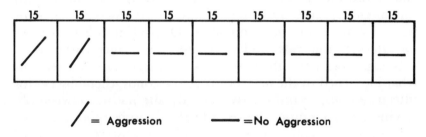

/ = Aggression   — =No Aggression

Even if several aggressive responses occurred during a single
interval, only one mark would be placed in that time block. In
general, only one occurrence of the target behavior(s) is recorded in each interval. Thus, the length of each interval
should be adjusted to the usual rate of the target behavior. If
the target behavior often occurs two or more times in each
interval, the therapist should decrease the interval length. For
example, if he has selected thirty seconds as the interval size,
and finds that the target behavior, e.g. aggression, often occurs
more than once each interval, his measurement is not reflecting
the problem accurately, i.e. aggression, is actually occurring
more frequently than his records indicate. In this case, the
interval is decreased to, for instance, ten or fifteen seconds. Five

seconds is generally the shortest interval size with which an observer can reliably keep up. On the other hand, one or two minutes is probably the longest interval that one should use. (If the target behavior rarely occurs more than once in a two minute period, one should probably change the recording procedure, e.g., to Event Recording or Time Sampling described below.)

With this method of recording, the task of the observer is to closely observe the client during the observation period and record in each interval whether or not the target behavior(s) occurred. This involves reading a stopwatch or listening for an auditory signal to keep track of the passage of time intervals as well as observing the individual's behavior. When using this method, the observer can usually do nothing except observe and record during the observation period. One problem with this method is that the observer may fail to observe a behavior while recording on the record sheet. One solution is to observe for *alternate* intervals, and to record in the intervening intervals, e.g. observe for fifteen seconds, then record for five seconds what happened in the previous fifteen seconds, then observe for fifteen seconds, record for five, etc. By alternating between observing and recording, the record is likely to be more accurate.

With the interval recording method, an observer can record more than one behavior simultaneously. For instance, one might record four different types of aggression, by assigning a distinct symbol to each.

B = Biting
S = Scratching
K = Kicking
P = Pushing

15	15	15	15	15	15	15	15	15
B S	K	K						

In this example, biting and scratching occurred during the first fifteen seconds; then the client kicked at some time during the next two intervals. Breaking a large category such as aggression into parts and recording each is more precise than simply recording "A" for any form of aggression. Similarly, an observer can record totally different types of behavior simultaneously. For instance, social interaction, appropriate use of materials, tantrums, and self-injury may be recorded at the same time by an observer using the interval method. The rule concerning recording of only one type of behavior in a single interval still applies when several behaviors are recorded simultaneously. In the example above, biting and scratching may be recorded in the same interval since they are recorded as separate behaviors. However, even if kicking occurred twice in an interval, that behavior would only be recorded once per interval.

The interval recording procedure is most useful with behaviors that occur relatively frequently, i.e. that have a moderate or relatively high rate. Because there is a limit as to how short one can practically make the intervals (probably five seconds), very high frequency behaviors cannot be recorded with accuracy using this method. On the other hand, it is not economical to assign an observer to conduct two 30-minute observation periods each day using this method, if the behavior is likely to occur only once or twice in that time. No specific, numeric guidelines are available. The therapist simply uses this method when it will reflect the behavioral problem accurately, while not wasting an observer's time.

When calculating reliability, the data records of the two observers are compared interval by interval. For instance, in the records below, both Observer 1 and 2 marked toy play as occurring during the first fifteen-second period. However, in the second interval Observer 2 noted the behavior, whereas Observer 1 did not. In the third interval, neither observer recorded the occurrence of toy play.

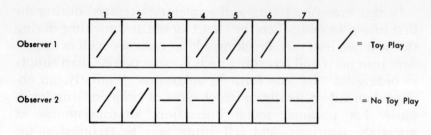

The observers agreed in Intervals 1, 3, 5, and 7 about whether or not toy play occurred. However, they disagreed about its occurrence in Intervals 2, 4 and 6. In calculating reliability, first total the number of agreements and disagreements, then use these in the following equation:

$$\frac{\text{Total number of agreements}}{\substack{\text{Total number of agreements} \\ \text{+ total number of disagreements}}} \text{ X } 100 = \% \text{ reliability}$$

For instance, in the example above, reliability is calculated:

$$\frac{4}{7} = .57 \text{ X } 100 = 57\%$$

Time Sampling

This method involves briefly observing and recording behavior each time a certain period of time elapses. In this case, the observer sets a timer for the desired sample duration, e.g. five minutes, and then "goes about his business" until the timer signals that the interval has elapsed. The observer immediately locates the individual, observes his behavior, and then records what the client was doing when the observer first located him. The observer's recording can be restricted to a particular behavior, i.e. whether it was occurring or not (event recording) or can consist of recording anything that the client was doing at the time of observation (narrative recording). One can also record whether a behavioral product has been left or not, for instance if the client has had a toileting accident since the last time sample was taken. It is also possible to conduct interval recording in conjunction with time sampling. For instance, when the timer signals that a time sample is scheduled, an observer can record the individual's behavior for one or more intervals. The observer then resets the timer, for example, to five minutes, and performs other duties until it signals again. In some cases it may be helpful to vary the sample size each time to prevent the observed client from predicting when the observations are scheduled, and thus altering his behavior. For instance, one might set the timer for five minutes the first time, ten minutes the second, nine the third and two the fourth. In this way, the client can be observed on an *average* of five minutes, rather than every five minutes. Of course, even if the time the individual is observed is varied, if the observer's behavior is conspicuous the client may be able to detect when he is observed and alter his behavior during the observation.

When using the time sampling method, reliability is calculated in the same way as for the interval method. As usual, the observers must have recorded that the *same* behavior occurred at the *same* time to be counted as an agreement.

Test Method

Most of the preceding measurement techniques are relevant to problems of *how often* or *how long* the client engages in an appropriate or inappropriate behavior. In some cases, the individual's problem is how *well* he does something, e.g. how completely he dresses himself, or how accurately he performs academic tasks. In this case, the test method may be most useful. As with all methods, one must first define the target response, specifying what constitutes an accurate or successful performance. The definition usually includes how much time the person will be allowed to complete the behavior. For instance, the definition of putting on shorts might be:

> Putting on pants such that one leg is in each leg-hole and the waist-band of the pants is within one inch of the individual's waist. (Allow three minutes.)

Next, a test procedure is designed. This test should closely resemble the situation in which the target behavior will occur after training. Details that require attention include: what verbal and other cues (if any) will be allowed, e.g. the words "put your pants on," and/or pointing to the pants; and in what room and with what furniture and materials the test will be conducted. Next, the observer brings the client to the test situation, presents the materials, and cues and observes him for the allotted time. Finally, he scores his behavior. One of two types of scoring is used most frequently:

a. Assign a "pass" or "fail" grade on the basis of whether or not the client performed the target behavior satisfactorily.
b. Assign a number representing the *degree* of success the individual had in performing the skill.

In the latter case, for instance, the therapist might arrange a scale from one to five with a score of one indicating the worst performance, and five representing the best. In this case, the observer assigns the score of one, two, three, four, or five depending on the quality of the performance. Of course, each behavior for which a score is assigned must be defined clearly.

The primary disadvantage of a "pass" or "fail" score is that usually behavior is not extreme, i.e. very good or very bad, but somewhere in between. In short, "pass-fail" scoring does not provide a very precise picture of the behavior. The assignment of a number on a scale provides a more sensitive picture of how well a client performs the behavior, depending on how many points or gradations appear on the scale (there are usually three or more). However, it is frequently difficult to obtain high reliability between two observers on precisely what number should be assigned. Of course, this depends upon how well each gradation is defined.

Reliability is calculated the same way as for the interval and time sampling methods. In this case, agreement is either:

• both observers marking "pass"
• both observers marking "fail", or
• both observers noting the same score on a rating scale

Automatic Recording

All of the previous recording procedures have involved a human observer with either paper and pencil or some other manual recording device. One of these (or in some cases, variations or combinations of them) will be adequate for any measurement problem. The therapist should be aware, however, that behavior can also be recorded automatically by electromechanical equipment. For instance, measurement of the target behavior of sitting in a chair in a classroom might be done by arranging an electrical switch which is activated by the weight of a person sitting on the seat. While activated, the switch would run an electric clock. Automatic recording frees a human from the observing task, thus eliminating the worry about staff economy while monitoring performance almost continuously. Further, automatic equipment is highly accurate when it is working properly (i.e. it is highly reliable), and not likely to fail in human ways such as becoming distracted or tired or showing a bias. On the other hand, it is not always possible to use automatic equipment for recording: for some situations it may be too expensive, cumbersome, conspicuous, fragile, or complicated; for some behaviors there has not yet been developed a means of automatic recording. For instance, in the case of appropriate social interaction, even if a client is wired in such a way that each time she touched another human a response was recorded, the equipment would include things that all would agree are *not* appropriate social interaction, e.g. slapping someone, and exclude behaviors that are, e.g. smiling at someone. In this case, automatic recording would not be a valid measure of social interaction, i.e. it would not measure what it was intended to measure because it included behaviors that most would agree were not social interaction and excluded responses which were. However, advancements in electronic technology are diminishing previous restrictions on the use of automatic recording.

METHODS OF RECORDING GROUP BEHAVIOR

The preceding techniques are designed to measure the target

behavior(s) of an individual. Other observation procedures are useful when attempting to measure the behavior of an entire group, e.g. disruptive behavior in a classroom, or the number of children playing appropriately with toys in a dayroom. The therapist must define group target behavior in observable, objective, and specific terms just as for an individual. One of several measurement procedures can be employed.*

Group observation involves observing the entire group simultaneously and noting *any* instance of the target behavior. The measurement technique could be either *event recording,* the *interval method,* or *duration recording.* For instance, an observer could watch an entire room and record with a tally mark (event recording) when any person aggressed. Alternatively, he could mark in an interval if anyone aggressed (interval method), or he could run the stopwatch as long as any aggression occurred (duration recording). Noting *which* person performed the behavior provides more precise data. In applying one of these three methods to an entire group, the therapist must be careful to keep the observation task manageable. The following factors, when excessively increased, may extend the requirement beyond the capabilities of an observer:

   a. number of persons observed: It is almost impossible for one observer to record the behavior of more than twenty or thirty individuals.
   b. frequency of the target behavior: For instance, if aggression occurs very frequently, one observer may not be adequate.
   c. size of the room in which the clients are located: If it is too large, the observer may miss behavior occurring in one section while recording behavior in another.
   d. the number of behaviors to be recorded: If the observer must record several different behaviors by different clients simultaneously, she may not be able to keep up.

Of course, all these factors "interact", e.g. by reducing the number of persons observed, the observer can probably record a

---

*Refer to previous sections in this chapter for complete explanations of procedures used with individuals which are identical to those used with groups.

larger number of behaviors. In any case, the therapist can test the limits of the observer by conducting a reliability check. If the reliability score is low, he either modifies the definition or reduces the amount the observer is required to watch.

Another method of group recording involves counting the tangible *products* of group behavior. This is identical to the procedure applied to individual behavior. If, for instance, the therapist is interested in teaching children to pick up toys in the playroom after the play period, then he might count the number of toys left on the floor after clean-up. To insure that this measure directly reflects clean-up behavior and not just how many toys were taken from the boxes and shelves in the first place, he should count the number of toys out of place before clean-up. Of course, this measure does not provide information on how many or who participated, but when modifying group behavior, this information is sometimes irrelevant.

In some cases, the therapist can arrange *automatic* recording of group behavior as for an individual child. For instance, if he is interested in the number of persons entering an area of a playroom where crafts are taught, the therapist might partition this section off, and install a turnstyle at the door. This device can then count how many times it operates each way (indicating children entering and leaving).

Another technique for measuring group behavior is the *subject sample*. When employing this procedure, a list is first drawn up of individuals to be observed. This can include all or part of the clients in the setting. If the observation is to include a representative sample of all types of individuals in the group, frequently these are selected "blindly," e.g. their names are drawn from a hat. Alternatively, preliminary measures of clients' behavior can be compared, and an equal number of those receiving the best, worst, and intermediate scores can be selected for the subject sample. On the other hand, depending on the aims of treatment, a sample of the group may be selected *because* they are not typical. For instance, it may be appropriate to select five students demonstrating the most severe behavior problems in the class, if the treatment program is directed specifically at decreasing classroom disruption. The observation should be begun by locating the first client on the list (if there is any deviation from the prescribed order, the therapist may be accused of biased recording, i.e. only observing a subject when he is seen emitting the target behavior!). Then the first individual is observed for a specified time. There are two general ways of prescribing this duration: a fixed amount of time is selected, e.g. five seconds, during which each client is observed momentarily, or observed "until you can see what he/she is really doing." The difficulty with the latter method is that the observer may watch the individual *until* he engages in the target behavior and thus bias the record. At the time that each person's behavior is measured, the observer may: record whether or not a particular behavior is occurring (event recording), describe any behavior that the client is engaging in at the time of the observation (narrative recording), note the presence or absence of a behavioral product (product recording), or record for one or more time periods by the interval method. After the behavior of the first client is recorded, the second client on the list is located and observed and his behavior recorded. In the same manner, each individual is observed sequentially. Then this process is repeated as many times as is allowed by the observation duration.

Subject sampling makes the observation task more manageable, especially when dealing with many persons and several behaviors. Further, it enables the therapist to construct a behavioral picture of both the entire group *and* each individual in it.

Another frequently used procedure is *time sampling*. As when dealing with an individual, the observer sets the timer for a particular duration and, upon a signal from the timer, observes the clients, records their behavior, and then resets the timer. One of the following methods is usually employed when the timer signals that the observation should begin: (1) recording the products of the group's behavior, e.g. the number of toys left out of place, (2) conducting a subject sample (in conjunction with either event recording, narrative recording, product recording, or interval recording) or, (3) counting the number engaging in the target behavior (event recording). The latter method closely resembles a group measurement procedure called the PLA-Check (Risley and Cataldo, 1973). This was developed to assess the extent of participation in planned activities. It consists of counting the total number of individuals in a room (or area of a room) and then counting the total number of clients who are actively participating in a specific activity. For instance, an observer would first count the students in a classroom, and then the number of individuals who were playing with the toys that had been provided. It may also be appropriate to use the PLA-Check method to record behaviors other than participation in activities. For instance, when the timer indicates that a time sample should be taken, the observer could record the number of individuals aggressing, *not* participating in the scheduled activities, eating with spoons, or self-stimulating (after noting the total number of residents present).

SUMMARY OF RELIABILITY

Reliability is a measure of the extent of agreement between observers. This is obtained by the simultaneous but independent recording of behavior by two observers.* Reliability checks indicate the accuracy of the overall measurement system, including the adequacy of the following factors:

1. the definition of the target behavior(s)
2. the extent of observer bias
3. the method of recording
4. the manageability of the recording task, e.g. the number of behaviors or individuals observed simultaneously.

A high score (usually about 80%) on a properly conducted reliability check indicates that the measurement system is accurate, and that others could successfully duplicate (replicate) the behavioral measure. Conversely, a low reliability score (below 80%) indicates that something is wrong with the measurement

---

*See Chapter 2 for a description of how to conduct reliability checks.

system and that others may not be able to replicate it. If this is the case, one or more of the factors listed above may be inadequate and need to be modified.

Reliability is typically calculated in one of two ways. One method consists of comparing the total number of responses recorded by each observer, and dividing the larger total of one observer into the total responses recorded by the other observer. This quotient is then multiplied by 100 to convert it into a percentage. Thus, the equation is:

$$\frac{\text{total responses recorded by observer with smaller score}}{\text{total responses recorded by observer with larger score}} \times 100 = \% \text{ reliability}$$

A more accurate reliability estimate can be obtained by comparing the observers' recording of each response and deciding whether or not they agreed as to *if* the behavior occurred and *when* it occurred. The number of agreements and the number of disagreements is then totaled. In this case, the equation is:

$$\frac{\text{total number of agreements}}{\text{total number of agreements} + \text{total number of disagreements}} \times 100 = \% \text{ reliability}$$

As described previously, the type of measurement technique employed typically dictates which equation can be employed.

The technology of obtaining and calculating reliability is rapidly being expanded and refined. However, for most clinical purposes, these methods of determining reliability will be adequate.

REFERENCES

Risley, T., and Cataldo, M. F.: Evaluation of planned activities: the PLA-Check measure of classroom participation. In Davidson, Clark, and Hammerlynck (Eds.): *Evaluation of Social Programs in Community, Residential and School Settings.* Champaign, Research Press, 1976.

Chapter 4

SELECTING A METHOD OF REPRESENTING THE DATA

AFTER the first one or two observation periods, the therapist should select a way of quantifying the information (data) that is being collected. It is very difficult to look over observation records and obtain a clear view of the information it contains. One usually needs a summary version of the data that can be readily read and understood by all.

Each measurement technique allows for several ways of *quantifying* the target behavior, i.e. describing the behavior in terms of numbers. Even if the therapist adequately defines the behavior, it is very difficult to communicate without such numbers. For instance, the statement: "Johnny's tantrums are really going away," will leave everyone unclear as to how frequently Johnny had a tantrum before and after treatment, even if "having a tantrum" is well-defined. *Numbers* will serve as a clear and precise basis of communication, and will enable all to evaluate if improvement is occurring, and if so, how much. "Johnny had tantrums four to six times per day before treatment was begun, and following treatment the rate was reduced to one or two times per day" is a clearer and more precise statement of improvement. The following measures are ways of quantifying the information from each of the measurement techniques, i.e. converting the observation records into numbers to describe the target behavior. Of course, there are other ways of quantifying the information from each observation method. Those included in this discussion are considered by this author as representative and/or the most frequently employed. Most students and staff who employ behavior modification need not learn which methods of calculating data fit with each measurement procedure. They can simply use this chapter as a reference when the need arises to quantify data.

31

QUANTIFYING AN INDIVIDUAL'S DATA

Narrative Recording

Information from this observation method is difficult to quantify. It is assumed that the therapist will use narrative recording only as a preliminary step before using another measurement procedure, and will not need to carefully quantify the target behavior from the narrative records. However, the therapist should be aware that he can count the *number* of responses or an approximate *frequency (rate) of response* from these records. The two measures will be described next.

Event Recording (For an Individual or a Group)

Data from this method are usually quantified in one of two ways. In the first, the *number* of tally marks, i.e. the number of times the behavior occurred during the observation period, are counted. For instance, if the therapist is recording a client's aggressive responses from 8 AM to 5 PM each day, after each observation he simply counts the number of aggressive episodes recorded on the sheet during that time. He keeps a table, similar to the following:

Monday:	8 aggressive responses
Tuesday:	5 aggressive responses
Wednesday:	4 aggressive responses
Thursday:	9 aggressive responses

The problem with counting the number of responses is that the behavior is often not recorded the same amount of time every day. For instance, if it was possible to observe the individual for eight hours on Monday and he aggressed seven times, but on Tuesday he was at the dentist for two hours and his score for that day was three aggressive responses, what could you conclude about the difference? Not much. A visitor looking at the client's data might say "Wow, Johnny was much better Tuesday." However, the therapist would know that the decline could be due to the fact that he could not observe the child for two hours, or that he did not have an opportunity to aggress because he was out of the situation in which the behavior usually occurred. In general, when the number of responses is charted, the same amount of time every day must be spent observing. Since this is usually inconvenient, if not impossible, the therapist should generally convert the data into frequency of response.

With the *frequency* measure, the therapist can correct for observation periods of differing durations. In this case, the total number of responses is added, e.g. eight aggressive responses, and divided by the amount of time the person was observed, e.g. eight hours. The result is the frequency of response (responses per unit of time), e.g.:

$$\frac{8 \text{ aggressive responses}}{8 \text{ hours}} = 1 \text{ aggressive response per hour}$$

Thus, the client aggressed at a rate of *once per hour* on Monday. The response frequency is calculated in the same way for Tuesday as for Monday. If he aggressed three times and was observed for six hours, his frequency of aggression was:

$$\frac{3 \text{ aggressive responses}}{6 \text{ hours}} = .5 \text{ aggressive responses per hour}$$

Any type of time unit can be employed in the denominator: seconds, minutes, hours, days, or weeks. However, it is important that the *same* unit of time (minutes, hours, days, or weeks) is always used throughout all calculations that are to be compared with each other. This will avoid attempting to compare something such as three smiles per hour with seventeen smiles per day. In each case, the following equation is used to calculate frequency.

$$\frac{\text{number of responses}}{\text{time (observation duration)}} = \text{frequency (rate) of response}$$

Frequency is one of the more useful and relevant measures of behavior.

Recording Products of Behavior (For an Individual or a Group)

Data from this method can be quantified into at least three measures. *Number of products* can be counted as were number of responses in event recording. For instance, the number of toys left out of place after clean-up can be counted as a measure of tidying. However, when using this measure one must insure that an increase or decrease in the number of products correctly reflects changes in the problem behavior. For instance, if fifteen toys are left on the floor Monday and three on Tuesday, it might be concluded that on Tuesday everyone did a better job of cleaning. However, if it was noticed that on Monday fifty toys had been taken from the shelves, and Tuesday only three had been removed, the therapist would realize that Monday was actually a better clean-up day. To better reflect this difference, a *percent* measure should be used.

With a *percent* measure, the therapist can correct for differences in the opportunity to engage in the behavior (and thus leave a product). The general equation is:

$$\frac{\text{total number of behaviors (or products)}}{\text{total opportunities to perform behavior (or leave a product)}} \times 100 = \text{percent of products}$$

For instance, a count of the total number of toys on the playroom floor before clean-up indicates the total opportunities to clean-up, and is used as the denominator. Then the total number of toys remaining on the floor after clean-up are counted. This number is divided by the denominator and the result multiplied by 100. The answer will be the percent of products observed (in the above example, toys on the floor). If on Monday, fifty toys were on the floor before clean-up and fifteen remained after, 30 percent of the toys were not replaced on the shelves.

$$\frac{15}{50} = .30 \quad X \quad 100 = 30\%$$

If on Tuesday, three toys were counted before and after clean-up, then 100 percent of the toys had not been picked up.

$$\frac{3}{3} = 1 \quad X \quad 100 = 100\%$$

Comparing these will now show accurately that Tuesday was a sloppy day!

Monday: 30 percent of the toys remained
Tuesday: 100 percent of the toys remained

If the individual always has the same number of opportunities to perform the response (e.g. if fifty toys are always on the floor before clean-up) then simply counting the *number* of products will be sufficient. If this is not constant, a percent should be used.

Amount (weight, volume, inches, etc) is often a good measure of the products of behavior. An obvious example of the use of the weight measure concerns programs for obesity. Since a product of overeating is weight gain, one could simply weigh the individual each day to measure progress.

Duration (For an Individual or a Group)

Information from this observation method is often summarized in one of two ways. If the records show several durations of the behavior for each observation period, then their *average duration* can be calculated.* For instance, assume that tantrums occurred four times on Monday with the following durations:

1st tantrum:	9:12 - 9:31	(19 minutes)
2nd tantrum:	11:02 - 11:16	(14 minutes)
3rd tantrum:	1:45 - 2:04	(19 minutes)
4th tantrum:	5:00 - 5:10	(10 minutes)
	total:	62 minutes

First add up the total minutes the client had tantrums. Divide this by the total *number* of tantrums (in this case, four).

$$\frac{62 \text{ minutes of tantruming}}{4 \text{ tantrums}} = 15.5 \text{ average minutes of tantruming on Monday}$$

---

*One can also use either of two other measures of central tendency: median or mode. These are presented later in this chapter.

The answer indicates that on Monday, the individual's tantrums lasted an average of fifteen and one-half minutes. This measure is only meaningful if the therapist has at least *two* or more durations to average together. If a client has one tantrum a day, it is not reasonable to refer to the duration of that tantrum as an average. In this case, the *percent of time* spent having tantrums would be most useful.

In calculating the *percent of time,* divide the total observation period (obtained from the beginning and end times) into the total duration of the target behavior and multiply the results by 100. For instance, if the person was observed for two hours on Monday, and had a tantrum once for five minutes and a second time for seven minutes, the equation is as follows:

$$\frac{12 \text{ minutes of tantruming}}{120 \text{ minutes (2 hours)}} = .10 \ \text{X} \ 100 = 10\%$$

This answer indicates during what percent of the observation period the client was performing the target behavior. In this case the person had a tantrum 10 percent of the time during which he was observed.

Interval Method (For an Individual or a Group)

These data are usually calculated as a *percent of time.* In this case, the number of intervals in which the target behavior occurred is counted, then this number is divided by the total number of intervals during which the client was observed, and multiplied by 100. For instance, if a child was observed for sixty minutes and recorded with thirty-second intervals, the denominator would be 120 intervals. If social interaction was recorded in sixty of those intervals, the numerator would be 60. The calculation would be:

$$\frac{60}{120} = .5 \ \text{X} \ 100 = 50\%$$

In other words, social interaction occurred 50 percent of the time that the person was observed. When using a percent, the therapist need not observe the same duration during all observation periods.

Time Sampling (For an Individual Only)

The information from this method is generally quantified into either a *number* or a *percent* measure. As mentioned previously, use of the *number* measure is limited to cases where the individual has the same opportunity to emit the behavior (and have it recorded) from one observation period to the next. With time sampling, the critical feature to hold constant is the number of times the client is observed. If this does not change, i.e. if the client has been observed the same number of times during each observation period, then the therapist can summarize the time sampling data into a *number* measure.

A *percent* measure is used most commonly when time sampling is employed. If, for instance, the therapist observes a child every five minutes for one hour a day, and records if he is engaging in toy play or not, the calculations are as follows: First, add up the total number of times he was observed, in this case 12. Next, divide this number into the number of times he was observed playing with the toy, e.g. 6. Finally, multiply that number times 100. The answer indicates that the child was playing with the toy on 50 percent of the occasions that he was observed.

With time sampling, as with other methods of measurement, one can calculate what *percent of time different behaviors occurred.* For instance, if when each time sample is taken, the therapist records which of the following four behaviors is occurring: playing with toys, sitting in a corner, aggressing, and self-stimulating, he can then calculate what percent of the time the child was engaging in each. For instance:

$$\frac{\text{number of times child was playing with toys when observed}}{\text{total number of times he was observed}} \times 100 = \begin{array}{l}\text{percent of} \\ \text{time in} \\ \text{toy-play}\end{array}$$

and

$$\frac{\text{number of times child was sitting in corner when observed}}{\text{total number of times he was observed}} \times 100 = \text{percent of time in corner}$$

etc.

Test Method

When using the *test method,* one of two types of scoring is used more frequently: (1) a "pass" or "fail" score is assigned, or (2) a number on a rating scale is recorded, representing the client's degree of success in performing the behavior.

"Pass-fail" scores are generally converted into either a *percent* or *cumulative correct* (or incorrect). If the therapist is interested in teaching a client to put on his shirt, he might arrange a test situation in which he hands him a shirt and tells him to put it on. (He should give him this test several times.) If a client has been given five tests, and if he passed two of these (i.e. twice the observer assigned a "pass" score on the basis of the definition of what constitutes proper putting on of a shirt), the therapist would then compute the *percent of correct responses* as follows:

$$\frac{2 \text{ (number of "pass" scores)}}{5 \text{ (number of tests)}} = .4 \times 100 = 40\% \text{ correct}$$

Similarly, if he wants to calculate the percent *incorrect,* the calculation is:

$$\frac{3 \text{ (number of "fail" scores)}}{5 \text{ (number of tests)}} = .6 \times 100 = 60\% \text{ incorrect}$$

With the test method, as with other methods of measurement from which a percent is obtained, percents are calculated with the formula:

$$\frac{\text{total number of responses}}{\text{total tests (opportunities)}} \times 100 = \text{percent}$$

A second method of presenting the data from tests is a

*cumulative graph.** In this case, each time a correct response occurs, i.e. each time the individual passes a test, "one" is added to the previous score of correct responses. If, for instance, the client passed the first test on putting on a shirt, a "one" is marked on his graph as shown:

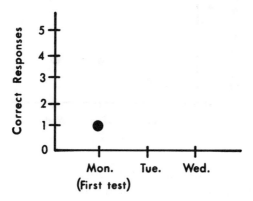

If he passes the second, add another "one" to the previous "one" and mark it on the graph as "two."

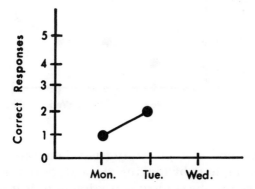

---

*This method is a way of *graphing* the data, not calculating it. Graphing procedures have not yet been described, and the reader may want to read this section after reading the general section on graphing, which appears later in this chapter.

If he failed the next test, add 0 to the previous score of "two." and mark another "two" on the graph.

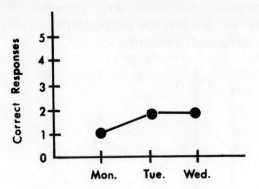

If he passed the fourth test, add "one" to his previous score of "two" and plot "three" as shown.

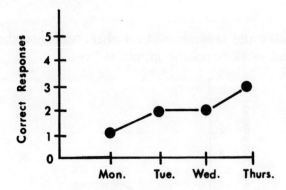

With this method of representing test data, one can see if the client is passing tests by looking at the *slope* of the curve. If the curve is going up, the student is passing tests; if it is running in a horizontal direction, he is not passing tests.

The second type of scoring used with the test method involves assigning a number on a scale representing the *degree* of success the student had in performing the skill. The data from this type of scoring can be summarized in several ways: (1)

*graph each score,** or calculate the (2) *average (mean)*, (3) *median,* or (4) *mode.*

In many cases, it is sufficient to plot each test score on a graph (with no calculations). For instance, if a student was tested on Monday, and was given a score of 5 (out of a possible 10) on the self-help skill of facewashing, the score could be plotted as follows:

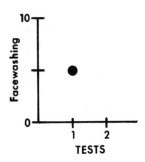

If his score was 10 on Tuesday, it would be plotted as shown, and a line drawn to connect the points.

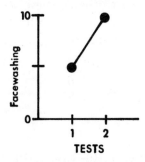

In this way, each score is graphed, and a picture of the client's skill at facewashing can be constructed.

---

*This is a method of *graphing* the data, not of *calculating* it. Methods of graphing have not yet been described. The reader may want to read this section after the general section on graphing.

AVERAGE (MEAN). If an individual has been given five tests on facewashing and thus been assigned five scores (from a scale ranging from 1 (worst), to 10 (best), his scores could be averaged. For instance, if the client has given the following scores:

$$
\begin{array}{lcl}
\text{Test 1} & = & 2 \\
\text{Test 2} & = & 4 \\
\text{Test 3} & = & 3 \\
\text{Test 4} & = & 2 \\
\text{Test 5} & = & 4 \\
\hline
& & 15 \text{ total score}
\end{array}
$$

the calculation would be:

$$\frac{15 \text{ (total score)}}{5 \text{ (total tests)}} = 3 \text{ (the average score)}$$

In this example, the individual received an *average (mean)* score of 3 on facewashing tests.

MEDIAN. If a person has been given five tests on a self-help skill, and consequently has been assigned five scores from a scale from 1 (worst) to 10 (best), these scores are rank ordered from highest to lowest (or lowest to highest). In this example, the client's rank-ordered scores might be:

$$
\begin{array}{c}
9 \\
6 \\
3 \\
1 \\
1
\end{array}
$$

Select the *middle* score, in this case 3; this is the *median*. (When an even number of scores is obtained, for example 9, 6, 4 and 1, calculate the *mean* of the two middle scores. In this example, the median is 5 (i.e. 5 is the average of 6 and 4).

MODE. This is simply the most frequently obtained score. For instance, in the following example, the mode is 1, since this score was obtained twice and the other scores were each obtained once.

3
1
1
9
6

Automatic Recording (For an Individual or a Group)

Electromechanical equipment can be programmed to yield any of the following measures: (1) *number*, (2) *frequency*, (3) *percent*, (4) *duration*, or (5) *amount*. In each case, the equation for calculating the data is the same as with previous measurement techniques.

QUANTIFYING GROUP DATA

Data from measurement techniques used with a group of individuals also must be quantified. Most of the measures calculated from group recording are identical to those used when the technique is employed with an individual. Consequently, much of what follows is a review of the preceding section; some is new material.

A. When observing an entire group simultaneously and recording any instance of a target behavior, the therapist should use a measure appropriate to whichever measurement technique he is using. If employing *event recording* on the entire group, a *number* or a *frequency of response* measure should be used. If an *interval method* is used for the entire group, a *percent* measure is appropriate. If *duration* recording is employed for the group, either *average duration* or *percent of time* should be calculated. Notice that all of these measures are identical to those used with an individual.

B. When *recording products of behavior*, use *number, percent* or *amount* as a group measure, as would be used for an individual.

C. The five measures used with *automatic recording* of an individual are also suitable for use with a group. These are: (1) *number*, (2) *frequency*, (3) *percent*, (4) *duration*, or (5) *amount*.

D. The *subject sample* method of measurement is only used with groups, and ways of quantifying this information have not yet been discussed. One of two measures is most useful: (1) *number* of persons engaging in the target behavior, or (2) *percent* of clients engaging in the target behavior.

The *number measure* can only be used if the same total number of clients are observed the same number of times during each observation. For instance, if on Monday the subject sample included fifteen clients each of whom was observed twice, this same number must be observed twice during every subsequent observation if the number measure is to be used.

The problem of day-to-day variation in the number of clients present is solved when you calculate what *percent* of the total number of individuals observed were emitting the target behavior(s). The equation is the usual one:

$$\frac{\text{number of individuals engaged in the target behavior}}{\text{total number of individuals observed}} \times 100 = \%$$

When using percents, the total number of people observed can change from one observation to the next.

E. When using the *time sampling method* with a group of individuals, the data should be summarized as *number* or *percent*. This is true regardless of which observation technique is being used in conjunction with the time sample: counting the number of clients emitting the target behavior (event recording or PLA-Check), conducting a subject sample, or counting the products of behavior. For instance, if, when the timer signals that an observation should begin, the therapist records the number of individuals engaging in the target behavior, the data can be summarized as either the *number* of clients, or the *percent* of clients emitting the behavior. In the latter case, the equation would be:

$$\frac{\text{number of individuals engaging in the target behavior}}{\text{total number of individuals observed}} \times 100 = \%$$

It is not necessary to calculate a percent for each occasion the timer goes off. Usually, several observations are combined, e.g. all observations for one day, before calculating a percent. For instance, if one observes ten individuals every five minutes for an hour each day (i.e. twelve times per day), 12 observations are multiplied by 10 clients to obtain the total number of opportunities to observe the target behavior, i.e. 120. This number is divided into all who were observed emitting the target behavior. For instance, if 6, 3, 5, 10, 1, 5, 4, 4, 9, 2, 1, and 5 clients were observed emitting the target behavior during each of the twelve time samples respectively, the total number of individuals observed engaging in the target behavior adds up to 55.

$$\frac{55}{120} = .45 \quad X \quad 100 = 45\%$$

In short, 45 percent of the individuals were observed engaging in the target behavior on that day. As mentioned previously, this same method of calculating percent can be used regardless of which observation technique is being used in conjunction with the time sample. As always, the percent measure is more satisfactory than summarizing the data as simply *number* emitting a target behavior or *number* of products.

Summary

In general, the behavioral *data* obtained from each measurement technique can be *quantified* into specific *measures* reflecting the observed target behavior.

Quantifying an Individual's Data

1. Narrative recording
   a. Number
   b. Frequency
2. Event recording
   a. Number
   b. Frequency of response
3. Recording products of behavior
   a. Number

    b. Percent of products

    c. Amount (weight, volume, inches, etc.)

4. Duration

    a. Average duration

    b. Percent of time

5. Interval method

    a. Percent of time

6. Time sampling

    a. Number

    b. Percent of response

7. Test method

    a. "Pass-fail" scoring

        (1) Percent correct (or incorrect)

        (2) Cumulative correct

    b. Rating-scale scoring

        (1) Graphing each score

        (2) Average (mean)

        (3) Median

        (4) Mode

8. Automatic

    a. Number

    b. Frequency

    c. Percent (of time or of response)

    d. Duration

    e. Amount

Quantifying Group Data

1. When recording any instance of group target behavior, the data is calculated by one of the following methods:

    a. Event recording

        (1) Number of responses

        (2) Frequency of response

    b. Interval method

        (1) Percent of time

    c. Duration recording

        (1) Average duration

        (2) Percent of time

2. Recording products of behavior
   a. Number of products
   b. Percent of products
   c. Amount of products (weight, volume, etc.)
3. Automatic recording
   a. Number
   b. Frequency
   c. Percent
   d. Duration
   e. Amount
4. Subject sampling
   a. Number of individuals engaging in target behavior
   b. Percent of individuals engaging in target behavior
5. Time-sampling used in conjunction with one of the following:
   a. Event recording or PLA-Check method
      (1) Number of clients engaging in target behavior
      (2) Percent of clients engaging in target behavior
   b. Subject sampling
      (1) Number of persons engaging in target behavior
      (2) Percent of persons engaging in target behavior
   c. Recording products of behavior
      (1) Number of products
      (2) Percent of products
      (3) Amount

Notice that the number, percent, and frequency measures are used most frequently. The general equations for these common measures are:

Number: is not calculated; it is simply counted from the observation records

$$Frequency = \frac{\text{number of responses}}{\text{duration of observation}}$$

$$Percent = \frac{\text{number of responses or people responding}}{\text{total opportunities to respond}} \times 100$$

GRAPHING INDIVIDUAL AND GROUP DATA

After calculating a behavioral measure from the observation record, next the data is plotted on a *graph*. Graphs provide a picture of the target behavior, and allow the reader to notice changes in the behavior much more quickly and easily than would be possible from a simple listing of the numbers. For instance, two methods of displaying the same data are shown below. Table 1 presents the data in a table; Figure 1 shows the same data in a graph. After becoming accustomed to reading graphs, a few seconds of looking at Figure 1 would indicate that aggression is: (1) gradually increasing week-by-week, (2) always lower on Monday than later in the week, (3) the same on Tuesday as on Thursday, and (4) is always higher on Friday than earlier in the week. It would require several minutes of studying Table 1 to discover the same information.

Table I

Day	Frequency of Aggression
M	1
Tu	2
W	3
Th	2
F	4
M	3
Tu	4
W	5
Th	4
F	6
M	5
Tu	6
W	7
Th	6
F	8

In most graphs, a measure of the target behavior is shown on the vertical line (the ordinant), and observation periods are shown on the horizontal line (the abscissa). The point where the vertical line meets the horizontal line is the zero mark. The top point on the vertical line should represent the maximum

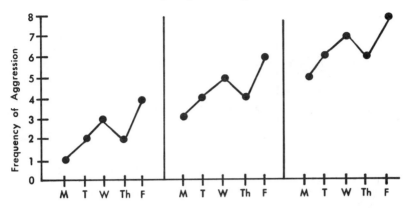

amount of behavior that could possibly occur (in your judgment). Next, evenly space the intermediate points (those representing the occurrences of the behavior which lie somewhere between zero and the maximum level) along the vertical line. One should use graph paper with evenly spaced divisions already printed along the horizontal and vertical lines. Each division should represent some convenient amount of behavior, e.g. one response per minute, one response per hour or 5%. (There are numerous other details that one will learn to consider as experience is gained in graphing. They will not all be discussed here.)

In the example on the next page, frequency of aggression is shown on the vertical line. The client who is being observed never engages in more than fifteen aggressive responses per hour, so the top number is set at fifteen. Each division on the vertical line (between 0 and 15) represents five aggressive responses per hour. Each day that the individual is observed is written along the horizontal line. If the client is observed *twice* on Monday, the therapist can plot the data from each observation period, or combine the observations when calculating the data into one number for the entire day. If each observation period is plotted separately, label the horizontal line "Observation Periods" rather than "Days."

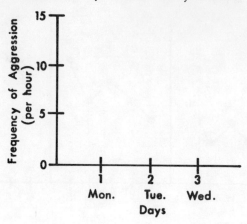

After arranging the format of the graph, plot the data calculated from the observations. If on Monday the individual engaged in aggressive behavior at a frequency of ten responses per hour, mark the point where ten and Monday meet, as shown.

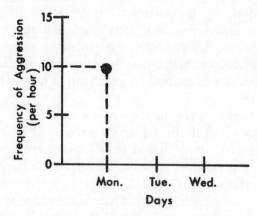

If on Tuesday, the client aggressed three times per hour during the observation period, find where Tuesday and three meet, and mark it with a point. Next draw a line between the points.

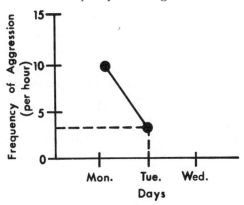

Plot each day's data in the same way.

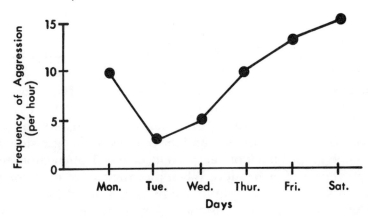

This is called a *noncumulative graph* and shows clearly that when the line goes up, the behavior is increasing; when it goes down (toward the horizontal line) the behavior is decreasing. When the line runs parallel to the horizontal line, it shows that the behavior is not changing from one observation period to the next. In this example, the individual rate of aggression is increasing, i.e. his problem is getting worse.

A second kind of graph, called a *cumulative graph* was described previously in this chapter, under methods of calculating data from the "Test Method." Although there are many types of graphs, these two will probably be adequate for most clinical purposes.

In the example above, the frequency of responses was plotted. In the same way, one can graph *any* measure of target behavior that was discussed in the sections on quantifying individual and group data: number, percent, frequency, average, median, mode, amount, etc. In each case, the measure of behavior is shown along the vertical line.

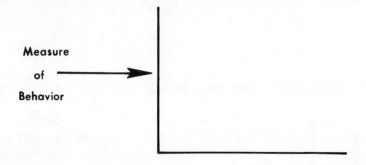

When measuring several behaviors simultaneously, they can often be plotted on the same graph, if they are calculated into the same type of measure. For instance, one can plot the *frequency* of social interaction and the *frequency* of aggression on the same graph, but not the *percent* of social interaction and the *frequency* of aggression. When plotting two or more target behaviors on the same graph, assign each a distinctive type of line and/or symbol. For instance: aggression = ●—————● , and social interaction = ▲—————▲ . These can then be plotted together. Be sure to include a "key" indicating what behavior each type of line represents, for example:

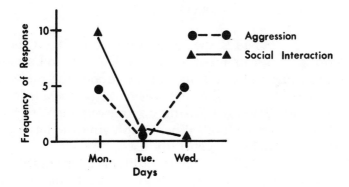

Chapter 5

MEASURING THE TARGET BEHAVIOR

BASELINE

AFTER the target behavior has been specified and defined, a measurement technique selected, and a method of summarizing and graphing decided upon, the therapist is ready to take a baseline. The terms *baseline* or *operant level* are normally applied when utilizing any measurement technique *other* than the test method. When employing the latter procedure, the term *pretest* is generally used.

"Taking a baseline" involves recording behavior until a clear picture is obtained of its level of occurrence before treatment. Two of the three reasons given earlier as to why behavior is measured relate directly to baseline measurement. A baseline allows the therapist to assess the extent of the problem, e.g. to determine how frequently Johnny has tantrums or how much of the day Susie plays appropriately. A baseline also serves as a basis of comparison with the measure taken during and after treatment, to evaluate if the target behavior is changing. The objective in taking a baseline is to allow the therapist to predict what would have happened to the behavior (i.e. whether it would have increased, decreased or remained at the same level) if no treatment was introduced.

Baseline measurement should be done when, where, and under the circumstances in which the problem normally occurs, i.e. the times and places in which appropriate behavior should but does not occur, or when and where an inappropriate behavior is exhibited. Similarly, the general situation that typically exists when the problem occurs should be determined. This situation includes all or most of the physical and social features of the setting. For instance, baseline observations should be conducted when the usual number of persons are present, and when the situation includes the typical arrangements of furniture, toys, and other materials. Similarly, all involved with the individual should act naturally, i.e. they should behave toward the target client and others just as they do when no observer is present. Further, all recording (during baseline, as well as during and after treatment) should be conducted in a manner that will not alter the situation in any way. For example, if the therapist feels that the observer may distract the target client or others, he should try to conceal the observer or in other ways make every effort to assure that he is as inconspicuous as possible.

In summary, baseline observations should measure the target behavior at the time, in the place, and under the conditions in which it is normally exhibited. After all of these dimensions are determined, they should remain unchanged during the baseline period and throughout the course of treatment.

Baseline observations should be continued until the graphs show either: (1) that the behavior is "stable", i.e. it is not steadily increasing or decreasing, *or* (2) the behavior is changing in a direction opposite to that expected after treatment is in effect. In the first case, it should be determined if the behavior is not changing. The graph will indicate this through the position of the data points, i.e. whether they are within a close range of each other. Behavior which is not changing at all appears on the graph as a horizontal line, as shown:

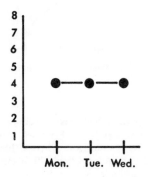

The following graph also shows data that appears to be stable, i.e.

the target behavior is not increasing or decreasing.

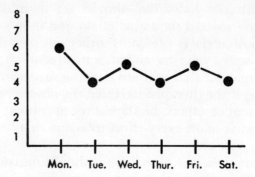

However, the following graph displays data reflecting a "variable" or "fluctuating" baseline, i.e. one that is changing widely.*

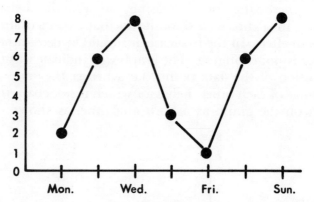

---

*In many cases, whether or not the behavior is changing is an opinion, judged simply by looking at the graph ("eyeballing"). In other cases (usually for research purposes), the behavior modifier employs a numerical criterion for changing conditions. For instance, the therapist might say: "A condition will be changed (in this case, baseline will be stopped) when aggression does not vary more than 10 percent up or down for three consecutive days." However, the use of such numerical criteria is generally too strict for most programs which are intended to improve the client and document the result, but not necessarily to submit the study for publication.

In the case of the second guideline, baseline is continued until it is determined that the behavior is changing in a direction opposite to that expected after treatment is in effect. For instance, if it is expected that treatment will *increase* an appropriate behavior, e.g. social interaction, and the behavior is *decreasing* steadily, i.e. the individual is interacting less and less, then treatment procedure may be implemented. Similarly, if the baseline measure reveals that the behavior is increasing, and the treatment objective is to decrease that response (in other words, reverse the trend) then the baseline can be stopped and treatment begun. The following graphs show increasing and decreasing baselines. In each case, it would be appropriate to discontinue baseline and start treatment.

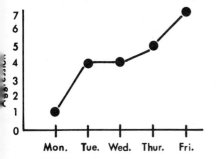 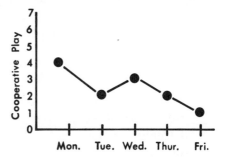

In general, it is desirable to conduct at least three baseline observations or pretests. Further, these observations should typically be conducted on three separate days, regardless of how many times per day the behavior is observed. It is difficult, if not impossible, to obtain an accurate, representative picture of behavior within less than three observations. The more variable the behavior, i.e. the more the data fluctuates up and down on the graph, the *longer* the baseline must be run before starting treatment.

While taking baseline and calculating and plotting each day's data on a graph, the therapist should also be observing environmental events which occur before and after the target behavior. For instance, if social interaction is being measured, the therapist should note if the availability of toys appears to increase the child's social contacts, or if he is more likely to interact if certain children or adults are present. It is particularly important to notice the *consequences* of the target behavior. In this example, the observer records what happens to the individual when he interacts socially: do other children play with him or shove him away; does the teacher attend to him during these times or ignore him? In general, the observer notes any environmental event which seems to regularly precede and/or follow the target behavior (or a response which resembles the target behavior). This information will provide valuable conjectures about environmental events (including physical objects, and adult and child behavior) which might be altered to bring about improvement in the target behavior during the treatment phase of the program.

CONTINUED MEASUREMENT DURING TREATMENT AND MAINTENANCE

As mentioned previously, baseline measurement enables a prediction of the level of behavior which might have been seen if treatment had not been introduced. After treatment is begun the therapist will compare the actual measure of the behavior during treatment to what he predicts the behavior would have been if no treatment were given. The difference between the behavior predicted by the baseline data and the actual behavior is a measure of the effect of treatment.

The measurement system must remain unchanged throughout baseline and treatment to reduce the chance that a change in the target behavior could actually be due to a change in some aspect of the recording technique. Specifically, the following aspects of observation generally should be specified before baseline and then held constant throughout the program (baseline and treatment):

1. The definition of the target behavior(s)
2. The type of measurement procedure, e.g. event or interval recording
3. The features of the specific measurement procedure: For instance, with interval recording the size of the interval

should not be altered; with subject sampling, the same
number of people should be observed each time.

4. The number of times per day the observation is conducted
5. The time of day it is conducted
6. The situation in which the client is observed
7. The duration of each observation period: It was previously
   stressed that if the therapist is using a measurement technique which yields either a *frequency* or *percent* measure,
   the duration of the observation need not remain the same
   from one observation period to the next. However, it is
   good practice to hold the duration as constant as possible,
   primarily to avoid adjusting the length of the observation
   according to the occurrence of the behavior, e.g. short-
   ening the observation if inappropriate behavior is not observed.

In general, continued measurement during treatment will
reveal if the target behavior is changing, and if so, how much.
For instance, the following graph shows that during baseline
(before treatment) aggression occurred between eight and ten
times per day.

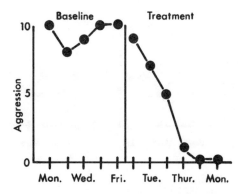

After treatment was begun, the behavior decreased to zero
within five days. Thus, examination of this graph indicates
that aggression declined. Similarly, the following graph displays an increase in appropriate play during the course of treatment.

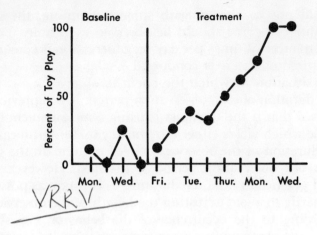

VRRV

On the other hand, the following graph shows a behavior which has not changed following implementation of a treatment procedure.

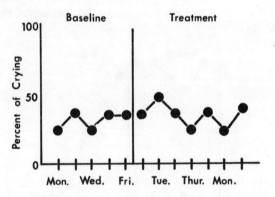

Of course, continued measurement will also reveal if a behavior is changing in a direction *opposite* to that considered desirable, for instance, if an inappropriate behavior is increasing.

How much a behavior must change to be considered improved depends on many factors, such as the seriousness of the behavioral problem, e.g. severe aggression usually must decrease to zero before the problem is considered remedied, and the requirements of the individuals who specified the target behavior in the first place, or who are now interacting with the client. For instance, if the individual now cleans his room 75 percent of the time when told to, this may satisfy the child's parents. Other parents may expect their child to complete the task 90 percent of the time. Similarly, if a child now breaks one toy a day (instead of five broken before treatment) the staff may feel that the behavior has improved sufficiently; others may not. In short, measurement of the behavior can tell the therapist if the behavior is changing, and if so, how much. Those responsible for the individual must decide when the improvement is sufficient to warrant ending formal treatment and beginning a maintenance program.

A maintenance program is usually arranged to insure that the behavioral improvement continues, but without the extensive time and effort typically involved in intensive treatment. Although treatment can and should be phased out, the target behavior must be periodically measured to evaluate if improvement has continued under a maintenance regime. During the maintenance program the measurement system can be altered somewhat. The same *measure* of the behavior, e.g. number, frequency, percent, or duration that was used during baseline and treatment should continue to be used in the maintenance program. The same *method* of measurement, e.g. interval or event recording, should also be employed. However, the *frequency* with which the measurement is taken may be reduced. For instance, instead of recording the behavior daily, measurement can be decreased to once or twice a week. How often the behavior is recorded depends chiefly on two factors: It should be frequent enough for the therapist to obtain a clear picture of the behavior, i.e. whether it is increasing, decreasing, or remaining unchanged, while at the same time not so frequent that measurement interferes with other staff duties. In short, measurement during a maintenance program should provide information as to whether the behavioral improvement is continuing, without requiring an unrealistic amount of time.

SELECTING AND APPLYING THE TREATMENT PROCEDURE: INCREASING BEHAVIOR

WHILE baseline is being conducted, the therapist should design a treatment procedure, i.e. a method for changing the target behavior, such as increasing an appropriate behavior and sometimes decreasing an inappropriate behavior. In this section, procedures are presented designed to increase desirable behavior. Such responses typically include social interaction, self-help skills, language, and academic behaviors. In some cases the objective might be to teach an appropriate behavior which does not presently occur at all. As an alternative, the aim may be to further increase the occurrence of a behavior which occurs at an unacceptably low rate. Finally, it may be necessary to direct treatment to the maintenance of a previously increased behavior, so that it will continue to occur at a high level. "Increase" might be translated specifically as an increase in the *number, frequency, percent, duration,* or *amount* of the target response. The procedures for increasing appropriate target behaviors are described in this chapter.

INCREASING BEHAVIOR BY POSITIVE REINFORCEMENT

A *positive reinforcer* (sometimes informally called a reward) is an event (stimulus) which when presented immediately following a response increases the strength of that response. *Event* refers to some noticeable change in a person's environment, such as someone saying "Good!" *Any* change in the environment that an individual is capable of noticing is an event, but only *some* events affect the client's behavior. *Increase in strength* refers to an increase in the number, rate, percent, duration, or amount of the behavior.

62

Positive reinforcers are events that in casual conversation are sometimes called "fun," "pleasant," or "satisfying." For instance, many of us enjoy (are positively reinforced by) praise, attention, money, promotions, and affection from loved ones. When a response is followed by one of these events, that response tends to be repeated in the future. For instance, if praise is a positive reinforcer for an individual, and every time he correctly answers a teacher's question the teacher says "Good boy, that's right!" then the student will be more likely to answer correctly in the future.

In summary, the *definition* of a positive reinforcer is an event (stimulus) which, when presented immediately following (contingent on) a response, increases the strength of that response. The term *contingent* means simply that there is a specified, dependent relationship between the response and the event (in this case, the positive reinforcer) that follows it.

How does one determine if an event is a positive reinforcer? The *only* way to tell for sure is to use it: consistently present it contingent on a response and see if that response increases in the future. If it does, the event is a positive reinforcer. Increasing the strength of a response by presenting a positive reinforcer immediately following that behavior is called *positive reinforcement*.

There are two kinds of positive reinforcers: (1) unconditioned (also called *primary*) reinforcers and (2) conditioned (also called *secondary*) reinforcers.

Unconditioned Reinforcers

An *unconditioned* (primary) *reinforcer* is an event which can function as a reinforcer (to strengthen behavior) without any special training. These are usually events which are basic to our physical survival, such as food and liquid. For example, milk functions as an unconditioned reinforcer for any newborn, i.e. the event (milk) is automatically reinforcing to all infants.

When using a primary reinforcer in training to increase a target behavior, the reinforcer must often be withheld for a time to enhance its effectiveness. For instance, one would not work for food directly after a hearty meal, nor will most children. Likewise, a drink of water will probably not strengthen a response that it follows if the client has just been given a large amount of liquid. To insure that food or liquid will function as an effective reinforcer, the individual should be somewhat *deprived* of it, i.e. the reinforcer should be withheld for a period of time prior to its use. The *deprivation* period should be adjusted to the individual. Some individuals will respond for food only after one to three hours of not eating; others always seem deprived and will work for food (especially favorite foods) without an arranged deprivation period. A client should not be deprived of water and milk, but other liquids such as colas and juice can usually be withheld for training purposes.

When an individual has received many unconditioned reinforcers, and finally the response which produces the reinforcer ceases (he stops working to get them), he is likely to be *satiated*. *Satiation* refers to a decrease in the potency of a positive reinforcer and typically accounts for the common observation during a training session that the client "fills up" and no longer responds for the reinforcer. In this case, the reinforcer should be withheld until it again increases in potency, i.e. until the person is sufficiently deprived, at which time he will again work to obtain it. When using unconditioned reinforcers, their effectiveness in strengthening behavior will vary with this deprivation/satiation cycle.

Conditioned Reinforcers

The second kind of positive reinforcer is a *conditioned* (secondary) *reinforcer*. A conditioned reinforcer is one which becomes effective as a reinforcer after special training. As a general rule (with very few exceptions) an event which does not function as a positive reinforcer can acquire a reinforcing function by being associated (paired) with something that already is a reinforcer. The kind of association that is most effective in making a nonreinforcer into a positive reinforcer involves presenting the nonreinforcer just before the presentation of an already established reinforcer. For example, praise is probably not an unconditioned reinforcer; it often becomes a conditioned reinforcer because it frequently is followed by some other reinforcer, such as food.

In *every* program designed to increase behavior, it is desirable to establish and use conditioned reinforcers. First, an event can be selected and established as a conditioned reinforcer, which can be presented *immediately* following an appropriate behavior without requiring the client to be oriented toward that stimulus. For instance, verbal praise can be presented to the client without necessarily being in close proximity or directly facing the individual. The therapist can say: "Johnny, that's good" from across the room, immediately following an appropriate response. (As will be discussed later, immediacy is one of the most important rules in employing reinforcement.) Second, a conditioned reinforcer can be far more convenient and economical to use than most unconditioned reinforcers. Whereas food and liquid are often unwieldy in training situations, social praise and tokens can be established as conditioned reinforcers and used easily, even with a group. Similarly, most common conditioned reinforcers are far less expensive than the continual use of unconditioned reinforcement. Indeed, social praise is free! Third, events which are reinforcers to most of society can be established and employed as conditioned reinforcers, thus increasing the chances that desirable behavior will be maintained in the client's natural community. With individuals who have not adjusted adequately to the "usual" environment in society, it is often necessary to use standard social reinforcers. For instance, most of us are reinforced by praise, approval, and affection. Since these are often the only consequence for socially appropriate behavior, clients who do not find these events reinforcing are likely not to develop or maintain desired responses. These events should therefore be established as reinforcers.

Although technically almost any event can be established as a conditioned reinforcer, those which best fit the above criteria and are most frequently employed are social approval, tokens (plastic chips which function as money), and activities (games and privileges). In many individual's histories, one or more of these types of stimuli have been *previously* established as conditioned reinforcers. Thus, the therapist may be able to use the event as a reinforcer without having to pair it with an already effective reinforcer. To determine if a stimulus is a reinforcer, it should be presented immediately following appropriate behavior on a consistent basis, and measured if that behavior increases. If it does, the therapist may continue to use that reinforcer to both increase and/or maintain behavior. In this case, although the therapist need not pair the reinforcer to make it effective, this can be done occasionally to maintain its effectiveness.

On the other hand, if the consistent, contingent use of the event does not increase the target response, that stimulus is probably not a reinforcer (or a very potent one) and requires training (pairing with an already effective reinforcer). If such training appears necessary, an already effective reinforcer should be selected. Although an event must be employed to determine conclusively that it is a reinforcer, in some instances "educated guesses" can be used to identify potential reinforcers. For instance, if a client indicates (verbally or gesturally) that he likes something, e.g. consistently consumes a particular food or engages in a specific activity when given a choice, the preferred event may be a reinforcer. (These factors are more fully described later.) The already effective reinforcer used in the pairing procedure is usually an unconditioned reinforcer, but may be a previously established conditioned reinforcer.

In the following description of the pairing procedure, the target response is smiling, the nonreinforcer which is to be made into a conditioned reinforcer is praise such as "Good boy," and the already effective reinforcer is bites of food (after a period of deprivation).

When the target response (smiling) occurs, the therapist immediately presents the nonreinforcing stimulus ("Good boy") and then quickly presents a small bite of food. The pairing procedure entails *first* presenting the nonreinforcer, and *then* the already effective reinforcer. It is important to notice that the nonreinforcer and the effective reinforcer are not presented simultaneously. However, the bite of food should follow "Good boy" immediately, i.e. within one to two seconds, just as "Good boy" should follow smiling immediately. This pairing procedure is employed each time the behavior occurs. After repeated pairings, the nonreinforcing stimulus will become a conditioned reinforcer, i.e. it will increase a response when presented contingently, and/or it will maintain a behavior which has previously been increased, without presentation of the unconditioned reinforcer.

After the nonreinforcer acquires conditioned reinforcing potency, the already effective reinforcer can be reduced gradually in one of two ways: in the case of token reinforcement, the therapist should gradually increase the time between delivery of the conditioned reinforcer (token) and delivery of the established reinforcer; in the case of *any* conditioned reinforcer, the therapist gradually decreases the number of times the conditioned reinforcer is followed by the established reinforcer. In the latter case, the number of times each conditioned reinforcer is followed with an already effective reinforcer is decreased to every other time, then every third time, etc. With either procedure, the change must be made *gradually*. If the conditioned reinforcer begins to lose its ability to increase and maintain behaviors that it follows, either the delay between the conditioned reinforcer and the already effective reinforcer should be shortened, or the number of times an unconditioned reinforcer follows the conditioned reinforcer (*re-pairing*) should be increased. In short, even after a nonreinforcer becomes a conditioned reinforcer, it will not remain so unless it is intermittently re-paired with an already effective reinforcer.

As mentioned previously, the most common events to be established as conditioned reinforcers are social events (*socials*) of various kinds, including tactual stimuli (e.g. pats, hugs and strokes) and verbal stimuli (words and phrases denoting enthusiastic approval, e.g. "That's very good", "Good boy", "Wonderful" and "Terrific"). It is recommended that the praise statement include a description of the behavior being reinforced, for instance, "I like the way you are peddling that tricycle!" or "You turned in your assignment on time, that's great!" Such statements are called *descriptive praise* in contrast to *general praise*, for example "Good boy", as exemplified earlier. Although positive reinforcement will be effective in increasing a behavior even if the individual is not told what behavior he is being reinforced for, nevertheless adding a description of the appropriate behavior may enhance the effectiveness of reinforcement. Since it is sometimes impossible to determine how much language a retarded client understands, it is desirable to use descriptive praise with even profoundly retarded individuals.

Every attempt should be made to vary the content of each social reinforcer presented, while insuring that each contains some clear and enthusiastic gesture of approval. Most of us would quickly tire of being repeatedly told "Good." As mentioned previously, it is important to use social stimuli which are as similar as possible to those the individual is likely to encounter in other situations and with other people.

A final point about social reinforcement deserves mention here. Although social approval and affection are common reinforcers for many in our society, negative social attention may also be a reinforcer. It is not uncommon to see children or even adults deliberately behave in such a way as to receive disapproval. Disapproval is a form of attention, and may be a reinforcer for one individual, just as praise is for another. Clearly, disapproval cannot be used as a reinforcer in a training program, but the therapist should be aware of its possible effects, particularly in increasing and maintaining *undesirable* behavior.

Another widely used conditioned reinforcer is the token. Tokens can take many forms, e.g. poker chips, coins, checkmarks, and slips of paper. Just as in the case of socials, the token is established as a conditioned reinforcer by being paired with an already effective reinforcer. In this case, when the appropriate response occurs, the person is handed the token immediately, then the token is reclaimed and an already effective reinforcer is given (usually a bit of food or liquid). Notice this sequence:

1. The appropriate behavior occurs.
2. Hand the individual a token (always accompanied by

social praise, e.g. "You closed the door, thank you, here's your token."

3. Immediately take the token back.
4. *Then* hand the client an unconditioned reinforcer (or an already established conditioned reinforcer). This is called a *backup reinforcer*.

This process is repeated many times. Next, a delay is gradually introduced between receiving the token and trading it for the already effective (backup) reinforcer. Gradually, the individual must receive two, then three, then four tokens, and so on before redeeming them for the backup reinforcer.

Token reinforcement has been used very successfully with a variety of populations, e.g. grade school students, retarded individuals, and psychotic adults. It is a convenient and effective system of reinforcement if run properly, e.g. if a wide enough variety of backup reinforcers are available for which tokens can be redeemed.

A thorough description of how to design, implement, and maintain a token system is presented later in this manual. For the purpose of the present discussion, several things about token systems should be noted. First, presentation of a token can be made into a conditioned reinforcer. Tokens are typically nonreinforcing before training (their contingent presentation would not increase a behavior). Second, after repeated pairings with already effective reinforcers, they acquire reinforcing power, i.e. they can strengthen a behavior when they are presented immediately following each occurrence of that behavior.

A third type of frequently used conditioned reinforcer is activities, e.g. games, playing with toys, watching movies, taking bus rides, and participating in recess. Most people have had previous experiences which have established some (or many) of these events as conditioned reinforcers. For instance, even with many profoundly retarded individuals presenting a toy or allowing access to a playground following an appropriate behavior will increase the strength of that desirable response. If an activity is shown *not* to be a reinforcer, it can be paired with an already effective reinforcer and acquire reinforcing potency. In this case, when an appropriate behavior occurs, the therapist should immediately present the activity, e.g. present the client with a game, and while he is handling or playing with the game, present him with an already effective reinforcer such as giving him attention or bites of food. After repeated pairings of this sort, the game will acquire reinforcing power. The therapist should then be able to gradually reduce the number of times the game is paired with attention or food. Eventually, only occasional pairings of the game and food will be necessary to maintain the activity as a conditioned reinforcer.

Since some delay is usually inevitable between the occurrence of an appropriate behavior and presentation of a reinforcing activity, a signal should always be presented immediately following the behavior which indicates that the activity will be presented. This signal can either be verbal ("Johnny, that's good; now you can go to the playground") or tangible (presentation of a token which he later hands to the therapist to gain access to the playground). This signal is, or will become, a conditioned reinforcer because it, too, is paired with the already effective reinforcer that is being paired with the activity. It will "bridge" the delay between the desirable behavior and delivery of the activity; hence it is sometimes called a *bridging stimulus*.

Activities as reinforcers are very useful in most training settings, because they are usually available anyway, but given free (noncontingently). By simply rearranging things a bit, i.e. by providing these activities following appropriate behavior, they can become a powerful and economical method of increasing target behavior. Further, as in the case of socials, many activities which are not reinforcing for a client should be made into reinforcers simply because they are reinforcing for much of society. For instance, a retarded child is likely to be considered "more normal" if he is reinforced by ("enjoys") playing with toys. Examples of activities which often are (or can be made into) conditioned reinforcers, include:

1. access to activities (bus rides, TV, movies, swimming pool and playground)
2. helping teacher (run errands, collect paper and erase blackboard).
3. access to play materials (puzzles, paints, scissors and

chalk).

4. privileges (being first in line, wearing star on forehead, having name on blackboard as a "good guy").

On the other hand, engaging in a reinforcing activity often interrupts a training session. For instance, teaching a person to wash his hands by using thirty-seconds access to a toy as a reinforcer for each correct response involves stopping often and waiting out each thirty-second period of reinforcement. Similarly, letting a child run out to the playground following each correct arithmetic response is hardly a practical procedure. Activities should therefore generally be used as reinforcers (1) in combination with tokens, i.e. the client receives tokens for separate correct responses and then trades the tokens for the activity at the end of the training session; or (2) later in training where a reinforcer for each correct response has been gradually reduced and the individual receives reinforcement only following a large amount of appropriate behavior, e.g. after washing his hands completely or finishing an entire assignment in his workbook.*

Using activities as reinforcers can perhaps be described as using a favorite behavior as a reinforcer. This concept is technically called the *Premack Principle* (named after the man who formally described it). It states that if two behaviors are observed to occur at different rates in the "natural," unrestricted environment, then the opportunity to engage in the more frequent behavior can be used as a positive reinforcer to increase the rate of the less frequent behavior. For example, if the therapist observes that a person seldom reads newspapers, but spends most of his time reading comic books, he can increase his newspaper-reading behavior by making the opportunity to read comic books, i.e. the availability of comic books, contingent upon newspaper reading. Thus, immediately after reading a newspaper (or a portion of it) the individual could be presented with a comic book. If reading newspapers increases in frequency (and/or duration), reading comic books is a rein-

---

*See section on "Intermittent Schedules of Reinforcement" and "Maintenance of Behavioral Improvement" for a more complete description.

forcer. Similarly, if a retarded individual spends most of his time sitting when given a choice of several activities, sitting may be a reinforcer which can be used to strengthen other, low-rate behaviors, such as playing with toys or interacting socially.

Deprivation and satiation, described under unconditioned reinforcement, also apply to conditioned reinforcement. After repeated delivery of socials, tokens (or their backups), and activities, these may gradually lose reinforcing power and the appropriate behaviors for which they are presented will then decrease (the client will become satiated). A period of deprivation should revive their reinforcing potency. However, socials, if varied in their content and occasionally re-paired with already effective reinforcers, *may* not be subject to satiation.

In general, it has been emphasized that the only conclusive method of determining whether an event is a reinforcer is to use it contingently and consistently with an appropriate behavior. However, a great deal of training time can be wasted by trying one ineffective reinforcer after another. It is often possible to *informally* identify a potential reinforcer by the following guidelines: first, one should consider an event's biological significance to the individual (and his species). As mentioned previously, food and liquid are very basic reinforcers to living animals (including humans). Second, it may be possible to use a "pleased reaction" as the basis of selecting a potential reinforcer. If a person laughs or smiles while receiving an item, it may be a reinforcer if presented contingently. Third, if the client verbalizes an interest in or attraction to a particular item or event, it may be a reinforcer. The difficulty with the latter two methods of identifying potential reinforcers is that what we *say* (gesturally or verbally) and what we *do* are often quite discrepant. A person may request an event, and/or laugh and smile when receiving it, but still not work to obtain it. Similarly, an individual may not show interest or concern in an activity, but respond consistently to earn access to it. For instance, he may routinely behave appropriately all day to earn enough tokens to watch TV only to sleep in front of it! A more reliable (accurate) estimate of a person's reinforcers may be what he consumes or does at a high rate when given a choice.

Regardless of what the client says, or the emotion he shows, the therapist should observe what he *does* when given unrestricted access to a variety of activities. Similarly, he may note what the individual eats, buys, or otherwise selects when given a choice. Fifth, it is often possible to use parental or staff suggestions when selecting a reinforcer. Those who are most familiar with a person sometimes provide excellent guidelines concerning potential reinforcers. Finally, possible reinforcers for a particular person can sometimes be identified on the basis of what many of an individual's age and level of functioning find as reinforcers. For instance, many children like candy, access to a playground, and attention. Thus, events such as these are likely reinforcers for a particular individual. It should again be emphasized that the above are only guidelines in the preliminary selection of potential reinforcers. An event must be *used* contingent on an appropriate behavior to demonstrate that it is, in fact, a reinforcer.

Factors Influencing the Effectiveness of Reinforcement

There are several factors which directly influence how effective unconditioned or conditioned reinforcement will be.

IMMEDIACY. The immediacy with which the reinforcer is delivered following an appropriate behavior is one of the most important features in the use of positive reinforcement. The therapist should not present either an unconditioned or conditioned reinforcer at all if he cannot do so very quickly following the target behavior. With a delay of even three seconds, the client may have stopped performing the desired response (the one that the therapist intended to reinforce) and be engaging in some other behavior which may be less appropriate. If, at that point, the therapist delivers the positive reinforcer, he may strengthen the less desirable behavior. For this reason, it is desirable (essential!) to use social reinforcement in training. When using socials, even if the client is not looking at the therapist, he can hear immediately that he has behaved correctly (unless, of course, his hearing is impaired). This is in contrast to the delay that is frequently involved when placing food in the client's mouth (even if the food is in the therapist's hand when the desirable behavior occurs).

Delayed reinforcement often functions in a manner similar to *noncontingent reinforcement* (also called *uncorrelated* or *response-independent* reinforcement). In the case of noncontingent reinforcement, a reinforcer is delivered without regard to the occurrence (or nonoccurrence) of a behavior, but solely on the basis of time. For example, Christmas and birthday presents are things which probably would serve as reinforcers if they were given only following the occurrence of certain behavior, but which are normally given noncontingently, i.e. at certain times of the year without regard to the preceding behavior. Similarly, snacks are sometimes scheduled at specified times each day, and given regardless of whether or not an individual has behaved appropriately. When reinforcers are presented noncontingently and frequently, *superstitious behavior* is likely to develop. That is, a particular behavior may sometimes be occurring when a reinforcer is delivered, even though that reinforcer is not intended to follow that response. It may thus coincidentally strengthen the behavior that it happens to occasionally follow. This process is called *accidental reinforcement*. Superstitious behavior is thus developed or maintained by an accidental association between its occurrence and the delivery of a reinforcer. Rain dances, the wearing of lucky charms, and other rituals are examples of such superstitious behavior. They are developed and maintained because they are accidentally reinforced by noncontingent reinforcement. For instance, rain falls periodically and independently of a rain dance, but at least occasionally such a rite may directly precede a shower. Thus the superstitious behavior of rain dancing may be intermittently (and accidentally) reinforced.

Delayed reinforcement may similarly generate superstitious behavior (either desirable or undesirable responses). For instance, if reinforcement is delayed by even two or three seconds, it may accidentally reinforce a person for *ceasing* the appropriate behavior or engaging in an undesirable response.

NUMBER OF REINFORCERS DELIVERED. Within limits, the higher the number of reinforcers that have been presented following the behavior, the stronger the response will be. This does not mean that simply practicing the response will necessarily help the person learn it. The strength of a response is increased by reinforcement. It is important to remember, however, that with the delivery of each reinforcer, the individual may become a little more satiated and after repeated reinforcement may cease responding *temporarily*. However, after a deprivation period, the client should begin again to respond for the reinforcer. These temporary cycles do not contradict the notion that the response increases in overall strength with continued reinforcement.

CONVENIENCE. If a reinforcer is not convenient to carry and deliver, a therapist will be less likely to reinforce appropriate behavior. For the sake of immediacy, therapists should carry reinforcers with them in the training situation. When this situation includes a large room and/or many clients, food and liquid are often messy, unsanitary, and cumbersome reinforcers. M&M's,® tokens and other lightweight, nonmessy items are generally convenient reinforcers. Of course, social reinforcement is most convenient of all!

DEPRIVATION. The therapist should only use events as reinforcers which can be withheld for training purposes (deprivation), or which need not be given noncontingently (free). For instance, clients should receive a certain amount of water and milk each day. However, an individual can be deprived of a nonessential liquid such as soda. Such reinforcers can then be used only in training situations, i.e. restricted at other times, and thus are more likely to function effectively.

If the target behavior is not increasing steadily, lengthening the deprivation period may enhance the effectiveness of the reinforcer. For instance, if raisins are used as the reinforcement, but the response for which raisins are given is not improving, the therapist might lengthen the time between training sessions.

Another method of forestalling satiation is to vary the content of reinforcement frequently. For instance, if food is used as a reinforcer, it is desirable to change the reinforcing food regularly. How frequently this is done depends on the client's behavior, i.e. if the response for which food is given begins to decline (or if the person accepts the food less enthusiastically), changing the reinforcer may be desirable.

Finally, an individual is less likely to become satiated with a reinforcer which is presented on an "intermittent schedule," than one which is presented following each appropriate response. Such periodic use of reinforcement will be described later in this chapter under "Intermittent Schedules of Reinforcement."

SIZE OF REINFORCEMENT. The size of each reinforcer should be large enough to be truly reinforcing, but small enough to delay satiation as long as possible. The proper amount for each person is determined by trial and error. The size of each bite of food can generally be increased or decreased easily. However, dividing a reinforcing activity into parts is often less convenient. For instance, the therapist can easily vary the duration of a bike ride, but varying the duration of a movie is sometimes impractical. In this case, tokens are a practical way of providing reinforcers following single, appropriate behaviors. When enough are accumulated, these may be traded for the entire activity, e.g. the movie.

CONSISTENCY. When a target behavior is first being increased it must be reinforced *each time* it occurs. If not, the response will develop very slowly, if at all. After the response is well established, reinforcement is gradually reduced (see "Intermittent Schedules of Reinforcement").

The above points pertain to both unconditioned and conditioned reinforcement. The following factors relate specifically to conditioned reinforcement: socials, tokens, and/or activities.

NUMBER OF PAIRINGS. The greater the number of pairings between the conditioned reinforcer and the already effective reinforcers, up to a point, the more effective the conditioned reinforcer will be in increasing and maintaining appropriate behavior. The number of pairings needed will vary in different cases.

POTENCY OF THE ESTABLISHED REINFORCER. The effectiveness of the conditioned reinforcer depends upon the effectiveness of the established reinforcer with which it is paired. For instance, if the individual becomes satiated with food, he may also cease responding for tokens which are paired with food (unless tokens are also paired with other reinforcers). For this reason, it is best to pair a conditioned reinforcer with as wide a variety of powerful, established reinforcers as possible. In this case, if one reinforcer is ineffective, e.g. due to satiation, the conditioned reinforcer can be paired with another, currently effective reinforcer. Conditioned reinforcers which are paired with a wide variety of established reinforcers, are called *generalized reinforcers*.

It may also be true that a conditioned reinforcer which is paired with an *unconditioned* reinforcer, e.g. food or liquid, is more effective than one that is paired with another conditioned reinforcer.

TIME BETWEEN CONDITIONED REINFORCER AND BACKUP. When the nonreinforcing stimulus is first being paired with the established reinforcer, the former should be immediately followed by the latter. With tokens, a delay is then gradually lengthened (to a point) between delivery of the tokens and redeeming them for already effective (backup) reinforcers. In this case, a decline in appropriate behavior for which tokens are given may indicate that this delay is too long and should be shortened.

FREQUENCY OF RE-PAIRING. To retain its reinforcing power, the conditioned reinforcer must be re-paired, intermittently at least, with established reinforcers. If behaviors which produce the conditioned reinforcer begin to decline, increasing the number of times a conditioned reinforcer is followed by the unconditioned reinforcer may restore the behavior (and the effectiveness of the conditioned reinforcer).

Shaping

Throughout the preceding discussion, the therapist was instructed to *wait* for the appropriate target behavior to occur, and then reinforce it with a conditioned and/or unconditioned reinforcer. Often, however, the target response *never* occurs. In these cases, he might watch the client carefully and be ready to reinforce the appropriate behavior, but not have an opportunity to do so because that individual never engages in the behavior. For instance, if the therapist wants to strengthen the response of sitting in a chair throughout a movie, and the person currently wanders around the room constantly during the show, the therapist might wait forever to provide reinforcement for sitting through the entire event. In such a case, he should use the procedure of *shaping*. In general, shaping involves the development of a target behavior by initially reinforcing a different but similar behavior, then differentially reinforcing successive approximations to the desired target behavior. The specific steps by which behavior is shaped are as follows:

1. Identify a behavior that the individual currently performs relatively often, which at least roughly approximates the desired target behavior. In the example above, the therapist might observe that the closest the client comes to sitting in his chair is walking past it at a distance of two to three feet.

2. Reinforce this approximation (response which resembles the target behavior). For example, whenever the individual passes his chair within two to three feet, the therapist should present him with a reinforcer *quickly* so that the approximation of being near the chair is reinforced. To insure that reinforcement is immediate, use verbal social approval and, if that is not a reinforcer (or a powerful one), also use a material reinforcer, e.g. tokens or bites of food. When shaping, use a reinforcer that does not take a long time to consume. For instance, if playing with a toy for thirty seconds is used as a reinforcer, most of the training session may be spent waiting while the child plays with the toy. On the other hand, raisins can be eaten quickly, without re-peatedly interrupting the training session. (Of course, if playing with a toy is the only effective reinforcer the child will respond to, use it!)

3. *At the same time*, withhold reinforcement for behaviors that are *less* similar to the target behavior. For instance, if the client consistently approaches his chair within two to three feet, the therapist reinforces this approximation and does not reward him for passing within four or more feet.

4. At the same time one approximation is being reinforced, *also* reinforce any closer (better) approximations which happen to occur. For instance, while the therapist is reinforcing him for approaching a chair within two or three feet, if he passes within one foot of it, that behavior should be reinforced. Of course, if the client displays a behavior which is even *more* similar to the target behavior, it should be reinforced. For instance, he should also be reinforced for touching the chair, standing with his back to it, and of course sitting in it! In general, the therapist watches for the emergence of new, closer approximations, and reinforces them when they occur.

5. When a closer approximation(s) begins to occur with some regularity, increase the criterion for reinforcement. That is, reinforcement should be discontinued for the previous approximation (the originally reinforced behavior which is less similar to the target behavior). This closer approximation may be *any* response that begins to occur consistently. It may be one that is only slightly more similar to the target behavior, or may actually be the target response itself. The client's behavior, i.e. which responses occur, and in what sequence, must determine the course of shaping.

However, just because a closer approximation occurs a few times (and is reinforced), it does not mean that the therapist should stop reinforcing the previous approximation. He must increase the rate of the closer approximation before discontinuing reinforcing a less similar response. For instance, as the client sits in the chair more and more frequently, he can stop reinforcing him for walking within one foot of the chair. If, on the other hand, the client continues to sit only rarely, reinforcing the previous approximation should not cease until sitting becomes more frequent.

6. While consistently reinforcing this relatively new approximation, *also* reinforce any closer (better) approximations which happen to occur. For instance, if the therapist is now reinforcing the individual for approaching within one foot of the chair, (and has stopped rewarding him for less similar approximations), he is also reinforced for *any* closer approximation (e.g. touching the chair).

7. In the same way, increase the criterion for reinforcement until the target behavior is developed, and occurs consistently.

8. If at any point in the development of the target behavior, the client stops emitting reinforceable responses, reduce the criterion for reinforcement is reduced so that he can once again be reinforced. For example, if the person is being reinforced for touching the chair, but for some reason ceases displaying this behavior, the therapist returns to reinforcing him for approaching it within one foot, then proceeds again to gradually increase the criterion for reinforcement.

In general, the shaping procedure is a method of teaching a behavior, i.e. one which does not presently occur. The person is initially reinforced for emitting behavior which even remotely resembles the target behavior, and is then successively reinforced for improvement. After this process is completed, reinforcement is only presented contingent on the actual occurrence of the target behavior.

The success of the shaping procedure depends upon several factors:

1. The *size* of each step: The individual's behavior should be the therapist's guide as to how large each increase in the standards of reinforcement should be. Novice trainers often make the mistake of raising the standards for reinforcement in too large of steps. If the therapist's standards are at a level at which the client rarely performs, he will be reinforced so infrequently that he will probably cease performing even behaviors that he previously emitted often. (For instance, if he consistently sits in a chair for ten seconds, and now the therapist waits to reinforce him until he sits for ten minutes, he will probably get up and start wandering again). If the therapist finds that he is not reinforcing the client for the new step, i.e. because he is not performing it often, he should *back up*, lower his standards, and reinforce a behavior that lies somewhere between the previously reinforced step and the one that the child is not yet performing.

Just as the therapist must be sensitive to the necessity of backing up to a step which is *less* similar to the target behavior, she/he must also watch for behaviors that are *more* similar. She/he should not stick to a prescribed sequence of approximations! For instance, if the therapist is reinforcing an individual for standing near the chair and suddenly he sits down in it, he definitely should be reinforced!

2. The *speed* with which the therapist moves from one step to the next: A new approximation should occur (and be reinforced) several times before the therapist stops reinforcing a less similar approximation. For instance, if the individual has sat on the chair for a full ten seconds only once or twice (and been reinforced each time) it may be too hasty to stop all reinforcement for sitting for less than ten seconds. On the other hand, the therapist should increase the standards as fast as the client's behavior will allow, and not reinforce a person on one step longer than necessary. Again, the individual's behavior must be the guide. After a closer approximation occurs several times (and is reinforced each time), then reinforcement is discontinued for the previous approximation. If the client does not perform this new step very often, the therapist should *back up*: return to the previous step and reinforce it further and/or reduce the size of the increase (this is the guideline mentioned above). If shaping continues for several training sessions, the therapist may have to back up briefly at the start of each session to a step below the one for which reinforcement was given at the end of the previous session. After "getting him started," the therapist rapidly increases reinforcement standards until it is possible to resume where he left off previously.

3. The effectiveness of the positive reinforcer: Of course, the success of shaping depends directly on the potency of the reinforcer used. All of the factors influencing reinforcer effectiveness must be considered if the shaping procedure is to be successful.

Shaping is used extensively in training, especially in combination with another procedure, "prompting and fading", discussed below. Almost any dimension of behavior can be (and often is) shaped in a well-designed training program. For instance, an individual can be shaped to respond for longer durations. Thus a client may be successively reinforced for sitting, playing, paying attention, running, or reading for longer and longer amounts of time. Similarly, a shaping procedure can be used to modify the amount (magnitude) of a response. For instance, an individual who whispers can be reinforced for successive approximations which finally result in an audible voice. On the other hand, a noisy class can be shaped into a quiet level of sound. The frequency (rate) of a response can similarly be modified by shaping. For example, a slow worker may initially be reinforced for completing an arithmetic assignment within fifteen minutes, then ten and finally within five minutes. Shaping also applies to alterations in the quality of performance. A student might receive an "A" grade, first for correctly spelling six words, next ten and then fifteen. Similarly, shaping can be applied to successively better penmanship, calisthenic performance, or speech enunciation. In the latter case, perhaps any vocal sound would initially be reinforced. Next, the student would be reinforced for longer and/or louder vocalizations. In a similar manner, vowel (and other) sounds could be shaped. Ultimately, the individual would only be reinforced for clearly enunciating words.

Prompting and Fading

In addition to shaping, another method of developing a response which occurs very infrequently, if at all, is called *prompting and fading.** With this procedure, a client is first provided with help in performing the responses (prompting) and reinforced when he does so. Next, this assistance is gradually removed (faded) while the individual continues to be reinforced for emitting the desired behavior. Finally, all extra help is withdrawn, and the person is reinforced only after he performs the response independently.

More specifically, a prompt is something which is effective in evoking the occurrence of the target response, i.e. every time the

---

*These procedures are often described as a method of establishing *stimulus control,* i.e. altering the occurrence of an existing response in different stimulus situations. However, several authors, including the present one, feel that the procedures are best described in the context of teaching new behavior.

prompt is presented, the target response is then emitted. For instance, one type of prompt involves physically moving the client through a response, such as the therapist placing her hand over the person's and moving him through the behavior of washing his face. Initially, a large prompt may be necessary to evoke the desired behavior, i.e. the client may require a lot of help. Regardless of the size of prompt, the individual is reinforced for each occurrence of the target behavior. The teacher then gradually reduces the prompt (it is faded out) at a rate that does not disrupt the target response, i.e. so the target response continues to be performed. During the fading process, the response continues to be reinforced each time it occurs. If at any point during fading the response ceases to occur, the therapist should back up to a previous fading step and employ a larger prompt. After responding is re-established, fading should resume at a slower rate. After such training, the target response should occur without any prompting.

The specific steps by which behavior is established by prompting and fading are presented below.

First, select a prompt which is already effective in getting the target response to occur. As mentioned previously, this means that every time the prompt is presented, the desired target behavior is then emitted. There are several types of prompts which can be used. Select one or more which is successful in evoking the target response *at least* 90 percent of the times that it is used.

One type of prompt is a verbal instruction. For instance, if the therapist wants a child to get dressed after getting out of bed in the morning, he might find that the prompt of telling the individual to dress (e.g. "John, get dressed") is effective in getting him to dress himself. In this case, the verbal instruction can serve as the prompt which the therapist will eventually fade out. A therapist need not always present the verbal instruction directly to the target student (the one requiring a prompt). If a group of individuals is participating in an activity together, he can locate a student who is behaving appropriately, and specifically in a manner that the target student needs to learn. He can then reinforce that appropriate behavior in such a way that the target student can see and hear. The reinforcement should contain a clear description of the appropriate behavior, as well as the specific reinforcer being presented (descriptive praise described previously). For instance, if a student is not using scissors properly, the therapist may prompt appropriate use of scissors by approaching another student and saying: "Susy, I like the way you are cutting only on the black line, here is some juice!" In this case, reinforcement of one student may also serve as an effective prompt in evoking appropriate behavior by another. This procedure is called *pointed praise* and will be described more fully later.

Another type of prompt consists of a gesture. For instance, if the therapist wants to teach a student to sit down immediately upon entering the classroom, he might find that pointing to the chair is an effective prompt. Similarly, if a client neglects to wash particular portions of his face, pointing to those areas may be effective in getting him to wash completely.

A third type of prompt involves arranging the environment so that occurrence of the target response is very likely. For instance, if the therapist wants to train the client to hold onto her purse, he might begin by using the prompt of taping or tying the client's purse to her hand, so that she cannot help but carry it with her. Similarly, if the therapist wants to teach a student to select his name printed on a card, from other names printed on other cards, he could begin training by modifying the cards in ways that make it very likely that the student would point to the correct card (the one bearing his name). For instance, the therapist could make the person's name very large in comparison to the other names, or written in very bright letters (with the other names printed in black), or the card on which the student's name appears could be made much larger or feature a brightly colored background in comparison to the incorrect cards. Making the correct answer much more distinctive than the incorrect answer does tend to make students more likely to respond correctly.

Thus, a prompt which consists of arranging the environment in ways that make the target response likely to occur, can do so by either:

1. physically insuring that the target response occurs, e.g. by tying a purse to a client's hand, or
2. making the correct answer very distinctive in comparison to the incorrect answer, e.g. larger, brighter or darker, so that it is more likely to evoke the target behavior.

A fourth type of prompt consists of physically moving the client's body through the target response; it is called *putting through*. For instance, if the therapist wants the client to spoonfeed independently, he might prompt this response by placing a spoon in the individual's hand, placing his hand over the client's, and pressing firmly enough so that the spoon remains in his hand. The therapist could then move the client's hand through the response of scooping the food and bringing it to his lips. Similarly, if the therapist wants the person to walk toward him when called, the therapist might have a teacher push the student gently from behind and steer him in the therapist's direction until the child stands in front of him.

A fifth type of prompt is *modeling*, i.e. demonstrating the correct response to the client by the therapist performing it himself. For instance, if a client is to be trained to wash his face, the teacher might initially use the prompt of washing her own face in the correct manner or having another student demonstrate the behavior.

A final type of prompt actually consists of a combination of several previously described prompts. It is called *priming*, and was developed for use with preschool students who demonstrated social and play deficits. In this case, another child is asked to approach the target child and play with her, thus prompting the desirable behavior. In a similar manner, other individuals may be useful in prompting a variety of appropriate behaviors, such as correct use of play materials and participation in group activities.

The type of prompt selected depends upon what works with each client. If one does not evoke a target response, another should be tried (but not necessarily in the order presented here). A verbal instruction or gesture may be the most convenient prompt to use. Modeling is also convenient, but some individuals do not have imitative skills. In addition, some situations, such as taking a shower, do not lend themselves to modeling. When done properly, arranging the environment and putting a client through the response are usually effective in evoking almost any response by any individual. (Of course, the therapist may be surprised to find that an arrangement of the environment which he thought would guarantee performance of the response does not do so.) The primary disadvantage of arranging the environment and putting through may lie in the difficulty of fading out these prompts. In terms of convenience, one might start with either a verbal instruction, gesture, or modeling, and if these are ineffective, another prompt can be attempted. Of course, more than one prompt can (and often should) be used at the same time to evoke a target response. For instance, the therapist might model *and* put the client through the response, if neither prompt is successful by itself.

Further, every effort should be made to use the *smallest* prompt possible which is successful in evoking the appropriate behavior. It should be remembered that such assistance will be faded out eventually, so it is desirable to use as little as possible in the first place. For instance, instead of fully putting the individual through a spoondip at the beginning of training, the therapist may find that only occasional guidance is required to evoke correct spoonfeeding.

Each time the response occurs following presentation of the prompt, it should be reinforced with a conditioned, and, if necessary, unconditioned reinforcer (e.g., praise and a bite of food).

Begin to *gradually* fade out the prompt. After reinforcing the client for performing the response several times with the full prompt, begin to make the prompt less conspicuous, i.e. provide the individual with less assistance.

In the case of a verbal prompt, the therapist can make it softer and softer, changing gradually from normal voice loudness to a whisper, then to mouthing the words with no sound, and gradually reducing the mouthing until no prompt is presented. Similarly, the teacher can reduce the number of words comprising the verbal prompt. For instance, the trainer can fade from "John, put on your shirt" to "John, shirt," to "Shirt," and then make the final word softer and softer until no verbal prompt is used.

A gestural prompt can be faded by making it less and less "complete." For instance, after initially touching an unwashed portion of the body, the teacher might only point to that area, then reduce both the size and duration of the point (e.g. instead of fully extending his arm and finger, begin to quickly gesture with only a partially extended finger and arm).

In a similar fashion, a modeling prompt can be faded by making it less complete. For instance, if the therapist is training the client to raise his arms at the command, "Raise your arms", he can use a modeling prompt by raising his own arms while presenting the verbal instruction. When fading, the therapist steadily reduces the "amount" of the demonstration, i.e. from raising his arms completely over his head, to raising them 3/4 of the way up, then to 1/2, next to only beginning to raise them, then to raising hands but keeping arms at sides, and finally to smaller and smaller hand gestures until the prompt is faded out completely.

With a prompt consisting of an arrangement of the environment which makes performance of the target response very likely, fading is accomplished by gradually removing the features which guarantee that the response will occur. For instance, if the therapist has tied an individual's purse to her wrist to insure that she carry it, gradually the length of the string can be increased until it is so long that it no longer aides the person in keeping her purse with her. Similarly, the therapist may have begun teaching a student to select his name printed on a card from other names printed on other cards, by making the correct card very distinctive in comparison to the incorrect cards. The therapist can then begin to fade out the difference between the correct and incorrect cards by, for instance, reducing the large size of the lettering of the student's name until it is the same size as the letters used in printing the other names. As an alternative, the therapist could gradually increase the size of letters on the incorrect cards. Similarly, the colors of the letters or background could be slowly faded into whatever colors are featured on the incorrect card. (Or colors could be gradually changed on the incorrect cards.) After fading, the cards should be identical in all respects except in the name which appears on each.

The prompt which consists of putting the person through the target behavior is faded out by providing less and less pressure in guiding the client's body. For instance, if the client is to be trained to wash his face, the therapist might begin by employing the prompt of putting him through that response. She starts by holding her hand over the child's and guiding the washcloth over all the necessary parts of his face. As he consistently performs the response with this prompt (and is reinforced each time), the therapist could begin to apply less and less pressure in moving his hand so that he must perform the response more and more independently. Instead of the therapist covering the child's hand with his, he might gently move the child's hand with one or two of his fingers; then gradually only touch the child occasionally throughout the facewashing sequence. Next, the therapist might move his finger with the child's hand movements, but not touch the child at all. Finally, the therapist can gradually move his hand away completely.

Priming by another individual may be faded out in a manner similar to the other types of prompts. In actual practice, however, priming is often used several times, and then eliminated abruptly when the client begins to show improvement.

Remember: Regardless of which type of prompt is employed, each time the target response occurs following presentation of the gradually diminishing prompt, it is reinforced with a conditioned and perhaps an unconditioned reinforcer, e.g. praise and a bite of food.

The prompt is faded at a rate that does not disrupt the target response, i.e. so the target response continues to occur. On one hand the prompt must be faded slowly enough, and in small enough steps so that the response is not disrupted. On the other hand, the prompt must be faded out fast enough to prevent the individual from possibly becoming dependent on the prompt, i.e. so accustomed to the extra help that its slightest reduction disrupts the target behavior. Fading should be done as fast and in as big of steps as is possible. If the target behavior stops, or begins occurring in a partial or incorrect form (for instance, instead of wiping off his entire face, the client begins skipping parts or "dawdles"), then the therapist can back up to a previous fading step where the prompt is more conspicuous and effective in getting the target response to occur. After responding is reestablished, the therapist again begins to fade out the prompt, this time at a slower rate and/or in smaller steps. It is best to avoid letting the person make many errors. After three or four consecutive errors have occurred, it is necessary to back up. Then, as soon as responding is reestablished, fading should again begin.

There are a number of factors influencing the effectiveness of prompting and fading, one or more of which should be altered if the procedure is not succeeding:

FADING TOO FAST. If the therapist is fading out the prompt too quickly, the target response will cease to occur, or will begin to occur in an incorrect form. It is desirable to reinforce an individual several (or many) times for responding correctly when given a particular amount of prompting, before reducing the amount of assistance. For instance, a student should respond correctly several consecutive times when given the prompt, "Wash hands" before the prompt is further reduced. If responding is disrupted, the therapist should *back up* to a previous fading step in which the response did occur, and then begin fading again at a slower rate.

FADING IN LARGE STEPS. If the therapist is fading out the prompt in too large of steps, the target response may also be disrupted. For instance, if he is beginning to fade out the instruction "Johnny, wash your hands", and reduces the prompt to "Hands", this reduction may be too large for one step. It is generally desirable to fade a prompt in very small steps, such as removing one word of a verbal instruction at a time. As before, if responding is disrupted, the therapist returns to using more assistance and then begins fading in smaller steps.

FADING TOO SLOWLY. If the therapist remains at a fading step for too long a time, the client may have difficulty performing the response with less prompting. The prompt should be faded as quickly as the individual's behavior allows (as long as he continues to perform the response correctly). As soon as the client performs the response consistently (several times) on one fading step, the therapist fades to the next step to see if he will respond correctly in this new situation. (If he does, the therapist reinforces him a few times on this step and then begins to fade again.) If not, the therapist backs up and then begins fading again as soon as possible. Actual experience with the techniques of prompting and fading, as well as their use with a particular individual, are necessary to acquire the *art* of fading at an appropriate rate and in acceptable step sizes.

FADING TOO MANY PROMPTS SIMULTANEOUSLY. As discussed, prompting often consists of more than one type of prompt. The therapist can simultaneously fade out as many of these prompts as the person's behavior will allow. For instance, if the therapist has established writing the letter *S* by modeling and putting the individual through the behavior, and he begins to fade both prompts at the same time, but the client's *S*'s become less accurate, it may be best to only fade one prompt at a time. The therapist might first completely fade out putting him through the response. After this prompt is eliminated, the therapist's demonstration can be faded out.

ALLOWING TOO MANY ERRORS TO OCCUR. It is best to avoid letting the individual make many errors. After two or three consecutive occasions in which the target response does not occur at all, or is performed in an incorrect form, the therapist should *back up*; then, as soon as correct responding resumes, he should begin to fade, more slowly, in smaller steps and/or eliminating fewer prompts simultaneously.

BACKING UP AND REINFORCING ERRORS. Although it has been stressed repeatedly that the therapist should back up if responding ceases or errors occur, therapists should be aware that returning to larger prompts (more assistance) may actually reinforce errors. Some research has shown that clients will work to receive an easier task. For instance, it may be possible that an individual will repeatedly emit errors in order to obtain more help (prompting) in performing a response. If the therapist finds that he must continually back up and provide the client with more prompting, and thus is not able to steadily fade the prompts, he may have fallen into just such a trap. In this case, the therapist should present a prompt which is only slightly smaller than the previously effective prompt, and then reinforce *any* attempt at responding correctly to this prompt. This is a shaping procedure (described previously) and is often used in combination with prompting and fading. Using shaping for more and more independent performance of a respone is *particularly* necessary with a client who is very dependent upon prompts.

STARTING WITH AN UNNECESSARILY LARGE PROMPT. Since the prompt must eventually be faded out completely, the less prompting that is done initially, the less fading will be necessary. Start with the smallest prompt which is effective in getting the target response to occur. For instance, instead of prompting the client by leading him by the hand into the dining room when the dinner bell rings, the therapist may be able to evoke the same response with only an occasional touch from behind (a smaller prompt). If this is the case, the therapist will have less fading to do.

USING AN INAPPROPRIATE PROMPT OR REINFORCER. When employing a prompting and fading procedure, the prompt which is selected for the individual must truly be effective in getting the target response to occur, i.e. the response should occur at least 90 percent of the time following presentation of the prompt. Similarly, fading will not be successful if the positive reinforcement procedure used in training is not truly effective, i.e. the person will cease performing the response, for instance because the reinforcer is not potent enough or is not presented immediately.

Using a Combination of Shaping, Prompting, and Fading

As mentioned in the previous section, prompting and fading are often used in combination with a shaping procedure. Specifically, a prompt may be successful in evoking a response which initially only approximates the desired target response. This response can then be reinforced. Over several presentations of the prompt, responses which more and more closely resemble the target behavior can be reinforced. Such shaping in the presence of a prompt can be used to avoid the use of large amounts of prompting, and facilitate fading prompts out. For instance, it is common to observe a client requiring extensive prompting to perform an entire, correct response such as writing his name. It is also likely that when prompting is reduced, even slightly, his performance may be disrupted at least somewhat. Rather than back up to full prompting, it is desirable to initially reinforce even a partially incorrect performance which is evoked by the reduced prompt. After this incomplete or incorrect behavior begins to occur consistently, responses will emerge which more closely approximate the desired target behavior. After these are reinforced several times, and occur regularly, responses which even more closely resemble the target behavior will appear. This shaping process will finally result in the emergence of the desired target behavior, which will now occur following a reduced prompt. Next, the prompt can be further diminished and the same shaping procedure can be employed if the reduced prompt initially only evokes an approximation to the desired behavior. In this way, shaping usually improves the possibility of fading out prompts.

Similarly, the success of shaping is often enhanced by combining it with a prompting and fading out procedure. For instance, instead of shaping a student toward sitting in a chair upon entering the classroom, training will probably proceed much more rapidly if prompting is initially employed and then faded out. For instance, the therapist might at first guide the student toward her seat, and then steadily reduce this physical assistance while reinforcing the student for sitting down more and more independently.

In general, shaping, prompting, and fading are typically employed together when teaching a new behavior, i.e. one that occurs infrequently, if at all.

Imitation

One type of prompt described previously consists of modeling, i.e. demonstrating the desired behavior for the client. However, this type of prompt is only useful for persons who imitate. A client is considered to have an imitative skill when he performs responses which are highly similar to behaviors just demonstrated by a model. For instance, if the therapist raises his right hand and the client immediately raises his right hand, and the therapist sits down and the individual then sits, and the therapist says "Ho" and he says "Ho" promptly, the client probably has the skill of imitation. The skill of imitating others can be very useful in teaching a wide variety of appropriate behaviors. Not only can an imitative student benefit from modeling prompts presented by a teacher, but more importantly he can learn from observing others without specifically arranging such training. In fact, it is generally believed that most normal children learn a large portion of their behavior through imitation. However, many retarded persons do not imitate, and must be taught to do so.

Such training should be started by teaching the imitation of a single, simple behavior. First the therapist demonstrates a behavior, for instance, raising his right arm, and says "Do this." Next, he waits for a few seconds to see if the child will perform a similar response. If the client does, he is reinforced with a social and, if necessary, a primary reinforcer. If the child also imitates other demonstrations correctly, he has a general imitative skill which can be used to establish many appropriate behaviors (discussed later). If he does not respond at all correctly, the therapist will have to teach the response with shaping and/or prompting and fading.

With shaping, after the model (the therapist) presents a demonstration, any response which resembles that demonstration is reinforced. For instance, after the therapist raises his arm, he reinforces the person for any response which resembles the therapist's response, e.g. raising the arm partially or waving it. As that approximation begins to occur consistently following his demonstrations of the behavior, the therapist will find that responses which are more similar to the demonstration also begin to occur. When he observes these closer approximations, he reinforces them. After one (or more) closer approximation begins to occur consistently following each demonstration, he stops reinforcing the previous approximation. For instance, while reinforcing the individual for raising his arm halfway following a demonstration of a complete arm extension, the therapist may notice that occasionally the client extends his arm 3/4 of the way up. This behavior is reinforced, but the therapist does not stop reinforcing a half arm-raise until the 3/4 extension has occurred following several demonstrations. When it has, he stops reinforcing the half arm-raise. This procedure is continued: presenting a demonstration, reinforcing a response which is similar to that demonstration, and gradually reinforcing responses which are more and more similar to the therapist's behavior. Finally, only a response which is basically identical to the therapist's demonstration is reinforced.

Prompting is also used in establishing imitation. In this case, the therapist demonstrates the response, and waits to see if the client will imitate it (and if so, reinforces him!). If not, the model (therapist) prompts the response. One type of prompt consists of putting the individual through the response. For instance, if the therapist has just raised his arm, he raises the clients's arm for him, and then reinforces that response. Next, he demonstrates the behavior again.

If necessary, the therapist again raises the client's arm and reinforces him. Gradually, he fades out the prompt, i.e. the amount of physical assistance, while of course, continuing to reinforce the person for correct imitations. For instance, instead of pulling the individual's hand all the way up, the therapist pulls it part of the way, and reinforces the client for completing the behavior. Next, the therapist only aids him in starting the response, then just touches his hand with one finger in an upward motion. If the client's imitations become incorrect while the prompt is being faded, he returns to giving more prompting until correct responding is re-established. Then he begins fading the prompt again, perhaps in smaller steps or more slowly. Finally, he reinforces the individual only when he imitates the demonstration without any extra prompting.

Another type of prompt is verbal. For instance, after the therapist raises his arm and says "Do this," the next prompt the client receives is verbal: "Raise your arm." If the individual responds appropriately, he is reinforced. As the therapist continues to demonstrate the behavior, he gradually fades out the verbal prompt, e.g. by making it softer and softer, or by gradually eliminating words or parts of words. For instance, when the client consistently raises his arm following the therapist's model and the prompt "Raise your arm," next he says "Raise arm" with each demonstration. If the individual continues to respond appropriately, he reduces the prompt further to "Raise." Next, either the therapist stops presenting that prompt with the modeled behavior or fades it out by saying "Ra" and then making it softer and softer. Finally, he reinforces the person only when he imitates the modeled demonstration without any extra prompting. Of course, a verbal prompt will only be useful with clients who can follow verbal instructions.

Prompting and shaping are usually employed together, i.e. responses which more and more closely resemble a correct, independently performed imitation are reinforced, while prompts are gradually faded out. Shaping is useful in establishing a vocal imitation, i.e. a sound or a word. In such cases a physical prompt can also be used as well, for instance by molding the client's lips to make an "O" sound. Prompts which involve putting the individual through the response are often used (in combination with shaping) to establish motor imitations, e.g. raising an arm, stamping a foot, turning in a circle and sitting down.

During imitation training, although an imitative response is reinforced when it immediately follows a model's demonstration, it is never reinforced when it occurs at any other time. For instance, if the client raises his arm more than fifteen seconds after the demonstration, or when the therapist has not yet raised her arm, she is not reinforced.

After one imitative response is established, a second, simple behavior can be trained by the same procedure. Continue training one imitative behavior at a time (and occasionally demonstrate the previously trained imitations, and reinforce the person each time he responds correctly).

After several imitative behaviors are trained, the therapist will notice that it takes less and less time to train each imitation. Finally, he will find that after individual imitative responses have been taught, the client will begin to imitate new behaviors the *first time* they are modeled. When the individual is able to perform many demonstrated behaviors on their first presentation, the person is said to have a general imitative skill. Further, correct imitations which are not reinforced can be maintained (will continue to occur), as along as other imitative responses are reinforced. For instance, while presenting a series of demonstrations which, if imitated, will be reinforced, the therapist can also occasionally present a demonstration to which a correct imitation will not receive reinforcement. Even though this imitation is not reinforced, it will continue to be performed as long as other imitations are reinforced.

The preceding discussion has concerned training a single response as an imitation. In addition, whole sequences of imitative responses can be established after the client has learned the general skill of imitating one response. The therapist can model two responses in sequence, e.g. raising his arm, then stamping his foot; and after the individual performs these two responses, he is reinforced. After the person acquires several two-behavior imitations and begins to imitate two-behavior sequences on their first demonstration, he is ready to learn three-behavior imitations, etc. The general skill of imitating several behaviors in a row is very useful since many appropriate behaviors contain several parts. Handwashing, for instance, involves: turning on the water, wetting hands, picking up the soap, soaping, putting down the soap, rinsing, and drying. In this case, if a client has acquired the general skill of imitating several behaviors in sequence, the model can demonstrate all the behaviors in order and, after the client has performed all of them in a similar fashion, he is reinforced.

Frequently, a response which is initially established as an imitative behavior is eventually trained to occur in other, non-imitative situations. For instance, after establishing the response "My name is John" by imitation, i.e. after the therapist says "My name is John," the client says "My name is John", the model can add an additional cue, and say "What is your name? My name is John." He is then reinforced for imitating both of these sentences. Next, the therapist begins to gradually fade out the words "My name is John," but continues to say "What is your name?" He may make the phrase "My name is John" softer and softer until it is barely audible, then just mouth the words, and finally not present it in any form. The individual continues to be reinforced for saying "My name is John" after the therapist says "What is your name?" If the client begins to respond incorrectly, e.g. begins to imitate "What is your name?" this cue should be presented more softly and the cue "My name is John" should be presented more loudly. After correct responding is reestablished, the latter cue is again faded out. In this way, a response which was initially established as an imitative response is gradually changed to a response to some other cue, for instance an answer to a question, identification of an object, e.g. the person is shown a picture of a cow and says "Cow," or performance of a motor response to a verbal cue, e.g. the client washes his hands when given the cue "Wash your hands".

Thus, the general skill of imitation enables the client to learn new behaviors very quickly, when simply waiting for the response to occur and then reinforcing it would not be successful (because the individual never performs the entire correct response), or without the time required to shape each new response.

Intermittent Schedules of Reinforcement

To this point, the discussion has emphasized reinforcing an appropriate or correct response each time it occurs. This "schedule" of reinforcement is called *continuous reinforcement* (CRF). Continuous reinforcement is always used early in training until a response is well established, i.e. until the client emits the behavior consistently. Then the therapist begins to reinforce the response only occasionally, i.e. on an intermittent schedule of reinforcement. There are four basic intermittent schedules: fixed-ratio (FR), variable-ratio (VR), fixed-interval (FI) and variable-interval (VI).

FIXED-RATIO. The *fixed-ratio schedule* (FR) provides for reinforcement following a fixed or constant number of responses. For instance, with an FR 5 schedule, reinforcement is delivered after every fifth response. Following reinforcement, the therapist waits until the client has completed the target response five more times, then reinforces him again. This process is continued repeatedly.

Each intermittent schedule of reinforcement produces a standard *rate* and *pattern* of responding.* FR schedules typically produce a pause immediately after each reinforcement, followed by a high rate of responding. (This is technically called "break-run" performance.) The larger the FR value, the longer the pause following reinforcement is likely to be. In addition, with larger FR values, the high rate following the pause may be interrupted by further brief pausing. This is technically called *ratio strain*. Generally if these breaks begin to occur, the FR is considered too large and should be reduced. In general, if the therapist wants the target behavior to occur at a high rate, often with a pause after reinforcement, he uses an FR schedule. For instance, if he wants students in a workshop program to take a break following reinforcement, e.g. receiving money after soldering twenty wires, then he should reinforce soldering on an FR schedule.

VARIABLE-RATIO. The *variable-ratio schedule* (VR) provides for reinforcement following a number of responses which changes from reinforcement to reinforcement, usually randomly. The number which is the average of all the different ratios, is used in identifying the schedule, e.g. a VR 10 schedule

---

*The characteristic patterns of behavior described under each intermittent schedule have been discovered in research with nonhumans. Other experiments have shown that humans may respond in slightly different ways under these schedules, but additional research is needed to clarify these differences.

means that, on the *average*, reinforcement is provided for every tenth response, but that sometimes more than ten and sometimes less than ten responses will be required for reinforcement. For example, if one wants to arrange a VR 5 schedule, he first arranges a list which is similar (but not necessarily identical) to the following:

First reinforcement:	after one response
Second reinforcement:	after seven responses
Third reinforcement:	after five responses
Fourth reinforcement:	after nine responses
Fifth reinforcement:	after two responses
Sixth reinforcement:	after eight responses
Seventh reinforcement:	after three responses
Eighth reinforcement:	after four responses
Ninth reinforcement:	after six responses

Then, the average is computed by adding all the numbers together and dividing the sum (in this case, 45) by the number of items in the list (in this case, 9).

$$\frac{45 \text{ responses}}{9} = 5 \text{ (the average number of responses emitted before reinforcement)}$$

If the average does not at least approximately equal the desired VR value, some of the numbers in the list can be changed, and the average computed again. After constructing a list that does average the desired value, the therapist follows it when reinforcing the client. In the above example, the first reinforcer is delivered after the individual has emitted the target behavior once, again after he has performed the target response seven times, and then following the fifth target behavior, etc. After completing the list, the therapist begins this same procedure again.

In many cases, a written list does not need to be constructed. A teacher can simply reinforce the student after differing numbers of target responses and informally try to keep the VR schedule near a certain average. This is, of course, much more convenient, and often just as effective.

There are two major guidelines for constructing a VR schedule;

1. The client should be unable to predict which ratio is next. There should be a sufficient number of ratios in the list, and/or the order of the ratios should be rearranged occasionally to prevent the client from learning the sequence. Further, there should be no pattern to the distribution of ratios, e.g. an increasing order, or long ratios always followed by short ratios.

2. Extreme ratio values, and many ratio values of a similar size should be avoided. For instance, do not construct a VR 10 schedule with nine ratios of one response each, and one ratio with ninety-one responses.

VR schedules also produce a characteristic rate and pattern of behavior. Under this schedule, responding continues at a very high rate with little or no pausing. If the client is not able to detect how many responses will be required for each reinforcement, he will respond at a high rate, even immediately following delivery of a reinforcer. Therefore, if the therapist wants the target behavior to occur at a very high rate with no pausing, he should use a VR schedule. For instance, if he wants students to perform a workshop assembling task very rapidly and consistently, he reinforces them (with, for instance, money) on a VR schedule.

FIXED-INTERVAL SCHEDULE. A *fixed-interval schedule* (FI) provides for delivery of a reinforcer for the first target response which occurs after a specified interval of time has elapsed. For instance, with an FI five-minute (FI 5-min) schedule, reinforcement is delivered following the first response which occurs after five minutes have passed since the last reinforcement. Responses which occur before this period of time do not "count," i.e. only the first response after the fixed period of time has elapsed earns reinforcement.

One of two patterns of responding are often observed under an FI schedule. Responding may temporarily cease following the delivery of a reinforcer and then gradually increase until it is occurring at a high rate at the time the reinforcer is delivered. (This is called the *fixed-interval scallop* because of the picture this pattern of responding makes on a cumulative recorder, an automatic recording device used primarily in laboratories.) Alternatively, the individual may simply not respond until after the time interval has elapsed, then responds once (or a few times) and receives his reinforcer. This is technically called a *low-rate solution*. The latter pattern is perhaps more likely seen with clients who develop a way of marking the passage of time, for instance by counting out the seconds between reinforcement. The client simply learns that responses occurring before a certain time interval has elapsed will not be reinforced, and that after the passage of this interval, only one response is required for reinforcement. He therefore does not respond until it seems that the interval has elapsed, then responds until his reinforcer is delivered. Therefore, if the therapist wants the target behavior to only occur after a fixed period of time elapses, or to begin to occur more and more frequently as the time for reinforcement draws closer, he should use an FI schedule. For instance, if one wants a person to take his own medicine every two hours, he places the medicine in a specified cup after the two hours has elapsed and reinforces the client for checking the cup for his pill and consuming it. The client will gradually learn to only check the cup as the two hours draw to a close, and may become so skilled that he will not check it at all until the time has just elapsed.

VARIABLE-INTERVAL SCHEDULE. A *variable-interval schedule* (VI) provides for reinforcement for the first response which occurs after a period of time has elapsed since the last reinforcement, and this time period is changed from one reinforcement to the next. The name of a VI schedule denotes the average duration of the intervals employed. For instance, with a VI five-minute schedule (VI 5-min), reinforcement is delivered following the first response which occurs after an average of five minutes. To accomplish this, a list is often arranged similar to the following:

First reinforcement:	for first response after an interval of six minutes.
Second reinforcement:	for first response after two minutes.
Third reinforcement:	for first response after three minutes.

Fourth reinforcement:	for first response after ten minutes.
Fifth reinforcement:	for first response after one minute.
Sixth reinforcement:	for first response after seven minutes.
Seventh reinforcement:	for first response after three minutes.
Eighth reinforcement:	for first response after twelve minutes.
Ninth reinforcement:	for first response after five minutes.
Tenth reinforcement:	for first response after one minute.

Next, the average is computed by adding all the numbers together and dividing the sum (in this case, fifty minutes) by the number of items in the list (in this case, ten).

$$\frac{50 \text{ minutes}}{10} = 5 \text{ (the average number of minutes which elapse before reinforcement)}$$

If the answer does not equal the desired VI average, some of the numbers can be changed in the list and the average computed again. After constructing a list that does average the desired VI value, the therapist follows it when reinforcing the client's target response.

In the example above, the first reinforcement is delivered for the first target response occurring after six minutes have elapsed; the second reinforcement follows the first response after another two minutes have passed since the first reinforcement. In this way, the therapist proceeds down the list reinforcing each response after the prescribed period of time has passed. After completing the list, he starts over.

In many cases, a written list need not be constructed. A therapist can reinforce a target response after differing periods of time, and informally try to keep the VI schedule near a certain average.

There are two major guidelines for constructing a VI schedule:

1. The individual should be unable to predict how long an interval of time must pass before the response is reinforced. (See a more complete description of this guideline under VR schedules.)

2. Extreme interval values, and many intervals of the same size should be avoided. For instance, a VI ten-minute schedule should not be constructed with nine intervals of one minute each, and one interval in which ninety-one minutes must pass before a response is reinforced.

As with the other schedules, the VI schedule produces a characteristic rate and pattern of responding. A target response which is reinforced on a VI schedule will be emitted at a moderate, steady rate. As with the VR schedule, if the client is not able to predict when the next reinforcement is due, he will continue to respond steadily, even after the delivery of a reinforcer. However, he responds at a lower rate than with the VR schedule. Therefore, if the therapist wants the target behavior to occur at a moderate rate with no prolonged pausing, he uses a VI schedule. For instance, if it is desirable for students to work consistently on arithmetic problems through a study hour, correct answers should be reinforced on a VI schedule. VI schedules are by far the most widely used because many behaviors are considered most appropriate when they occur at a moderate, steady rate.

Two rules must be followed when using any intermittent schedule:

1. After establishing the target behavior by reinforcing it on a CRF schedule, the therapist gradually increases either the length of time before a response is reinforced (if using a ratio schedule) or the length of time before a response is reinforced (if using an interval schedule). For instance, the therapist does not jump from CRF to an FR 150 schedule. Instead, he gradually increases the number of responses required for reinforcement. For instance, after reinforcing on a CRF schedule, he increases the requirement to an FR 2 and reinforces every other response until the client is responding satisfactorily on this schedule. Next, the therapist might increase the FR value to 3, and deliver a reinforcer after every third response. After deliv-

ering a few reinforcers on this schedule, the therapist might increase the schedule to an FR 5, then FR 10, etc. This process of increasing the schedule value, i.e. either increasing the number of responses required for reinforcement in ratio schedules or increasing the amount of time that must pass before a response is reinforced in interval schedules is technically called *thinning* the schedule. The size of each increase and how long the therapist spends on one step (i.e. how many reinforcers he delivers under a particular schedule value) depends on the situation. For instance, if the therapist is gradually increasing the number of completed arithmetic problems that are required for reinforcement, he might find that within five 1-hour class periods, the student is able to move from a CRF schedule (in which a reinforcer is given for the correct completion of each problem) to an FR 15 (in which a reinforcer is delivered following correct completion of fifteen arithmetic problems). The student's behavior must be the therapist's guide. If the target behavior is not reinforced for lengthy periods because it does not occur often enough, then it will decrease and may stop completely. If the therapist notices such a decrease while the reinforcement schedule is being thinned, he should back up and begin to make reinforcement available for a smaller number of responses (ratio schedule), or for a response occurring after a shorter period of time (interval schedule). After responding is re-established, the therapist begins again to thin the schedule, with a smaller increase in each step and/or a longer time at each step.

2. The schedule should be thinned to a point that maintains the rate and pattern of behavior that is desirable. Clearly, the less frequently the target behavior must be reinforced to be maintained, the more convenient the program will be to administer. On the other hand, reinforcement must be frequent enough to maintain the response at the proper rate. For instance, if the therapist is reinforcing a child for playing cooperatively with others, and gradually increasing the time between reinforcements on a VI schedule, the therapist may observe that an average interval of more than ten minutes will not maintain

the desired rate and pattern of behavior. For instance, instead of maintaining a moderate rate of cooperation with few or no pauses, the child may play alone and do other things which are not considered cooperative play. In this case, it would be appropriate to reduce the schedule to a shorter value, e.g. seven or eight minutes. In short, although the therapist can gradually change the schedule so that the target behavior is reinforced only intermittently, there is a point beyond which further thinning of the schedule will weaken the response that the therapist wishes to maintain. That point will differ with each individual, the target behavior, and the situation, and must be determined by simply thinning the schedule until the behavior appears to be decreasing to an undesirable level, then back up to a value which will maintain the appropriate behavior.

As mentioned previously, the therapist need not construct a written list of either number of responses required or amount of time which must elapse before a response is reinforced. Rather, the therapist can reinforce the target behavior according to an approximate average. Three guidelines should be followed when deciding which alternative to use:

1. If the teachers are not trained in the use of intermittent schedules, and are likely to either reinforce the behavior more or less often than is desirable, or are likely to either thin the schedule too rapidly or in steps which are too large, then a written schedule should be constructed including: the size of each increase to new schedule values, approximately how long to reinforce on each step, and the list constituting the final schedule.

2. Even with trained teachers, these written instructions are often useful in achieving consistency between therapists. For instance, if a child is being reinforced intermittently for cooperative play on first shift in a cottage, the second shift staff may not follow the same schedule without a clearly stated, if not written, account of the details of the schedule.

3. Reinforcing a target behavior on the basis of a written schedule can be complicated and awkward. The teacher may not be able to perform other duties while following a precise

schedule. Thus, if teachers can be adequately trained in the use of intermittent schedules, and a way of achieving consistency between trainers can be established, written schedules should not be necessary.

As mentioned, intermittent schedules are more convenient and economical than CRF. Their *primary* importance, however, lies in their effect on a person's behavior. After a behavior has been reinforced on an intermittent schedule (*particularly* a VR or VI schedule), it is likely that the client will continue to perform that behavior under conditions in which reinforcement is delivered very infrequently, if at all. Individuals will most certainly not remain in an environment in which each and every appropriate response is reinforced. If the therapist has used only CRF in reinforcing a target behavior, the client will quickly stop performing that behavior if reinforcement is not presented for every response. If, on the other hand, the schedule has been gradually thinned to only occasional reinforcement, the response will persist during periods of little or no reinforcement. In short, intermittent reinforcement results in a behavior that is highly durable under conditions of nonreinforcement. Technically, the procedure of not presenting a reinforcer following a behavior, is called "extinction." Behavior reinforced on a continuous schedule is not resistant to extinction, i.e. it will quickly cease when reinforcement is stopped. Behavior reinforced on an intermittent schedule is very resistant to extinction, i.e. it will continue for some time even if reinforcement is discontinued.

Not only are intermittent schedules useful in maintaining an increased target behavior, but they can explain why a behavior (appropriate or inappropriate) is maintained even though the therapist does not observe it being reinforced each time it occurs. For instance, if an individual hangs on and continually says inappropriate things to strangers, and he observes most strangers ignoring him, intermittent schedules may provide the answer as to why the client continues to emit this behavior. Every once in a while a stranger reinforces the client's pestering by, for instance, paying attention to him. In some cases, the behavior is reinforced so infrequently that the therapist might conclude that he is not being reinforced at all. A closer, longer observation will reveal that this is not the case. He is being reinforced intermittently by something or someone, or he would not continue emitting the behavior.

Combinations and Variations of Positive Reinforcement Procedures

Although the basic principles and procedures of positive reinforcement have been discussed, these are increasingly being employed in novel combinations. New methods of teaching appropriate behavior appear in the literature continuously; however, the following is a description of several of the better known procedures.

CONTINGENCY CONTRACTS. When dealing with individuals who demonstrate some language skills, teachers may find it helpful to arrange a written contract specifying the following: a description of the appropriate target behavior, the consequences for engaging in that behavior, and (when necessary), a description of an inappropriate behavior and its consequences. Sample contracts appear below:

> Each time Johnny Smith is in his seat within five minutes after the recess bell sounds, he will earn a star by his name. When he has earned three stars, he may be first in line for the next lunch.

> Susie Jones will earn two dollars for each pound she loses. If she does not lose any weight during a seven-day week, she must pay her mother four dollars. She must pay four dollars for each pound she gains.

> Mark Stevens will earn five minutes of recess time for each arithmetic problem he completes correctly. If he gets all problems right, he can hand out papers at the end of the arithmetic period.

> Tad Chapin can wear his watch as long as he keeps his glasses on. If he removes his glasses, his mother will take his watch for ten minutes. She will return his watch after he has worn his glasses for at least ten minutes.

Such contingency contracts are usually arrived at in a conference between teacher (or parent) and the student. Although their effectiveness does not depend upon the individual's participation in designing the contract, such involvement may in itself be a valuable educational experience for the student.

A contingency contract can be helpful in modifying behavior. However, it is critical that the teacher follow through with "promised" consequences for both appropriate and inappropriate behavior. For instance, the contingency contract can be read to the student at the start of each class, and then the teacher should actually use those contingencies throughout the remainder of the day. In short, contingency contracts are not intended to *replace* positive reinforcement or other consequences, but to state the rules clearly to the individual whose behavior needs changing.

It should be stressed that although contingency contracts may be helpful in changing behavior, they are not necessary. The procedures described in this book can be effective even if they are not described to the individual receiving treatment, or if that student does not know they are being used. For instance, they are successful with the severely and profoundly retarded individuals for whom verbal instructions may be meaningless.

GROUP CONSEQUENCES. When dealing with a group of individuals, a teacher may use group consequences. In this case, whether or not an individual student receives a consequence (such as a positive reinforcer) depends upon the behavior of the entire group. The "good behavior game" is an example of such group consequences. (Barrish, Saunders, and Wolf, 1969). A class was divided into two teams, and any instance of either talking out or out-of-seat behavior by any member of a team was marked on the board under that team's listing. The team with the smaller number of marks was awarded privileges such as lining up first and extra recess. Similarly, a consequence could be arranged in which the entire group receives a snack when the play area is cleaned up. In this case, an individual need not respond appropriately, i.e. help with clean up, but still may share in reinforcement so long as one or more other members of the group completes the job correctly.

Although group consequences have been used almost exclusively with normal individuals, they may prove equally effective with mildly and moderately retarded persons. They may not be useful with individuals who demonstrate few social or language skills, but little is currently known about their effects in these cases.

The major advantage of group consequences is that they may enlist the aid of peers in establishing and maintaining appropriate behavior of group members. However, when individuals within the group try to influence other members to respond appropriately so that all may receive reinforcement, care must be taken to insure that such persuasion is humane. Clearly, beating up a team member is an unacceptable method of peer control!

The chief disadvantage of group consequences is that the appropriate behavior of individuals within the group may not be reinforced because of misbehavior by peers. An individual may not receive reinforcement no matter how appropriately he responds, and thus his desirable behavior will decrease or cease. In this case, group consequences are neither effective nor fair. If one or more members of the group repeatedly prevents others from earning reinforcement, the misbehaving student may need to be removed from the group consequence program, and placed on an individual regime. A similar question of fairness is raised when certain events are used as group consequences. For instance, many would object to using academic grades as a group consequence. Similarly, major privileges, e.g. trips to the Ice Capades and other highly prized reinforcers such as a week's salary are often considered more appropriate for use in individual contingencies where an individual's ability to earn reinforcement rests solely on his own behavior. Nonessential, "small" privileges which are available more frequently are generally judged more appropriate for use in group consequences.

FEEDBACK, PRACTICE, and REASONING. As mentioned previously, teaching appropriate behavior is often best accomplished by a combination of procedures. In addition to combining positive reinforcement, shaping, and prompting, several other techniques are often also employed to teach desirable target behavior.

1. Feedback: A specific behavioral description of the appro-

priate (or inappropriate) behavior the student has just displayed; for instance: "Steve, you finished your arithmetic assignment in only five minutes."

2. Practice: A period of time in which the client rehearses the appropriate behavior, for example, "Please show me how you hang up your coat when you come into class. Good, now let's practice that one more time." When the person is practicing, the therapist should always provide positive reinforcement for any correct responding or approximations to appropriate behavior, as well as feedback for incorrect behavior.

3. Reasoning: A discussion of *why* a behavior is desirable (or why a behavior is inappropriate). This often includes a description of possible natural consequences of either action; for instance: "When you learn to go to the bathroom and not have accidents, everyone will enjoy being around you more and you can go to class in the school building."

These three techniques are often combined with prompting (such as verbal instructions and modeling), contingency contracts, and, of course, positive reinforcement procedures. In fact, the teaching instruction developed and described by the Achievement Place Research Project (Phillips, Phillips, Fixen and Wolf, 1974) consists of all of these and other components.

These techniques are intended to teach appropriate behavior, either during the individual's regular schedule, e.g. while he is in class, and/or during specially arranged sessions. For instance, if a student needs to learn to follow instructions, the teacher may find it most effective to conduct two or three intensive teaching sessions each day on this skill. (In addition to reinforcing appropriate instruction following at other times.) It is also possible to employ these (and other) procedures as a consequence for *inappropriate* behavior. For instance, immediately after a student tears a book, he can be prompted to practice appropriate use of materials, and be given feedback and reinforcement for doing so correctly. (A more thorough description of the use of these techniques for decreasing inappropriate behavior appears in the next chapter under Contingent Education.)

INCREASING BEHAVIOR BY
NEGATIVE REINFORCEMENT

A second method to increase an appropriate target behavior is called *negative reinforcement.* Negative reinforcement involves increasing the strength of a response by removing or postponing a stimulus (a negative reinforcer) contingent on the occurrence of that response. A negative reinforcer is an event (stimulus) which when removed or postponed immediately following a response increases the strength of that response. By an increase in strength is meant that it increases the number, rate, percent, duration, or amount of the behavior; in general, it increases the likelihood that the response will reoccur. Negative reinforcers are events (stimuli) which in casual conversation are sometimes called "unpleasant," "aversive," or "painful." They are events which the client will work to turn off, get away from, or avoid.

There are two negative reinforcement procedures: one provides for removal of (escape from) the stimulus contingent on the response (the *escape procedure*), and one involves postponement (avoidance) of the stimulus contingent on the target response (the *avoidance procedure*).

Escape Procedure

In this case, the negative reinforcer is presented to the individual, and when the person emits the appropriate target behavior, the negative reinforcer is immediately removed (turned off). Later, it is again turned on, and the individual must again perform the target response to escape the stimulus. For instance, if one has a toothache, any response, e.g. taking aspirin, which alleviates the pain (negative reinforcer) will be more likely to reoccur in the future when a toothache reoccurs. In short, taking aspirin is increased in strength because it removes (escapes) the negative reinforcer (toothache). Similarly, a child's crying is an unpleasant sound to many adults. A response which removes the crying, for instance handing the child a cookie, will tend to reoccur when the child cries again. Technically, the adult's response of feeding the crying child cookies is strengthened by turning off (escaping) the crying and will be more likely to be repeated when the child cries in the future. (The child's crying behavior is probably being increased by positive reinforcement, i.e. cookies contingent on crying).

In summary, the escape procedure involves the removal of a negative reinforcer contingent on a response with a resulting increase in the strength of the response. To use the escape procedure, the therapist first finds a stimulus which he thinks may be unpleasant (yet harmless) to the client. Next, he presents the stimulus, and if the desired target response is emitted, immediately turns the stimulus off. After doing this repeatedly, if the response increases and begins to occur dependably, that stimulus is a negative reinforcer and the response is being increased in strength by negative reinforcement. In short, it is not possible to determine if a stimulus is a negative reinforcer until the procedure is used consistently for a period of time.

Avoidance Procedure

In this case, the target response postpones (avoids) the negative reinforcer. If the target response occurs, the stimulus is not presented for a certain amount of time; if the response is *not* performed, the negative reinforcer is presented. Each target response postpones (avoids) the negative reinforcer for a period of time. For instance, if the response occurs, delivery of the negative reinforcer is delayed five minutes. Any occurrence of the target behavior during that five minutes again delays presentation of the negative reinforcer by five minutes. However, the client cannot accumulate time, e.g. he cannot respond ten times in rapid succession and avoid the negative reinforcer for a full fifty minutes; he must perform the target response at least once every five minutes. Avoidance procedures operate frequently in the "real world." For instance, paying bills is negatively reinforced by *avoiding* repossession and loss of utilities such as electricity. Observing posted speed limits is often negatively reinforced by avoidance of tickets. Similarly, receiving immunization may avoid contracting diseases, and thus an individual may consistently seek such medication.

In summary, the avoidance procedure involves the postponement of a negative reinforcer contingent on a response, with a resulting increase in the strength of that response. To use the avoidance procedure, the therapist first selects a stimulus which he thinks is unpleasant (yet harmless) to the client. Next, he decides how frequently the stimulus will be presented if the target response does *not* occur. Then, he presents the stimulus on that schedule *unless* the target response occurs. If the response does occur, it should delay the presentation of the event by a certain amount of time. After doing this repeatedly, if the response increases and begins to occur reliably, the stimulus which the response avoids is a negative reinforcer, and the response is being increased by negative reinforcement. The therapist cannot determine if a stimulus is a negative reinforcer until the procedure is used consistently for a period of time.

Unconditioned and Conditioned Negative Reinforcers

Just as with positive reinforcement, there are two types of negative reinforcers: unconditioned and conditioned.* An *unconditioned negative reinforcer* is an event which increases the strength of a response which escapes or avoids it, without previous experience with that event. Electric shock, and probably spanking are examples of unconditioned negative reinforcers. *Conditioned negative reinforcers* are stimuli which can be used to increase the strength of an escape or avoidance response after being paired with an unconditioned negative reinforcer, or perhaps with a previously established conditioned negative reinforcer. For instance, verbal reprimands and frowning are probably neutral stimuli (they have no effect on behavior) until they are paired with an unconditioned negative reinforcer. In pairing, the neutral stimulus is presented just before presenting the unconditioned negative reinforcer e.g. a spanking. After repeated pairings the unconditioned negative reinforcer need

---

*For a more complete description of unconditioned and conditioned reinforcement, and how to establish a conditioned reinforcer, see section on positive reinforcement earlier in this chapter.

not be presented every time; the newly established conditioned negative reinforcer can be used to *maintain* a previously increased response, or *increase* (establish) a new escape or avoidance behavior. Of course, the conditioned negative reinforcer must occasionally be re-paired with an unconditioned negative reinforcer (or with a previously established conditioned negative reinforcer) if it is to remain effective.

As stressed previously, the therapist must use negative reinforcement with a client to see if it is effective in increasing the occurrence of a response. Some commonly effective negative reinforcers include: verbal reprimands, e.g. "That's bad," other expressions of disapproval, e.g. frowns and shaking one's head, spanking (not allowed in some public institutions), or withdrawal of a positive reinforcer, e.g. taking a child's toy away (explained in the next chapter under Punishment). Negative reinforcement is not frequently used when designing a treatment program to increase an appropriate target behavior. Positive reinforcement is usually considered less traumatic, often equally effective and more publicly acceptable.

The escape procedure is used most commonly when a client has been excluded from an activity following an inappropriate behavior. (This is a "time-out" procedure and will be described more fully later.) Frequently, the individual is released from his room or chair and allowed to return to the activity, only after he has behaved appropriately for a certain period of time. In this case, the client can escape the negative reinforcer (social isolation) by engaging in the appropriate response of sitting quietly. (Of course, by being allowed to return to an activity, the person is probably also receiving positive reinforcement for being quiet.) The escape procedure may also be used by allowing a person to, for instance, leave class after completing an assignment or go outside after making his bed. Again, positive reinforcement may also contribute to an increase in the appropriate behavior in these examples. Further, some individuals who dislike being touched or helped may learn to perform a skill such as a housekeeping or self-help task by escaping the prompt of being put through the behavior.

Often, avoidance is used in combination with positive reinforcement. For example, the individual is praised if he comes when called (positive reinforcement), and reprimanded if he does not (negative reinforcement). Probably such a combination of procedures is more effective than either alone. Similarly, a student can be positively reinforced for behaving appropriately in class, and scolded, sent to the principal, or kept after class if he does not.

In addition to its therapeutic use, negative reinforcement can account for an increase or maintenance of undesirable behavior. When a teacher dismisses an unruly class, a parent gives a tantruming child a cookie, or a therapist stops a training session because a child is not being cooperative, the adults' behavior is probably being strengthened by negative reinforcement. In each case, the adult's behavior, e.g. of dismissing the class, is reinforced by escaping the unpleasant situation. Unfortunately, such procedures *also* reinforce inappropriate behavior by clients. For instance, rowdiness and uncooperativeness may be reinforced by being allowed to escape class or a training session (negative reinforcement) and therefore being able to engage in more enjoyable activities (positive reinforcement). Similarly, having a tantrum may be positively reinforced by a cookie. Thus, a "vicious cycle" is established; the teacher *and* student are being reinforced for inappropriate behavior, and the problem worsens. In cases such as this, the teacher must recognize that her escape and/or avoidance behavior is responsible for her student's inappropriate responding, and stop "giving in." Hopefully, improvement in the student's performance will positively reinforce the teacher's efforts!

INCREASING BEHAVIOR BY DISCONTINUING A PROCEDURE WHICH IS SUPPRESSING THE TARGET BEHAVIOR

In addition to positive or negative reinforcement, a third method for increasing an appropriate target behavior involves stopping a procedure which is suppressing the target behavior.

Later in this book several procedures will be described which can be used to decrease undesirable behavior. In cottages, classrooms, and homes, those surrounding the individual may inadvertently use one of these techniques with an *appropriate* behavior, and thus accidentally reduce its occurrence. Although a detailed description awaits the next section, several situations should be checked if an appropriate target behavior is emitted infrequently.

1. The individual is punished for the appropriate response: The therapist may notice that the client does emit the desirable behavior, but it is often followed by an unpleasant event. For instance, if he wants the child to play with toys more frequently, he might observe that occasionally the child does, but that frequently another child interrupts his play by pushing him away or hitting him. In this case, toy play may be increased simply by preventing the aggressor from hurting the child when playing.

2. The individual is positively reinforced for *not* performing the appropriate response: The therapist may notice that the client is more likely to be positively reinforced when he is *not* performing the target response than when he is. For instance, if the child rarely plays with toys independently, the therapist may observe that the parents pay more attention to him when he is sitting in the corner and *not* playing, than when he is playing. Often, untrained teachers reason that a person is "alright" and does not "need attention" when he is behaving appropriately, and thus only attend to him when he is emitting an undesirable response. An appropriate target behavior can sometimes be increased by stopping positive reinforcement for the undesirable behavior (in this case, sitting in a corner) *and* at the same time presenting it following the appropriate response (playing with a toy).

3. The individual is not given the opportunity to perform the appropriate response: The therapist may notice that the client is never put in a situation which requires that he emit the target response. For instance, if it is said that the person never puts on his own shirt, the therapist may observe that the staff always dresses him, and does not give him an opportunity

to put on a shirt by himself. Similarly, if the student has never answered questions in class, perhaps it is because he has a hearing loss, and the cue used with other students (such as "Tell me the time") is not appropriate to his physical capabilities. In cases such as these, the staff may only need to provide an appropriate opportunity, e.g. hand the individual the shirt, tell him to put it on, and then give him enough time to do so, or present a different, nonauditory cue, and he may perform the response or an approximation to it. He can then be reinforced, and a start made on increasing the occurrence of the response. Further, if a client is heavily medicated, he may be physically incapable of performing the response. A physician may be able to safely change medication to allow the client to behave in a more or less active manner. He may then emit behavior that no one suspected he had learned.

The preceding sections involve procedures for increasing a single response. Another technique, called *chaining* is employed to increase a complex behavior which is composed of many parts. This procedure is described later. Do not try to read it before reading Chapter 9, which deals with stimulus control.

REFERENCES

Barrish, H. H., Saunders, M. and Wolf, M. M.: Good behavior game: effects of individual contingencies for group consequences on disruptive behavior in a classroom. *Journal of Applied Behavior Analysis, 2*:119-124, 1969.

Phillips, E. L., Phillips, E. A., Fixen, D. L. and Wolf, M. M.: *The Teaching Family Handbook*, University of Kansas Printing Service, 1974 (revised).

Chapter 7

SELECTING AND APPLYING THE
TREATMENT PROCEDURE:
DECREASING BEHAVIOR

THE preceding chapter has discussed methods of increasing behavior which is considered appropriate and desirable. In some cases, treatment is also aimed at *decreasing* a behavior which is considered inappropriate and undesirable. Such behavior often consists of self-stimulation, aggression, self-injury, destruction of property, and other disruptive and dangerous acts. *Decreasing* means reducing the chance that the individual will perform the undesirable behavior in the future. For instance, the objective is *not* to interrupt the child's tantrum once he has started it, but to decrease the chance that he will even *start* to tantrum in the future. Some procedures that untrained teachers use to interrupt an inappropriate behavior, e.g. giving a cookie to a child having a tantrum, may stop that tantrum but *increase* the likelihood that the undesirable behavior will reoccur in the future.

The selection of a technique to decrease behavior must be done with caution. As will be discussed more fully in the latter portion of this chapter, such procedures differ widely in terms of effectiveness and appropriateness with certain individuals and behavior problems, ease of staff training and supervision, practicality, "normalcy," and extent of disruption to a client's overall program. Further, a great deal of professional, public, and legal discussion is currently directed toward using procedures which are most benign, i.e. least traumatic to the individual receiving treatment, most publicly and ethically acceptable, and least susceptible to abuse.

There is not universal agreement among professionals or nonprofessionals as to the relative severity, acceptability, and

118

danger associated with each treatment procedure. Nevertheless, the author has arranged the array of procedures to decrease behavior on the basis of *her interpretation* of current moral and legal thinking concerning which procedures are generally considered to be more, or less, restrictive and severe. Thus, the first techniques described are usually considered benign, publicly and ethically acceptable, and least susceptible to abuse and should therefore be considered first when attempting to decrease a behavior problem. The procedures presented later are usually employed only if less drastic techniques have proven ineffective and if the behavior problem is severe. An ordering of this type is necessarily imperfect, and will not elicit agreement by all professionals and nonprofessionals. Further, it risks misleading the student of behavior modification. These procedures have been ranked on grounds other than effectiveness in treating a behavior problem. Thus, the procedures discussed first are *not necessarily* the most effective; they are instead viewed as the most widely accepted for moral and ethical reasons. In addition, this sequencing of procedures *does not* mean that the effectiveness of techniques described later depends upon first implementing procedures appearing earlier in this chapter. The effectiveness of the most severe procedure, i.e. shock punishment, does not rely upon the prior use of, for instance time-out or overcorrection (less severe procedures).

An exception to this is the use of the first several procedures presented in this chapter. As will be emphasized, procedures such as positive reinforcement for appropriate behavior and discontinuation of reinforcement for inappropriate responding should be part of any program to decrease undesirable behavior, even if another more severe technique must also be employed.

Thus, when beginning a program to decrease an individual's behavior problem, the individual should first be placed in an environment which is as physically and socially stimulating as possible and in which positive reinforcement is available for appropriate responding. When an individual is provided with educational and play materials, can participate in a variety of activities, and receives attention and other forms of positive reinforcement for behaving appropriately, the necessity for instituting a program to decrease undesirable behavior may be reduced. Even when such an environment is not effective by itself in preventing or decreasing a behavior problem, it is usually considered a prerequisite step to instituting a program specifically designed to decrease undesirable behavior.

DECREASING BEHAVIOR BY EXTINCTION (NONREINFORCEMENT)

The procedure of extinction consists of discontinuing reinforcement of a behavior. For instance, while taking baseline on crying and whining, the therapist might notice that often when the client cries, a staff member approaches that individual and comforts him, e.g. hugs him or gives him a cookie. These events (hugging and giving cookies) are often positive reinforcers. Thus, although such comforting may temporarily stop this crying while the client consumes the cookie, the crying response will be more likely to reoccur in the future and the individual will begin crying and whining frequently. Simply stopping positive reinforcement (comforting) for crying may be effective in decreasing its occurrence. In this case, it is said that "the behavior is put on extinction," or that "the behavior is being extinguished."

Many events are positive reinforcers, and thus may be used inadvertently to strengthen an inappropriate behavior. Some of these are:

1. Material reinforcers, e.g. food and tokens.
2. Privileges and activities, e.g. access to games, toys, trips, and the playground.
3. Attention, e g. hugs, touching, and smiles. Since attention can take many forms, some therapists are surprised to find that simply looking at the client (even momentarily) can be a positive reinforcer. In addition, attention in the form of scoldings, frowning, holding the individual firmly, shaking, or sometimes even spanking can be positive reinforcers and strengthen an inappropriate behavior that it follows.

If any of the above are observed to follow the inappropriate behavior (even intermittently), they may be increasing or maintaining that behavior. If the extinction procedure is used, none of these events should be presented following the undesirable behavior.

Several factors must be considered before employing the extinction procedure.

1. After an extinction procedure is begun, the inappropriate behavior often *increases* temporarily before it declines. ("The problem gets worse before it gets better".) This increase is only temporary, perhaps lasting a few minutes or a few days, but if the inappropriate behavior is highly destructive or disruptive to the client or others around him, this temporary increase may not be safe or acceptable.

In addition, as the inappropriate behavior decreases, it often increases again at the start of each session. For instance, if the therapist is using extinction with an undesirable behavior which occurs in the dayroom, he may observe an increase in the behavior when the individual is first placed in the dayroom, *even though it was occurring very infrequently during the time in which he was previously in the dayroom.* Similarly, if he is using extinction for an inappropriate behavior which occurs throughout the day, he may notice that the behavior will steadily decline one day, but may occur frequently the next morning before beginning to decrease again. This is called *spontaneous recovery.* When the extinction procedure is used consistently, these spurts of inappropriate responses will become shorter and shorter, and will finally disappear.

2. The effectiveness of the extinction procedure depends directly on whether the therapist can *identify,* and then *control* the positive reinforcer maintaining the inappropriate behavior.

In some cases, even after extensive observations, the therapist simply will not be able to guess what reinforcers might be maintaining the behavior. Of course, if he cannot identify the reinforcer, he cannot withhold it following the inappropriate behavior.

At other times, even if the therapist identifies one (or several) possible reinforcers, he may not be able to control its occurrence following the inappropriate behavior. For instance, he may be certain that the reinforcer maintaining a client's aggession is the crying of the person receiving the aggression. In most cases, however, he cannot tell the recipient not to cry when attacked. Similarly, he may suspect that an individual's aggression is being strengthened by a trainer rushing over and pulling the aggressor away. However, one cannot ask the trainer to allow the victim to be hurt while the trainer ignores the behavior.

3. If the inappropriate behavior has been reinforced on an intermittent schedule, it will be very "resistant to extinction." (See the section on intermittent schedules of reinforcement in Chapter 6 for a complete description.) In short, it will continue for a long period under conditions in which it is no longer reinforced. In this case, the procedure of extinction will require a very long time to take effect (decrease the behavior), even if it is conducted consistently and properly. Similarly, if the extinction procedure is run inconsistently, i.e. on some occasions the response is not reinforced, and sometimes it is, this schedule of intermittent reinforcement may prolong the problem further, if not *make it worse!*

After weighing these factors, even if the therapist decides not to employ extinction as the main procedure, it should always be a part of *any* procedure that he selects to reduce an inappropriate behavior. When using one of the other methods for decreasing behavior, if the behavior continues to be reinforced, the therapist will have great difficulty in achieving the desired effect. In short, he should *always* try to identify and discontinue positive reinforcement for an inappropriate behavior ("put it on extinction") regardless of what other procedures are being used to reduce the occurrence of the behavior.

DECREASING BEHAVIOR BY DIFFERENTIAL REINFORCEMENT OF INCOMPATIBLE APPROPRIATE BEHAVIOR (DRI)*

A second procedure for decreasing an inappropriate behavior

---

*This procedure is also called *Counterconditioning.*

consists of presenting reinforcement for an appropriate behavior which is incompatible with the undesirable behavior. "Incompatible" means that the client cannot emit the undesirable and desirable behaviors at the same time. Thus, by strengthening the appropriate behavior, the therapist weakens the inappropriate behavior. If, for instance, the therapist's objective is to decrease the behavior of playing alone, he might reinforce the child for playing with other children since a child cannot engage in social interaction and isolate play simultaneously.

Other examples of inappropriate behaviors and more appropriate behaviors which might be incompatible with the undesirable behavior are:

Inappropriate behavior	*Appropriate behavior*
Aggression	•Playing appropriately with another child
	•Touching another child "lightly" and "gently"
Self-destruction	•Sitting quietly
	•Playing with a toy
Whining	•Verbalizing or vocalizing in a "normal" tone of voice

In the above examples, the therapist would reinforce the appropriate behavior in an attempt to reduce the inappropriate behavior. The use of this procedure requires (1) that a potent reinforcer be found and used consistently following the incompatible desirable behavior, and (2) that this behavior is truly incompatible with the undesirable behavior. An individual can do many things simultaneously or in rapid succession. If an appropriate behavior is reinforced and increases in frequency, and yet the undesirable behavior does not decrease, the therapist should either increase the appropriate behavior further, or look for another desirable behavior to reinforce, and similarly test it to see if increasing it will reduce the inappropriate behavior.

DECREASING BEHAVIOR BY DIFFERENTIAL REINFORCEMENT OF OTHER BEHAVIOR (DRO)

The procedure of differential reinforcement of other behavior

(DRO) consists of presenting the client with a positive reinforcer following a period of time in which he has *not* emitted an inappropriate behavior. For instance, if the therapist's objective is to reduce aggression, and he is going to use a DRO five-minute procedure, he delivers a positive reinforcer after every five-minute period in which *no* aggession occurs. If the person is aggressive at any time during the five minutes, the time before reinforcement is extended by five minutes. Thus, if the individual is aggressive after three minutes have elapsed since the last reinforcement, he must again wait five minutes (not eight minutes) before receiving another reinforcer. He will receive the reinforcer if he does not aggress during that time. If he does aggress, his time is again extended by five minutes. In short, with a DRO 5-minute schedule, five minutes must elapse between an aggressive behavior and presentation of a reinforcer. If the individual is *never* aggressive, he will receive a reinforcer every five minutes.

A DRO schedule can consist of almost any duration. Generally, the procedure is begun by reinforcing the client frequently, i.e. after very short periods of time, if the inappropriate behavior does not occur. Then the time between reinforcements is gradually increased until it is determined that the inappropriate behavior is beginning to reoccur. At that point, the DRO duration is reduced to the last value which was effective in keeping the inappropriate behavior at a low level. For instance, if the therapist's objective is to reduce an individual's self-destructive behavior, he begins by presenting a reinforcer following very short periods of time. For instance, he might present a bite of cookie after every fifteen seconds in which the client does not hit himself. (Of course, if he does hit himself, the delivery of this reinforcer is delayed by fifteen seconds.) In doing this, the therapist can simply count out the seconds silently, or use a stop-watch. After the client has earned many reinforcers on this schedule, and self-destructive responses rarely delay delivery of the reinforcer, the time between reinforcers can be gradually increased. For instance, next the therapist might reinforce him every twenty or twenty-five seconds for not hitting himself, and after a period in which he consistently earns reinforcement, with few self-destructive behaviors occurring, again increase the DRO duration by a small amount, e.g. to thirty seconds. In this way, the therapist continues to increase the DRO duration until the self-destructive behavior begins to occur more frequently (and thereby delays reinforcement more often). At this point, the DRO duration should be reduced to the value that was previously shown to decrease the occurrence of the response. After the DRO schedule has been established in the gradual manner described above, it may be possible to reinforce an individual once every hour or two for not engaging in the inappropriate behavior.

A number of factors should be considered before employing the DRO procedure.

1. The effectiveness of the procedure depends directly on the potency of the positive reinforcer employed. If a truly effective positive reinforcer cannot be located, the DRO procedure should not be attempted.

2. The DRO procedure can be costly in staff time if the client must be reinforced after very short intervals. Of course, this procedure (and most others in behavior modification) requires that the staff closely observe the client to detect any instance of the inappropriate behavior. In addition, the therapist must time the periods between reinforcements as well as deliver reinforcers. If the individual must be reinforced frequently, e.g. every five minutes, to maintain the desired reduction in the inappropriate behavior, the DRO procedure may not be practical.

3. When using DRO, only the behavior which will delay reinforcement is specified. If that behavior has not occurred during the required time, the reinforcer is delivered regardless of what the client is doing (as long as he is *not* engaging in the one behavior specified as the inappropriate behavior). The contingency can result in reinforcement of almost any other behavior, *appropriate* or *inappropriate*. Thus, if the individual emits high rates of a variety of inappropriate behaviors, it is best either not to use a DRO procedure, or to include more than one response as the target inappropriate behavior which will delay reinforcement.

MISCELLANEOUS PROCEDURES FOR
DECREASING BEHAVIOR

Most procedures discussed in this book have been thoroughly researched. After proving effective with a variety of individuals and in a variety of settings, these techniques have been incorporated into the formal behavior modification technology (and thus appear in this book). There exist numerous other procedures which have not received a great deal of research attention, but are used widely by parents and others and *appear* to be noncontroversial and benign, i.e. their potential for abuse and violation of client's rights seems to be very small. These are therefore presented in the following section, with the caution that all of their effects have not been systematically evaluated (at least with the retarded). Nevertheless, a decision may be made to try one or more of these procedures before resorting to more restrictive methods of decreasing behavior.

Placing the Child in a New Environment

Research with animals has shown that changing stimuli can, by itself, temporarily alter behavior. Translated to humans, this may mean that placing a client in a different, novel situation may result in a decrease in an inappropriate behavior that the person has been displaying. For instance, when a retarded individual is moved to a new residence, e.g. cottage or home, it is sometimes observed that initially his behavior often changes markedly. Aggression and other inappropriate behavior may cease, and desirable responses may emerge. Similarly, when a client is taken from his cottage to a classroom in another building, the undesirable behavior which he emitted in the cottage may not be observed. Thus, it may be useful to attempt such an environmental change to decrease unacceptable behavior. However, the beneficial changes which may result from placing an individual in a new situation will be temporary unless other procedures to maintain the improvement are used in that new situation. For instance, the first day that a student begins attending classes in a school building, the teacher should take advantage of the temporarily reduced level of unacceptable behavior by teaching and reinforcing appropriate behavior, as well as reinforcing the student for *not* emitting undesirable responses (the DRO procedure). The proper use of these reinforcement procedures may prevent the development of inappropriate behavior in this new situation. In a similar way, changing a student's teacher, or even changing furniture and other decor in his usual environment *may* result in a decline in a behavior problem. Once again, however, the improvement is likely to be temporary unless other procedures such as reinforcement for more appropriate behavior are employed by this new teacher or in this redecorated situation.

In some cases, it may be useful to change a particular aspect of an individual's environment to produce improvement in a behavior problem. For instance, if it is observed that an individual typically selects smaller persons to aggress against, the aggressor may be moved to a residence in which larger individuals live.

Clearly, such environmental changes may not always be practical. However, in some cases such "fresh starts" may avoid the use of much more elaborate, and perhaps restrictive procedures to handle a behavior problem.

Distraction

Parents and others often attempt to distract a misbehaving child, i.e. to direct the child to a more appropriate alternative activity. For instance, the parent of a one-year-old may be observed to remove the child from crawling on the dog and give him a toy or other interesting objects to play with instead. Similarly, a retarded individual might be distracted from tearing a book by providing him with an alternate activity such as a puzzle. Although widely used, this procedure has not been researched. Distraction appears to be an easy technique to try, but *may* be ineffective; frequently one observes that the client returns repeatedly to the inappropriate activity. Further, since this procedure typically includes a great deal of adult attention, and often results in the individual receiving an attractive toy or activity to distract him, its use is likely to reinforce the unacceptable behavior, i.e. the problem may get worse. In light of this problem, it may be more reasonable to use distraction *before* an inappropriate behavior actually occurs. For instance, if the parent/therapist observes a child approaching a china cabinet, he leads him to an area containing toys. Although this use of distraction may reinforce approaching the china cabinet, it avoids reinforcement of breaking dishes!

Attending to the Victim

Some research has shown that an undesirable behavior, such as aggression, can be reduced by withdrawing the recipient of the aggression and attending to him, while ignoring the aggressor. For instance, immediately upon observing one client hit another, the therapist might lead the victim away and comfort him. In addition to providing the necessary check to insure that the recipient is not hurt, such a procedure serves to interrupt an aggressive episode, increases the chances that the aggressor is not reinforced by the therapist's prolonged attention (the extinction procedure), and may be unpleasant for the aggressor to observe. Of course, if the aggressive individual receives sufficient reinforcement from the reaction of his victim (e.g. crying) and/or from the mere approach of the therapist, the procedure will not be effective. Further, care should be taken to insure that a person does not *provoke* an attack by another to gain the staff's attention. Obviously the usefulness of this procedure has limits. It is hardly reasonable to comfort a torn book! Nevertheless, attending to *anything* other than the misbehaving client (when possible) is a necessary and desirable procedure.

Physical Removal of the Target, Object, or Person

Parents and others frequently control a behavior problem by

removing the object or person typically involved in the child's undesirable behavior. For instance, many parents and teachers routinely put fragile and dangerous objects out of the reach of children. In this case, they physically prevent the child from performing an undesirable response. Similarly, an individual's aggression may be reduced by separating him from his usual victim, e.g. placing the students in different classes. Such physical restraint prevents the response from occurring; it does not teach the student not to emit the inappropriate response. However, in some cases this kind of physical prevention may be useful, for instance when a teacher does not have enough time to conduct a training program with a student, when a person never demonstrates the undesirable behavior except toward one person or object, or when it is too dangerous to permit even one occurrence of the response, e.g. swallowing poison.

Pointed Praise

This procedure has been demonstrated effective in decreasing inappropriate classroom behavior by normal and mildly retarded individuals. In this case, when a teacher observes a student engaging in an unacceptable behavior such as wandering around the classroom, he immediately locates another student(s) who is behaving appropriately (sitting and studying). He reinforces that student for his appropriate behavior in such a way that the misbehaving student can hear and see. It is recommended that the reinforcement include a clear description of the appropriate behavior as well as the specific reinforcer being presented (*descriptive praise*). For instance, the teacher might say "John, I like the way you are sitting and studying. Here are five tokens for doing such a good job." This procedure has several advantages: (1) it may remind the misbehaving client specifically what is the appropriate, alternative behavior and the reinforcer for that behavior, (2) it reinforces other individuals for their appropriate behavior (including ignoring the disruptive individual), and (3) it increases the chances that the teacher will not reinforce the misbehaving student by, for instance, scolding, since he is busy attending to other students. Of course, this.pointed praise procedure must be accompanied by positive reinforcement for appropriate behavior when it occurs. For instance, if the individual is rarely or never reinforced for sitting, he will not sit when pointed praise is used during his wandering. Initially, the person should be reinforced *immediately* upon ceasing the inappropriate behavior and beginning the desirable response. For instance, if Johnny returns to his seat after others have been praised for sitting, the teacher should immediately reinforce him. He should also be rewarded for sitting at times *other than* immediately after returning to his seat. Later, he should be reinforced for engaging in the desirable behavior for longer and longer periods. For instance, after immediately rewarding him several times for returning to his seat following pointed praise to others, the therapist next requires that he sit for several seconds before receiving reinforcement. After reinforcing him several times for sitting this duration, he next requires that the child sit for a minute or two before being reinforced. (See the section on shaping in Chapter 6 for a further description of this procedure.) In short, care must be taken to not accidentally reinforce an undesirable behavioral sequence of first emitting the inappropriate behavior then switching to a desirable response.

DECREASING BEHAVIOR BY DIFFERENTIAL REINFORCEMENT OF LOW RATES (DRL)

Some behaviors are inappropriate only because they occur at an excessively high frequency (rate). For example, interrupting a teacher's lecture to ask questions is often desirable, but if the interruptions occur too frequently, they disrupt the lecture. A DRL procedure is designed to *maintain* the occurrence of a behavior, but to maintain it at a *low rate*.

With a DRL schedule, a response is reinforced any time it follows the previous response by some specified period of time. For example, if the therapist is training the pupils to ask questions, but not more than one a minute. He might use a DRL one-minute schedule as follows: Start a stop-watch; when the timer reaches the one-minute mark, the next question from the student will be reinforced (for instance, by the therapist answering it). Next, the time is immediately reset to start again at zero; any time a question occurs before the timer reaches the one-minute mark, it is reset to zero, timing is started again, and the question is not reinforced. Thus, only questions that follow the previous question by at least one minute are reinforced. In practice, the procedure can be conducted with less precision, by the teacher estimating the passage of time, rather than going through the cumbersome procedure of resetting a timepiece. If the procedure is conducted properly, the result will be a low (about one per minute) but steady rate of question-asking behavior.

It is important to learn the difference between DRL, DRO, and FI schedules. With a DRL schedule, a specific target response is reinforced only if it occurs after a period of time during which that response did not occur. If a response occurs before the time interval passes, the timer is reset, and reinforcement is delayed. The client must then wait until the prescribed amount of time has elapsed, and *then* respond, to receive reinforcement. Thus, the target response is maintained at a low rate. With a DRO schedule, reinforcement is only presented following a period of time in which the target behavior has *not* occurred. Therefore, a DRO schedule is designed to decrease the target behavior to zero. In the case of both FI and DRL schedules, the client is reinforced for the first response which occurs after a specified interval has elapsed. With the FI schedule, responses which occur during the fixed interval do not count toward earning reinforcement, nor do they delay the presentation of the reinforcer. Only the first response which occurs after the fixed interval has elapsed is reinforced. Thus, responding under an FI schedule tends to gradually increase between reinforcements. That is, immediately after one reinforcement the individual may not respond, but will gradually begin to respond more and more frequently as the time for the next reinforcement draws near. Finally, after the fixed interval elapses, and the next response is reinforced, he will again cease responding temporarily and then will begin to respond more and more rapidly as the time for reinforcement again approaches.

A variation of the DRL schedule may be easier for staff to employ. In this case, reinforcement is delivered if the number of responses which occur in a specified period of time is less than a prescribed limit. For instance, a parent might reinforce a child if he breaks two or less toys in a day. Similarly, a class of students might receive a snack if fewer than seven disruptive behaviors occur during the morning class period. (This is an example of DRL schedule applied to group consequences.)

CONTINGENT EDUCATION

In recent years an array of procedures have been designed to decrease undesirable behavior by teaching other, appropriate behavior. These techniques differ in three major respects from the procedure entitled Reinforcement of incompatiable appropriate behavior (DRI) described previously: (1) It is employed even when an appropriate behavior occurs so infrequently that it could rarely, if ever, be reinforced, (2) it consists of extensive verbal instructions, the opportunity to practice the appropriate behavior and other features which are not typically a part of the DRI technique, and (3) such training is often conducted contingent on the occurrence of the *inappropriate* behavior, i.e. immediately after emitting the undesirable behavior the client receives *contingent education.*

Although some of these techniques have not been employed extensively with lower functioning retarded persons, they have yielded impressive results with youths with behavior problems who live in group homes.* Some of the features of contingent education (and the term itself) have been specifically proposed for use with the retarded by a panel of experts reviewing behavior modification techniques in residential institutions (Risley, Twardosz, Friedman, Bijou, Wexler, et. al., 1975).†

---

*The description of these procedures is not intended to reflect precisely the techniques used, for instance, in Achievement Place Homes, but represents this author's compilation of their techniques with others which fall logically into the same category.
†This report includes three procedures under the "contingent education" title: contingent observation, overcorrection and educational fines. The former procedure is described in this section; the latter two are described later. The author had taken this liberty in the interests of clarity, since no formal systematization has yet been incorporated into the behavior modification literature.

Contingent education may include one, but often consists of a combination of several components.

1. Feedback: A specific behavioral description of the inappropriate behavior, for instance, "Mary, you just stepped on the dog." In addition, feedback may be given by modeling the inappropriate behavior for the individual (see below).

2. Instruction: A description of the alternative appropriate behavior, for instance, "Rudy, in the future please shut the door quietly when the others are studying."

3. Reprimand: A statement conveying disapproval, for instance "I am very disappointed." Such a reprimand should be said in a serious, but unemotional manner, and should not imply a condemnation of the individual, e.g. "You are a bad person."*

4. Reasoning: A discussion of *why* a behavior was inappropriate or *why* an alternative behavior would be appropriate, often including a description of possible natural consequences of either action, for instance, "When you throw blocks they can hit other people. The others will stop playing with you if you hurt them."

5. Modeling: A demonstration of the alternative appropriate behavior, for instance, "Gary, here is the way to ask someone to return your book: 'Mary, I was using that book, please return it and I will give it to you when I'm finished.' " When a person is participating in a group activity such as table games and he behaves in an inappropriate manner, the effectiveness of the modeling procedure may be enhanced by removing the individual from the activity and requiring him to sit and watch his peers modeling correct behavior. For instance, immediately after Fred screams or throws toys, the therapist might explain that he must learn how to play by watching others. He should be placed in a chair and required to sit while the therapist reinforces others for appropriate use of materials. After Fred is quiet and indicates (verbally or gesturally) that he is ready to play in an acceptable manner, he is allowed to rejoin the

---

*Technically, a reprimand is a punishment procedure (which will be described later). However, since it is sometimes used with contingent education, and since if it is used properly it is considered a mild procedure to decrease behavior, it is also presented in this section.

group. This procedure combines elements of modeling with *time-out from positive reinforcement,* a procedure which will be described more fully later.

6. Practice: A period of time in which the client rehearses the appropriate behavior, for instance, "Please show me how you clear your desk during clean-up time. Fine, now let's practice that one more time." While the person is practicing, the therapist should provide positive reinforcement for any correct responding or approximations to appropriate behavior, as well as feedback for incorrect behavior.

7. Contingency statement: A description of the inappropriate behavior, the consequences for engaging in that behavior in the future, and a description of a more appropriate behavior and its consequences. For instance, "John, you just threw a block at Sue and that's wrong; if you do it again, you will have to go to your room for ten minutes. If you play nicely with her, you can continue playing outside."

8. Positive reinforcement for appropriate behavior: If the individual engages in desirable behavior, e.g. practices the appropriate alternative, or corrects the immediately preceding inappropriate behavior, he should be reinforced. Reinforcement may be given for simply paying attention to the contingent training. For instance, a therapist might praise the client for making eye contact or watching a demonstration of acceptable behavior.

There is much overlap in the procedures described above; for instance, contingency statements contain a great deal of feedback, correction, and instructions. The distinction between these methods is not of great importance, since several are usually combined into a single consequence for inappropriate behavior. Indeed, the "teaching instruction" developed and described by the Achievement Place Research Project (Phillips, Phillips, Fixen, and Wolf, 1974) consists of most of these components. Even though several of these components may be combined, the entire consequence need not take more than one or two minutes, and often requires less time. Thus, a contingent education procedure can be employed even when there are few staff and many clients to train.

When using these procedures, it is desirable to require the individual to indicate that he has attended to and understands the consequence. For instance, if the individual is verbal, he can be asked to repeat what the therapist has said. A nonverbal person may simply be asked to nod or otherwise gesture an acknowledgement. Of course, a decrease or alteration of the inappropriate behavior is the best and ultimate test of whether or not the client has understood the consequence.

In addition to the use of these techniques as a consequence, i.e. immediately following inappropriate behavior, they are also recommended as a teaching device to be used before trouble starts, for instance, at the beginning of a class period or at the start of the day at home. At that time, the student can be instructed to, for instance, practice sharing or proper use of materials and be reinforced for engaging in these behaviors.

These procedures are not intended for long-term use. They are employed most appropriately during the initial period of treatment, when it may be assumed that the client engages in undesirable behavior because he has not learned appropriate alternatives. How long such contingent education procedures should be employed before resorting to another procedure to decrease behavior differs with individuals and situations. However, even with individuals showing severe behavioral deficiencies, several days of consistent use of contingent education should indicate whether or not the procedure is effective. If an undesirable behavior is not decreasing, another technique should be tried. Indeed, since these methods typically include a great deal of adult attention *their contingent use may actually reinforce an unacceptable behavior,* i.e. the problem may get worse. Nevertheless, these procedures (and those described previously) should be employed first to insure that a behavior problem is not occurring simply because of the absence of positive reinforcement for more appropriate behavior and/or a lack of training of acceptable responding.

DECREASING BEHAVIOR BY SATIATION

Another procedure which is sometimes used to decrease an

inappropriate behavior is called *satiation*. As the reader will recall from the discussion on positive reinforcement, satiation refers to the gradual decline in a response which is maintained by positive reinforcement as the number of reinforcers that the client earns accumulates. For instance, if an individual earns food for performing a response, e.g. smiling, he will gradually stop responding as he earns more and more food. In other words, he will work for food while he is hungry (deprived), but as he "fills up," i.e. becomes satiated with food, the response will cease. Satiation interferes with training an appropriate behavior by positive reinforcement, and various techniques are used to avoid it. On the other hand, satiation can be put to constructive use to decrease an inappropriate response.

First, the therapist identifies that reinforcer which might be maintaining the inappropriate response. This is done by observing the client and noting what consequences occur, at least occasionally, following the inappropriate behavior. Then he provides the individual with an abundance of this possible reinforcer and attempts to satiate him on the item or activity. With a material reinforcer, he simply continues giving the client a large amount of the item, e.g. food or tokens, noncontigently ("free") until he shows no more interest in it, e.g. stops eating. With reinforcers in the form of activities and privileges, the therapist allows the client continual access to the event, e.g. lets him stay on the playground as long as he wants.

Ayllon (1963) decreased towel-stealing in a psychotic woman by providing her with large quantities of towels. Periodically throughout the day, an attendant would bring a large stack of towels into the woman's bedroom and hand them to her. As the number of "free" towels accumulated, the response of hoarding and stealing towels decreased. In fact, the woman began to complain about the amount of folding she had to do and began returning the towels to the laundry. Ayllon attributed the decline in this stealing behavior to satiation of the reinforcer (towels) that maintained the inappropriate behavior.

Satiation is not a widely used procedure for decreasing inappropriate behavior, perhaps because of the following considerations:

1. To use this procedure, the therapist must first identify the positive reinforcer maintaining the undesirable response. As mentioned when extinction was discussed, this is not always possible.

2. Even if the therapist can locate the reinforcer, sometimes it is not feasible to provide the client with large amounts of the item or activity. For instance, large amounts of sweets may result in tooth decay, poor nutrition, and excessive weight, and thus satiating an individual on candy to decrease an undesirable behavior which is maintained by candy may have unhealthy side effects. Other reinforcers are dangerous or destructive. For instance, if a client is reinforced by drawing blood, the therapist obviously cannot allow him to aggress or engage in self-destructive behavior until he satiates on that reinforcer. Other reinforcers are simply not practical to present in abundance. For instance, if the therapist determines that the reinforcer maintaining "playing hooky" from class after recess is continued access to the playground, he can probably not allow the child to remain on the playground as long as he likes each day until he becomes satiated.

3. Social reinforcement (e.g. praise, hugs, and smiles), if varied in their content and occasionally re-paired with already effective reinforcers, *may not* be subject to satiation. Although further research may clarify whether or not this is the case, one should be aware that this information is not yet available and consequently not use satiation of social reinforcement as a tested procedure for decreasing an undesirable behavior maintained by social attention.

A rather popular notion asserts that an individual behaves in inappropriate ways because he needs more attention. It is sometimes assumed that if "TLC" (tender loving care) is heaped upon the client, his inappropriate behavior will decrease. Many view this as a fallacy. A person may behave inappropriately because he is getting TLC (reinforcement) following *that undesirable* behavior, not because he is getting too little attention. In this case, the therapist should discontinue reinforcement for the inappropriate behavior (extinction procedure), and also either: (1) provide TLC (reinforcement) for appropriate behavior which is incompatible with the inappropriate behavior, or (2) provide reinforcement for *not* emitting the undesirable behavior (the DRO procedure). The point is that simply increasing the overall amount of attention the client receives will probably not decrease the inappropriate behavior, and may increase the undesirable response by accidental positive reinforcement. That is, by providing a great deal of noncontingent reinforcement, the attention may occasionally follow the inappropriate behavior, and thereby make the problem worse. In short, the practice of TLC has not been shown to be a reasonable way to reduce a behavior problem, unless it is used contingently in one of the two ways described above.

4. With powerful reinforcers, satiation may be very slow in taking effect. For instance, it may take a child a very long time to satiate on hearing a favorite story or playing on the playground.

5. Satiation *may* be permanent in some cases, but more generally seems to be temporary. After the client becomes satiated on a reinforcer, and ceases performing the response which resulted in the item or event, a period of deprivation occurs in which the individual will not work to receive that reinforcer. As that period continues, he becomes more and more likely to perform the inappropriate response which results in the reinforcer. Finally, when he is again fully deprived, the response will occur repeatedly until the client is again satiated on the reinforcer. At this point, the response will again cease *temporarily*. For instance, if the therapist wants to decrease food stealing by satiating the individual on food, he might provide the client with large amounts of food. Although this may be effective in decreasing food stealing, it will only work until he begins to become hungry again. When that occurs, he is likely to resume stealing. Since most want inappropriate behavior to be decreased permanently, and not reappear in cycles, satiation may not be useful if the improvement it produces is not permanent.

6. If a reinforcer is given almost continuously and noncontingently, e.g. every few seconds, it may accidently be presented

following an inappropriate behavior and thus strengthen that response. In this case, one inappropriate behavior may decrease (by satiation) and another increase (by accidental reinforcement).

7. When an individual is satiated on a reinforcer, that reinforcer cannot be used to increase and/or maintain more appropriate behavior. In this case, the therapist must find another reinforcer to train desirable responses, a task which is sometimes difficult.

To avoid this and other problems with a satiation procedure, it is probably advisable to use reinforcement of an incompatible behavior or some procedure other than satiation to decrease a behavior problem.

DECREASING BEHAVIOR BY OVERCORRECTION

The procedure entitled *overcorrection*, which was developed by Azrin and his colleagues, (e.g. Foxx and Azrin, 1972; Webster and Azrin, 1973) actually consists of several techniques and is based upon a variety of behavioral principles.

In general, a misbehaving individual is required to (1) restore his environment to a state which is better than it was before his inappropriate behavior disrupted it (restitution), and/or (2) intensively practice appropriate alternative behavior (positive practice).

Restitution

When using restitution (also called restitutional overcorrection), the teacher must first identify what environmental disturbance results from a student's inappropriate behavior. For instance, aggression may cause physical injury to others, and throwing furniture can result in destruction of property. The next step in employing a restitution procedure is to specify what the individual must do to correct, indeed *over*correct, the environmental disruption caused by the inappropriate behavior. For instance, if a student marks on a wall with a pencil, he may be required to wash that wall, as well as all other walls in the classroom. The following are examples of the use of restitution with several undesirable behaviors:

1. If an individual disturbs the physical environment by, for instance, throwing a chair or turning over a bed, he is required to correct the particular disturbance he caused, e.g. restore the chair to its correct position, as well as straighten all other objects in the room.

2. If an individual eats or mouths inappropriate material or objects (including biting people), he is required to destroy the germs invariably associated with such behavior by cleansing his mouth with an oral antiseptic (typically one which is unpleasant tasting).

3. If an individual aggresses against another, he is required to correct (overcorrect) the discomfort incurred by his victim. In this case, he must assist in providing medical treatment, and filling out the necessary reports (either verbally, gesturally, or in a written fashion).

4. If an individual has screamed or otherwise created a noisy disturbance, he is required to correct and compensate for such disturbance by remaining exceptionally quiet. He must lie on his bed for fifteen minutes to two hours, and must be quiet and calm for at least five to fifteen minutes before being allowed to get up.

5. Further, some inappropriate behavior appears to result from an agitated, distraught state. Thus, overcorrection can be directed toward this agitated state rather than the other behavior which tends to accompany it, such as self-injury, aggression, screaming, and tantrums. In this case, when the therapist observes the student either becoming extremely distraught, or immediately after a specific inappropriate behavior occurs, he leads the individual to bed and requires him to lie down for fifteen minutes to two hours. (Again, the student must remain quiet for at least five to fifteen minutes before being allowed to get up.) Such a required relaxation procedure fits the overcorrection rationale because extended relaxation corrects the agitated state and compensates others for the disruption by

providing all with a period of peace and quiet.

Restitution should be effortful and of an extended duration. Typically, an individual should be required to work steadily and vigorously for at least thirty minutes. During this time, the therapist should minimize reinforcement, i.e. not praise the student or attend to him any more than is necessary to insure continued performance. (Other important features of the restitution procedure are presented at the end of this section.)

Positive Practice

As mentioned, positive practice (also called positive practice overcorrection) requires that, following an inappropriate behavior, an individual intensively practice appropriate alternative behavior. Often, the student is required to practice a behavior that is the opposite of the undesirable response. Some features of the positive practice procedure also consist of restitution. For instance, when an individual is required to straighten all objects in a room after he has turned over a chair, he is not only correcting his disruption, but practicing appropriate use of furniture. Other undesirable behaviors, such as autistic self-stimulation and nervous habits such as fingernail biting, do not disrupt the environment and thus the restitution procedure is not applicable. In these cases, positive practice would be used by itself.

The following are examples of the use of positive practice with several undesirable behaviors:

1. If an individual self-stimulates by moving her head from side to side repetitively, she is required to practice holding her head still, and moving it for functional reasons, e.g. when told to do so. Thus, the therapist instructs the student to move her head up, down, or straight-ahead, and maintain each position for several seconds.

2. If an individual self-stimulates by repetitive hand clapping, he may be required to practice holding his hands still and to move them only for functional reasons, e.g. when told to do so. Thus, the therapist instructs the client to, for instance, hold his hands out in front of him, to put them into his pockets, and

to sustain each position for several seconds.

3. If an individual displays a nervous habit such as a thumb-sucking or fingernail biting, she is required to practice placing her hands at her sides, grasping objects, clenching her fists, or opening and closing her hands.

Unlike restitution, positive practice is not intended to be very effortable, time-consuming, or unpleasant. Typically, the student is asked to practice for five minutes, and is not expected to expend a great deal of effort.

When employing restitution and/or positive practice, several guidelines should be followed:

RELATION BETWEEN BEHAVIOR AND CONSEQUENCE. It is recommended that the overcorrection procedure should relate directly to the misbehavior. For instance, rinsing out the mouth with a mouthwash is only suggested as a consequence for oral behavior such as inappropriate mouthing of objects and biting. Oral hygiene training is not recommended for other types of undesirable behavior such as turning over furniture or repetitive hand clapping. Recent research indicates that arbitrary overcorrection (such as washing an individual's mouth with mouthwash for turning over furniture) can be effective in reducing an inappropriate behavior. However, those who have developed the overcorrection procedure contend that one advantage of using a consequence which is related directly to the misbehavior is that it makes sense to the public and staff and avoids the impression that the individual is being punished.

IMMEDIACY. Overcorrection should follow the inappropriate behavior immediately. Regardless of whether restitution or positive practice (or both) is employed, it should begin within seconds after the undesirable behavior occurs.

DURATION. As mentioned previously, the restitution procedure is usually of an extended duration, generally continuing for thirty minutes. However, a shorter version of restitution may be tried in which an individual briefly corrects the specific disruption caused by his behavior, without engaging in *overcorrection*. For instance, following a toileting accident, a child may be required to wipe up the accident, change and wash his pants, and wash his hands. Such a procedure generally requires no more than fifteen minutes. Although a brief correction procedure of this type violates the rule that overcorrection should be effortful, it has been used with some success and may be more practical for staff. If this type of brief restitution does not show effects after several applications, the therapist should change to a full restitutional overcorrection regime.

The duration of positive practice, on the other hand, is usually short. Unlike restitution, positive practice is not intended to be unpleasant, and thus the misbehaving individual is only required to practice appropriate alternative behavior for approximately five minutes.

EFFORT. Restitution should be very effortful; the misbehaving client should be required to actively work without pausing for the full duration of the restitutional period. However, when a positive practice procedure is used, the individual should not be required to expend a great deal of energy, but merely to practice appropriate behavior several times during the five-minute period.

POSITIVE REINFORCEMENT. Although restitution is designed to be unpleasant and positive practice is not, in *both* cases positive reinforcement should be minimized as much as possible. If the client is praised or excessively attended to during overcorrection, the procedure will not have its intended effect (to decrease inappropriate behavior). Indeed, even if a therapist conducts overcorrection properly and does not reinforce the client deliberately, his mere presence and close attention in getting the client to perform the overcorrection may *in itself* be too much reinforcement. Thus, if restitution or positive practice is not successfully decreasing the inappropriate behavior that they follow, the therapist should try to further minimize reinforcement that may accompany either procedure. If the behavior problem is still not improving, overcorrection should be terminated and another procedure attempted.

ENSURING THAT THE INDIVIDUAL WILL PERFORM OVERCORRECTION. Although positive reinforcement should be minimized during overcorrection, the therapist must employ some technique to assure that the misbehaving individual will engage in the procedure. To do this, three types of prompts are recommended: verbal instructions, gestures and physical guidance (putting through). First, the therapist should verbally and gesturally direct the activities of the student to insure that he continues working and performs the task satisfactorily. If these prompts are not successful, the therapist may need to physically guide the client (put him through the behavior). As always when using prompting, he uses the *least* amount of assistance (the smallest prompt) which is effective in evoking correct performance. Then, he tries to fade assistance as rapidly and completely as possible. (A more thorough description of prompting and fading appears in the section on positive reinforcement in Chapter 6.) For some individuals, being put through a behavior is unpleasant and they may learn to avoid much manual guidance by responding independently. For others, some form of prompting may continue to be necessary indefinitely.

DISRUPTIVE BEHAVIOR DURING OVERCORRECTION. If an individual refuses to perform the overcorrection regime (for instance by "going limp") or aggresses against the therapist, the overcorrection period is extended until the client has cooperated for the full duration of overcorrection. For instance, if a student attacks the therapist after fifteen minutes of restitution training, the entire procedure should begin again for thirty minutes. Similarly, if an individual lies on the floor and refuses to move, the period of positive practice is extended again by five minutes.

If the individual behaves in a highly disruptive or dangerous manner during overcorrection, he may be required to lie down on his bed and relax for thirty minutes to one hour. After he has remained calm and quiet for at least the last five minutes of the required relaxation period, he should be required to resume overcorrection for the full prescribed duration.

Although overcorrection has been extensively researched, its effects have not been fully documented with a large number of individuals in a variety of settings. Consequently, it may be best to employ the procedure with the specific behaviors for which Azrin and others have used overcorrection. These include: turning over and throwing furniture; aggression; mouthing objects; incontinence (toileting accidents); stereotyped self-stimulation; dropping, spilling, and drooling food; nervous habits such as tics and nailbiting; screaming; crying; and tantruming.

Further, since these procedures are relatively complex, it is recommended that the articles referenced at the end of this chapter be read carefully before attempting to implement overcorrection. These references will expand and refine the brief description provided above. They will also clarify the many procedures upon which overcorrection is based. These include: time-out, extinction, and punishment.

DECREASING BEHAVIOR BY TIME-OUT
FROM POSITIVE REINFORCEMENT

If none of the previously described techniques have proven effective in reducing a behavior problem, the therapist may have to employ *time-out from positive reinforcement,* often simply called *time-out.* Time-out consists of presenting a stimulus following an inappropriate response, e.g. "Johnny, no," and then discontinuing for a time positive reinforcement for all behavior. The procedure of time-out assumes that the client is being reinforced, and that the brief discontinuation of the reinforcement contingent on an inappropriate behavior will decrease that undesirable behavior. Such reinforcement may consist of socials, food, or tokens, or may simply derive from engaging in some enjoyable activity. Regardless of the type of reinforcers that the individual was receiving, during the time-out period he should receive as little reinforcement as possible for any behavior. Various forms of time-out are used to remove positive reinforcement during this period. In the following discussion, these are arranged in an order from least to most restrictive. As mentioned previously, it is desirable to use the least restrictive, most innocuous form of *any* procedure to decrease behavior before resorting to more drastic methods. The form of time-out can range from a therapist simply turning away from a child for a few seconds to secluding a client in a locked room for several minutes. Clearly, the former procedure is much less restrictive and controversial than the latter. Thus, when beginning a time-out program, a therapist should first attempt to use the forms of time-out described earlier in the following discussion before employing the time-out procedures discussed later.

Methods of Time-Out

A simple form of time-out consists of the therapist simply turning or walking away following an inappropriate behavior. For instance, immediately following an aggressive act, the therapist presents a stimulus (cue) that time-out is beginning, e.g. "No, Mary", and then does not reinforce Mary for any behavior during a certain period of time. (Turning or walking away may prevent accidental reinforcement in the form of remaining close to, looking at, or speaking to that person.) This type of time-out is used in a situation in which there are very few other sources of reinforcement besides those which the therapist delivers, for instance, when the client and therapist are alone. Clearly, if the therapist walks away but the client can continue to receive reinforcement from other individuals or materials, this will not effectively accomplish the desired interruption in positive reinforcement.

In situations in which other individuals and interesting activities are present, a second form of time-out may be most appropriate. A client who behaves in an unacceptable manner is instructed to sit in a chair away from the activity for a period of time. Often this form of time-out is effectively combined with a modeling procedure in which the person is asked to sit and watch other individuals act appropriately. While the client is observing, the therapist reinforces others for acceptable behavior. Although this procedure was described previously in this chapter under "Contingent Education-Modeling," it combines features of time-out since reinforcement from the therapist and the opportunity to participate in the activities is removed for the time during which the client is sitting.

If an individual's inappropriate behavior does not decrease, perhaps because he is not learning appropriate behavior by observing his peers, or because he is receiving too much reinforcement from other individuals or from watching the activity, another form of time-out may be employed. The time-out chair may be placed behind a screen or otherwise out of sight (and hearing) of the area in which the group is located. However, in this form of time-out, the client is still in the same room with the others and not *physically* prevented from returning to the activity.

If the individual continues to be disruptive while in the time-out chair (for instance, screams and throws materials) or refuses to remain seated, he may be taken to another room such as his bedroom or a hall. This area should be as free of distractors (reinforcement) as possible. While in this room the client should be checked regularly, preferably in such a way that he cannot detect being observed.

A final, more restrictive form of time-out may be employed if none of the preceding types of time-out are effective, if they are impossible to use because, for instance, the individual will not stay in his bedroom voluntarily, and if the inappropriate behavior is severe. For instance, milder forms of time-out may not be reasonable for a client who throws dangerous objects, breaks windows, or hits other individuals. For use in these cases, time-out may be conducted in a locked room. As with other forms of time-out, the client is first given a cue that time-out is beginning and is then confined in either a bedroom, hall, or other room where reinforcers are at a minimum. If the person is highly destructive when in time-out, and is likely to injure himself or extensively destroy property, a special time-out room may be necessary. Such a room should be clean, well-ventilated and lighted, and should allow the individual to sit and stand comfortably. It should also permit frequent but unobtrusive observation (for instance, through a peephole). However, it should not contain furniture or materials with which the client can play or injure himself. When a person is likely to hurt himself, it may be wise to restrain him in a chair or on a bed while in time-out.*

---

*As will be emphasized later, the use of locked or restrained time-out may be prohibited in certain facilities and states.

As stressed previously, when a client is placed on a time-out program, the therapist should first attempt to either turn away, or to place the individual in a chair from which he can observe the others behave appropriately (or, if necessary, place him behind a screen to further block reinforcement). If the behavior problem does not decrease after these forms of time-out have been employed consistently, *or* if the person refuses to sit or is too disruptive or dangerous, placement in another area of the school or living unit may be a possibility. Finally, if this form of time-out is not effective, or if it is impossible or dangerous to conduct time-out in this manner, the client may have to be locked or otherwise restrained in another room. While it is recommended that each form of time-out be tried in sequence, it is important to note that exposing an individual with a behavior problem to increasingly more severe forms of time-out *may* make that individual less and less sensitive to even the most restrictive time-out procedure. Although research is needed in this area, gradually increasing the intensity of time-out is similar to a procedure known as *desensitization* in which an individual is successively exposed to something which is unpleasant to him (for instance, a dog) first in small amounts and then in greater and greater amounts until that individual no longer finds the maximum amount of the event, e.g. a dog jumping on him, unpleasant. In a similar way, gradually exposing an individual to more and more severe forms of time-out may desensitize him to even the most severe time-out procedure. It is therefore recommended that each form of time-out be tried consistently for a brief period of time, such as one to three hours. If the inappropriate behavior is not noticeably reduced, or if it is clear that it will be impossible to conduct mild time-out either because the client refuses to cooperate by sitting or staying in his room or because he behaves in a disruptive or dangerous manner while in time-out, the therapist should change to a more severe form of the procedure.

It may also be desirable to combine two or more forms of time-out for a given individual. For instance, immediately following an inappropriate behavior, the client may be placed in a chair and given an opportunity to observe the others. If the individual leaves the chair, screams, or becomes aggressive, he may *then* be placed in his bedroom. If he leaves his bedroom or engages in dangerous or destructive behavior, he may be confined in a special time-out room. These "backup" methods of time-out may teach the person to remain in his chair. If it does not, i.e. if on each occasion when time-out is used, the client repeatedly must be placed in his bedroom or a time-out room, then the therapist should discontinue trying to put the client in the chair. In this case, when an undesirable behavior occurs, the client would immediately be placed in his bedroom or a time-out room. Similarly, if the individual is consistently self-injurious while being placed in his bedroom or routinely refuses to stay there voluntarily, he may be restrained or placed in a time-out room without first sending him to his bedroom.

Conducting Time-Out

Regardless of the form of time-out being employed, on each occasion that the client receives this consequence, a signal (cue) should first be presented to tell the individual that time-out is beginning. This signal should be given *immediately* following the undesirable behavior, i.e. within one to three seconds. The cue should be one that is easily perceived by the client and is used by all who employ the time-out consequence with that person. It is sometimes suggested that this cue consist of feedback, reasoning, or other components of contingent education described previously. For instance, immediately following an undesirable behavior, the therapist might provide feedback to the client describing the inappropriate behavior and its desirable alternative, e.g. "Leslie, you should use the scissors to cut paper, not Mary's hair." Next, a period of time-out, for instance observing the others from a chair, would occur. Cues such as this are designed to teach appropriate alternative behavior, and should be tried first when beginning a time-out program. However, since such instruction necessarily involves a great deal of adult attention which may be reinforcing, if the behavior problem does not improve, the therapist may change the cue to one that involves less attention. For instance, he might use a brief reprimand, e.g. "Mary, no!" to indicate that time-out is beginning. Changing the cue from one that attempts to teach desirable behavior, such as feedback or reasoning, to a brief reprimand should be done *first* before changing to a more restrictive form of time-out. Specifically, if a therapist is attempting unsuccessfully to decrease an unacceptable behavior by feedback followed by unrestrained placement in a chair, he should *first* change the cue from feedback to a brief verbal reprimand and continue using the chair time-out procedure *before* resorting to placement of the client in his bedroom or a time-out room.

Regardless of the type of cue employed to indicate the onset of time-out, the individual should *immediately* be timed out following the presentation of the signal. This is done even if he stops the inappropriate behavior after the signal is presented.

It is essential that the client be reinforced as little as possible with attention while being placed in time-out. As stressed previously, if positive reinforcement, e.g. attention, accompanies *any* procedure for decreasing behavior, that procedure will be less successful. Thus, if a contingent education procedure such as feedback is used immediately preceding time-out, the therapist should attempt to reinforce the individual as little as possible during that instruction. If such an interaction contains too much reinforcement and instead a brief reprimand is used to signal time-out, the therapist should *only* present the cue immediately following the inappropriate behavior, then lead the individual firmly but unemotionally to time-out, without looking at, talking to, or unnecessarily touching him.

During the time-out period, the client should be frequently but inconspicuously checked to insure that he is not hurting himself, in medical difficulty, or engaging in a behavior which might be reinforcing. Obviously, if his safety is in danger, he should be removed and cared for. If he is engaging in a harmful behavior, steps should be taken to prevent that activity, e.g. his hand and/or legs should be restrained in the time-out situation. After the therapist has observed that he will behave in a dangerous or reinforcing manner in time-out, the method used to restrict this behavior should be used on every subsequent time-out occasion.

The duration of time-out is usually from ten seconds to thirty minutes.* When beginning a time-out program, it is best to try a relatively short time-out period, e.g. one to three minutes. After using this duration consistently, if the procedure is not having the desired effect of decreasing an inappropriate behavior, a longer time-out duration may be used. It should be remembered that although time-out may be necessary to reduce a client's behavior problem, while in time-out (unless he is observing the appropriate behavior of his peers) he is not participating in activities that may be a valuable learning experience for him. Thus, the shorter the time-out period which is still effective in reducing unacceptable behavior, the better! The best and most effective duration should be established in the first day or two of the program, to prevent that individual from gradually adapting to longer and longer time-out periods.

Some have suggested that the duration of time-out be determined by the client's behavior. For instance, instead of specifying that time-out will last for five minutes, it might be arranged that whenever the individual is quiet and perhaps indicates (verbally or gesturally) that he is ready to behave in an acceptable manner, he is allowed to rejoin the activities. If this procedure is not effective in decreasing an inappropriate behavior (for instance, when a client consistently calms down after a few seconds in time-out and is thus "released," but continues to engage in the unacceptable behavior after returning to the activity) then a fixed duration of time-out, e.g. five minutes, should be employed. In this case, regardless of the person's behavior, time-out would continue for five minutes.

---

*When calculating the rate of an inappropriate behavior which is being treated with a time-out procedure, subtract the time that the client is in the time-out room from the total observation time. For instance, if the client is observed for one hour, and is timed out four times at five minutes each, twenty minutes would be subtracted from the sixty-minute observation period. Thus, the number of inappropriate responses (four) is divided by forty minutes, resulting in a rate of one response per ten minutes (or six responses per hour) for that day.

More frequently, the client is released from time-out when the time period is up *and* when the individual is quiet for some period of time. If the therapist removes that person from time-out when he is engaging in inappropriate behavior, for instance, screaming, swearing, or kicking, he will reinforce these behaviors and increase the likelihood that they will reoccur when the client is next placed in time-out. Since these behaviors are usually disruptive to others in the immediate area, it is desirable that they be eliminated. If, for instance, the client is to be timed out for fifteen minutes, the therapist should wait until he has been quiet for a certain amount of time at the end of the fifteen minutes, before releasing him. At first, the therapist may only require that the person be quiet for ten seconds before removing him from time-out. One should begin listening at fourteen minutes and fifty seconds to see if the client has been quiet for the last ten seconds. If he makes noise during that ten-second period, his release from time-out should be delayed by ten seconds. When the individual has been quiet for a full ten seconds, he is released. After several occasions in which he is consistently quiet for the ten seconds, the therapist might increase the time the client must be quiet to fifteen or twenty seconds. When he is consistently being quiet for this duration, the time requirement is increased again. Eventually, the individual should have to be quiet for at least one minute to be released.

After the client is released from time-out, activities should return to normal. He should not be comforted or shown extra attention, but any appropriate behavior which would normally be reinforced should be reinforced at that time.

Effectiveness of Time-Out

The *only* way to evaluate the effectiveness of time-out is to observe if its contingent use decreases the occurrence of the undesirable behavior. A client may laugh while being placed in time-out, but still cease emitting the behavior for which he is timed out. Similarly, an individual client may cry and scream when timed out, but the procedure may have no effect on the future occurrence of the behavior which results in the time-out.

Several factors determine whether or not the time-out procedure will be effective.

1. The reduction of positive reinforcement on the way to and during time-out will not decrease an inappropriate response if the person is highly reinforced on the way to or during time-out. Reducing reinforcement on the way to time-out has been discussed. Since even being led may be somewhat reinforcing, it is best to locate the time-out room or chair as close as possible to the situation in which the inappropriate response may occur. This is done so that there is as little contact as possible while the staff places the client in time-out.

It is equally important to block out as many sources of reinforcement as possible during time-out. This usually includes sounds and sights, but may also involve smells and touch. Of course, those stimuli which are reinforcing differ with individuals. For some, simply being removed from contact with others, even if the time-out room contains many other stimuli such as furniture and even toys, will be effective in decreasing an inappropriate behavior. With others, being placed in a time-out chair in the same room with other individuals but prevented from moving freely around the room and participating in activities, will be effective. If this is not successful in decreasing an inappropriate behavior, perhaps blocking the sight of the activities (by placing a screen around the chair) will enhance the success of the time-out procedure. Even if the client is placed in a time-out room, the therapist may have to eliminate the opportunity to hear what is going on, e.g. by locating the time-out situation in a remote part of the building. In other cases, *all* of these sources of reinforcement may have to be eliminated if time-out is to be effective. In summary, the more forms of positive reinforcement that can be eliminated, the more successful the time-out program is likely to be.

2. Time-out will not be effective if the client's usual situation is not more reinforcing than time-out. For instance, if a client is kept in a barren, noisy, smelly dayroom in which he receives no attention, being removed from this situation and placed in an empty, quiet time-out room may not be any

less reinforcing (and may be even *more* reinforcing). In short, the time-out situation must be less desirable to the client than the situation from which he is removed. As stressed previously, before attempting to use any procedure to decrease undesirable behavior, every effort should be made to make the individual's environment as reinforcing and stimulating as possible. For instance, adding music, toys, and other activities as well as reinforcement for appropriate behavior may, in itself, reduce a behavior problem. If it does not, the provision of such activities and reinforcement should be considered a necessary prerequisite to beginning a time-out program. Remember the procedure's complete name: Time-out *from positive reinforcement*.

3. The inappropriate behavior must be immediately followed by the cue which signals that time-out will begin.

4. The time between presentation of the cue signaling that the client will be timed out and actually placing the individual in time-out should be as short as possible. After presenting the signal, e.g. "Johnny, no," the client should immediately be placed in the time-out situation.

5. As with all procedures to decrease behavior, time-out should follow an inappropriate response *every* time it occurs.

6. As with most procedures, time-out may have to be used for some time before its effectiveness can be evaluated. If, for instance, an inappropriate behavior occurs two to five times a day, you may have to use the procedure for at least one week to determine if it is having the desired effect.

Finally, it should be emphasized that the time-out procedure should not be confused with long-term physical restraint. In the latter case, the client is tied continuously in a chair or bed, for instance, for self-destructive behavior, or placed in isolation in a room, e.g. to prevent aggression toward others. This procedure does work as long as the restraints are applied, but upon release the individual will resume the inappropriate behavior. Further, this type of restraint generally prevents all behavior, both appropriate and inappropriate, from occurring. This technique may also have serious physical side effects. In the case of time-out, although a client may be placed in an isolated room or tied in a chair this is done *immediately following an inappropriate response and for a short period of time.* Physical restraint is generally continued for lengthy periods of time and on a schedule which is independent of the individual's behavior. For instance, a self-destructive client is tied in bed until a staff member has time to watch him closely, then released for a few minutes until the staff member must attend to other duties. At that time, regardless of whether the person is being self-destructive or not, the individual is returned to bed.

DECREASING BEHAVIOR BY MEDICATION

The use of sedatives and other types of medication to suppress behavior problems is *not* presently considered by professional behavior modifiers to fall within the area of behavior modification. Nevertheless, the extensive use of drugs in controlling behavior deserves mention here, particularly since attempts to decrease undesirable behavior by medication are sometimes required before more restrictive behavior management procedures are employed. However, successful chemotherapy is presently limited by the following drawbacks. Prescribing medication to decrease an inappropriate behavior may have the undesirable side-effect of decreasing many appropriate behaviors as well. The client may no longer be aggressive, but he may also be unable to perform desirable, constructive behavior. In addition, if drug treatment is discontinued, all behaviors often return, whether appropriate or inappropriate. Medical and behavioral research may yield drugs which act selectively, i.e. decrease only an inappropriate behavior without producing a generally unresponsive state. Until such medication is available, many behavior modifiers view the use of drugs as an undesirable alternative to training the individual not to engage in inappropriate behavior.

DECREASING BEHAVIOR BY PUNISHMENT

Punishment can take many forms, ranging from mild to severe. Although in practice, mild forms of punishment are often tried before resorting to more restrictive forms of, for instance, time-out and overcorrection, *all* forms of punishment will be presented in this section. This represents a departure from the overall sequence of this chapter, in which milder procedures which should be tried first are presented before more severe procedures. However this organization is intended to give the reader an accurate conception of which procedures technically fall under punishment. As usual, the forms of punishment will be arranged in the order from mild to severe.

Response Cost

Punishment exists in two forms. One punishment procedure is called *response cost*, and involves withdrawal of a positive reinforcer contingent upon a response, which thereby decreases the strength of that response. With response cost, the client has a positive reinforcer in his possession, and when he emits an undesirable behavior, the positive reinforcer is taken away. For instance, if a child is playing with a toy, and hits another child, the toy is withdrawn for a brief period, e.g. two minutes. Similarly, if an individual is eating a meal, and throws or grabs food or engages in some other inappropriate response, his food is removed for a brief period, e.g. thirty seconds. The response cost procedure is often used with individuals who are on a token system. In this case, an inappropriate response results in the removal of a token(s), i.e. the person is "fined" tokens for unacceptable behavior.*

In order to conduct a response cost procedure, the individual must have some reinforcer(s) in his possession so that one or more of these reinforcers can be withdrawn contingent on an undesirable behavior. Ideally, a client will have received (and continue to be earning) these reinforcers contingent on appropriate behavior. However, there may be circumstances under which a client has not yet earned any reinforcers, for instance at the start of class. Thus, a response cost procedure could not be used, since the individual has no reinforcers to withdraw. In this case, it is desirable to give the client several "free" rein-

---

*See Chapter 8 for a complete description.

forcers. For instance, the therapist might give each individual a small bag of M&M's® at the start of the class period which they can keep (and consume at the end of class). If an inappropriate behavior occurs during class, one or more M&M's® are taken from the misbehaving student. Similarly, an individual might be given an allowance at the beginning of each week, portions of which can be taken back contingent upon undesirable behavior. Of course, the person *should* continue to earn reinforcers for appropriate behavior, for instance throughout the class period or the week at home. Therefore, the number of reinforcers given free at the beginning of these periods should be relatively small, so that the client will continue to try to earn additional reinforcers and so that he will not become satiated. Giving free reinforcers is only intended to allow the use of a response cost procedure for undesirable behavior which occurs *before* the individual has earned reinforcers for behaving appropriately.

The amount of the reinforcer which is removed, e.g. the number of tokens fined or the length of time the toy is withdrawn, should be kept relatively small for each misbehavior. Clearly, if the client loses all of his tokens for one transgression, he can then engage in other undesirable behaviors through the remainder of the day or week, and cannot be fined! On the other hand, the amount of the reinforcer which is removed in the response cost procedure should be large enough to truly "cost" the person something. For instance, removal of a toy for ten seconds may not be effective in reducing an inappropriate behavior when the child can freely play with that toy for a one-hour period. Similarly, ten tokens may not be an effective fine, when the individual has 10,000 tokens in his account.

When employing a response cost procedure, the reinforcer which is withdrawn following an undesirable response is often partially returned contingent upon acceptable behavior. For instance, if response cost is combined with practicing appropriate behavior (or other contingent education procedures), the client could be fined for misbehaving and then allowed to re-earn a portion of that fine for practicing an appropriate alternative behavior. As stressed previously, positive reinforcement for desirable behavior should be part of any program to decrease an inappropriate behavior; however, returning the reinforcer removed in response cost is not technically a part of the procedure.

Response cost combined with one or more contingent education procedures should be tried *before* resorting to either overcorrection, restrictive forms of time-out (such as placement of the individual in a locked bedroom), medication, or more severe punishment (described below). If the procedure is not effective in reducing an undesirable behavior, the therapist should try response cost *without* contingent education. If the behavior problem continues, he should *next* try one of the more severe procedures to decrease behavior.

In summary, a response cost procedure involves withdrawing either a conditioned or unconditioned reinforcer which the client has in his possession (e.g., a meal, toy, or token) contingent on an inappropriate response. The *only way* to evaluate if the procedure is successful in reducing an undesirable behavior is to try it consistently for a time and see if its contingent use decreases the target behavior. If it does not, it is not considered a punishment procedure, since punishment is technically defined as *both* a procedure, such as the response cost procedure, *and* as a decrease in the behavior which resulted in that procedure. Thus, the complete definition of response cost is *withdrawal of a positive reinforcer contingent on a response which decreases the strength of that response.*

Contingent Use of Aversive Stimuli

A second type of punishment consists of presenting a stimulus (event) contingent on a response which decreases the strength of that response. The stimuli used in this type of punishment are commonly called *aversive, noxious, painful,* or *unpleasant.* However, it is not necessary for an event to be painful in order for it to be a punisher; a frown is hardly painful, but its contingent use may be effective in decreasing a behavior. Such an aversive stimulus is presented immediately following (contingent upon) an inappropriate response in this type of punishment procedure. If that behavior decreases, e.g. if it occurs less frequently, then that stimulus is termed a punisher.

Perhaps the mildest form of punishment consists of frowns, reprimands, or other methods of showing social disapproval. Screaming and other harsh reprimands may also be punishers, but are usually not employed in public facilities. Although unemotional social disapproval should be tried first before resorting to more severe punishers, they may prove ineffective, i.e. they may be neutral. Further, since this is a form of attention, and attention is often a positive reinforcer, they may be counterproductive, i.e. not only fail to decrease the behavior that they follow, but may actually *increase* it.

Slaps and spankings are common punishers, but these are not typically allowed in many facilities.

Similarly, noise, such as the sounding of a loud horn, may be an effective punisher. The intensity (volume) of such auditory stimuli must be carefully adjusted to prevent physical damage to the ear. Further, this form of punishment is easily avoided by placing hands over the ears, may change intensity depending on the distance between the client and the source, and may not be practically employed in situations such as classrooms. These considerations, as well as possible public reaction to the use of noise, limits its desirability as a punisher.

Several unpleasant-tasting substances may also be punishers. For instance, chronic rumination (elective vomiting) was eliminated in a six-month-old infant by squirting a small amount of lemon juice into her mouth whenever this behavior occurred (Sajwaj, Libet, and Agras, 1974). Tobasco® sauce, Thumb® and Lavoris® may be similarly effective punishers. However, most unpleasant tasting substances are not intended to be swallowed (which is usually unavoidable even if they are only applied to the lips) and sometimes persist in the mouth for long periods, including times during which the individual is behaving appropriately.

The most severe form of punisher is electric shock. It involves touching the individual's bare skin for one or two seconds with an inductorium which delivers a painful, but harmless, electric shock. Although it has been shown to be an extremely effective punisher when used properly, it should only be used as a last resort, i.e. when all other methods for controlling the behavior problem have failed, or when the behavior is so dangerous that it must be eliminated immediately. Such behaviors include severe self-injury such as repeated and intense head-banging, and aggression which causes serious physical harm to others. Shock punishment is not allowed in some facilities. Its use should depend upon client or parental (guardian) permission, review by appropriate professional and nonprofessional persons, and administration and supervision by highly trained personnel.

Regardless of which of the two punishment procedures is employed, punishment should be preceded by a *conditioned punisher*. Recall that a conditioned positive reinforcer should always be presented prior to the delivery of an already effective reinforcer, to insure that the appropriate behavior is reinforced immediately, and to establish an event as a reinforcer which is convenient to deliver and used by a great deal of society. The same reasons exist for establishing and using a conditioned punisher. An event can be selected which is convenient to deliver, e.g. the word "No!" and can be delivered immediately following the inappropriate behavior, even if the already effective punisher will be slightly delayed, e.g. while one crosses the room to take a token from the client. Further, establishing a conditioned punisher will enable the therapist to minimize the number of times that a more severe punisher must be used. That is, after the conditioned punisher is established, it can be used *by itself* to decrease inappropriate behavior with only intermittent repairing with an already effective (and usually more severe) punisher.

A conditioned punisher is established by being paired with an already effective punisher. By such a pairing procedure, almost *any* stimulus can be made into a conditioned punisher. A conditioned punisher should be an event which is convenient to deliver, can be presented immediately, is easily perceived by the individual and is likely to be used by all others with whom the person has contact. Usually, social disapproval is the type of stimulus which best meets these requirements. Whether such disapproval takes the form of "No" or a brief description or explanation of an inappropriate behavior, e.g. "Johnny, don't throw blocks; you've hurt Susie", verbal disapproval is typically convenient to present immediately, and is easily perceived. Further, social disapproval is frequently used by society, and thus many agree that a person should learn the meaning of disapproval if that individual is to live in a natural, normal situation.

Since in many individuals' training social disapproval has previously been established as a conditioned punisher by being paired with an already effective punisher, it may not be necessary to specifically arrange such pairing. To determine if a stimulus such as "No" is already a punisher, the therapist should present it immediately following an inappropriate behavior each time that behavior occurs. If that response decreases, "No" is already a conditioned punisher and can be used by itself. In this case, although the therapist will not have to pair "No" with an already established punisher to make it effective, he should probably re-pair it with another punisher occasionally to maintain its effectiveness.

If the stimulus ("No") does not decrease the occurrence of the undesirable response after being used consistently, then it is not a punisher and pairing is necessary. If this is the case, an already effective punisher should be selected next. This can involve either presentation of an aversive stimulus or removal of a positive reinforcer (response cost). Of course, what constitutes an effective punisher will differ in individual cases. Although an event must be used to determine conclusively that it is a punisher, in many cases it may be sufficient to simply guess what stimulus might be an already effective punisher. If a client shows distaste or aversion to an event by whinning, crying, or avoiding it, that stimulus *may* be a punisher. A child's reaction is not necessarily a good test. For instance, some children react emotionally to spankings but their contingent use does not decrease a behavior, i.e. spanking is not a punisher for them; others seem unconcerned by a spanking, but cease emitting the punished response. Nevertheless, for many purposes, an individual's negative reaction to a stimulus may be a good starting place in identifying an effective punisher, and save valuable time which would otherwise be consumed in trying a variety of possible punishers before beginning the pairing procedure.

After locating a stimulus which the therapist suspects or knows to be an already effective punisher, the pairing procedure is begun. The stimulus ("No") is presented immediately following the inappropriate behavior, then the already effective punisher is immediately presented. For instance, if the client aggresses, "No" is presented clearly and firmly; *then* the person's hand is slapped.

This procedure is employed each time the behavior occurs. If the individual stops the undesirable response after the conditioned punisher is presented, the therapist *should deliver the already effective punisher anyway.* For instance, if the client aggresses against another client, the therapist says "No," and the client then ceases aggressing, the therapist should slap the individual's hand anyway. As long as the "No" is presented immediately following the inappropriate response, the already effective punisher can be *slightly* delayed and even presented at a time when the client has ceased the behavior. In short, after the undesirable response has occurred and the conditioned punisher presented, the person should not be allowed to avoid punishment by *any* means, e.g. ceasing the behavior, running from the therapist, or saying he's sorry.

After repeated pairings, the neutral stimulus ("No") will become a conditioned punisher, i.e. it will decrease an inappropriate response when presented contingent on that response. As this stimulus becomes a conditioned punisher, the already effective punisher can be gradually reduced by decreasing the number of times the conditioned punisher is followed by the established punisher. For instance, after following *each* conditioned punisher with the already effective punisher for a time, next follow the conditioned punisher with an established punisher every other time, then every third time, etc. The client should not be able to predict when the already effective punisher will follow the conditioned punisher. To accomplish this, re-pair the punishers on an *average* of, for instance, every third or fourth time. For instance:

First time client aggresses: a conditioned punisher *and* an already effective punisher are presented.

Second time the client aggresses: a conditioned punisher *only* is presented.

Third time client aggresses: a conditioned punisher *only* is presented.

Fourth time client aggresses: a conditioned punisher *and* an already effective punisher are presented.

Fifth time client aggresses: a conditioned punisher *only* is presented.

Sixth time client aggresses: a conditioned punisher *and* an already effective punisher are presented.

Seventh time client aggresses: a conditioned punisher *and* an already effective punisher are presented.

A conditioned punisher should *always* be used following *each* occurrence of an inappropriate response, and before *each* delivery of an already effective punisher (token loss, shock, spanking, or whatever). Ultimately, the already effective punisher should have to be used infrequently, i.e. the therapist can decrease inappropriate behavior by the contingent use of only the conditioned punisher. However, the conditioned punisher will not remain effective unless it is occasionally re-paired with an already effective punisher.

It is sometimes recommended that contingent education be used in addition to a conditioned punisher. For instance, as mentioned previously, response cost is often followed by a period of time in which the individual is asked to practice an appropriate alternative behavior and receives feedback and reinforcement for such practice. Similarly, social reprimands are sometimes combined with contingent education components such as reasoning, contingency statements, and feedback.* As was stressed, contingent education may consist of too much reinforcement following an inappropriate behavior, and thus the behavior problem may either not improve or become worse. If this is the case, contingent education should be eliminated, and either the response cost procedure or a brief verbal reprimand should be employed as the *only* consequence for the undesirable behavior. (Contingent education should be eliminated first, and response cost or reprimands tried individually *before* resorting to more severe procedures.) On the other hand, the author does not suggest combining contingent education with either spanking, noise, unpleasant tasting substances, or shock as a consequence for inappropriate behavior. The author knows of no research in this area, and thus makes this recommendation on intuition alone. If the behavior problem is so severe, and if all other procedures for decreasing a behavior have failed (including contingent education by itself and in combination with other procedures, such as time-out) then either spanking, noise, unpleasant tasting substances, or shock should be used by themselves. That is, when an inappropriate behavior occurs, the therapist should immediately present the conditioned punisher, e.g. "No," and then deliver one of the four types of punishers described above. After, for instance, spanking the child, the therapist should walk away and say nothing further to the child for two to five minutes (see below for details of the proper procedure following punishment).

In summary, punishment consists of either presenting an aversive stimulus contingent on a response, or removing a positive reinforcer contingent on a response (response cost), and thereby decreases the occurrence of that response. In either case, a conditioned punisher should be established and presented before each presentation of an already effective punisher. The only way to evaluate if punishment is effective is to observe whether it decreases the future occurrence of a response. As stressed previously, this does not mean interrupting the behavior, once started. Similarly, the therapist cannot use the

---

*See the section in this chapter entitled "Contingent Education" for a more thorough description of each of these procedures.

individual's behavior while being punished as an indication of whether or not a punisher is effective. As mentioned, a child may cry during a spanking, but that spanking may be ineffective in reducing the inappropriate behavior for which he is spanked. A child may likewise laugh during a spanking, but nevertheless cease emitting the undesirable behavior which resulted in this consequence.

It is important to stress the difference between negative reinforcement and punishment. Negative reinforcement consists of removing or postponing presentation of an aversive event contingent on a response and thereby *increases* the occurrence of that response. Punishment involves presenting an aversive stimulus or removing a positive reinforcer contingent on a response and thereby *decreases* the response. Thus, not only are the procedures completely different, but while negative reinforcement *increases* a response, punishment *decreases* behavior.

Effectiveness of Punishment

A number of factors influence the effectiveness of the punishment procedure.

IMMEDIACY. The inappropriate behavior must be followed by the punisher *immediately*. If punishment is delayed, it should not be presented at all, since the person may have ceased the inappropriate behavior, and may even be engaging in an appropriate response. This is why a conditioned punisher should always be used. It can be easily presented immediately following the undesirable behavior, and then followed, even after a short delay, by another punisher.

INTENSITY OR AMOUNT. For maximum effectiveness, an intense punisher should be used at its full strength whenever punishment is delivered. A mild punisher may decrease the behavior gradually and by a moderate amount, and will thus have to be used more often. Although intense punishment produces superior suppression of behavior, humanitarian considerations dictate that one use the *least* intense punisher, *which is still effective in decreasing a behavior*. Therefore, it is best to try milder forms of punishment first before resorting to more severe punishers. However, if punishment intensity is gradually increased, the client may adapt, i.e. become less and less sensitive to even the most severe punishment procedure. It is therefore recommended that each form of punishment be tried consistently for a brief period. If the inappropriate behavior is not noticeably reduced during that time, a more severe punishment procedure may be tried. Specifically, the therapist may first try either social reprimands or a response cost procedure. If a small token fine or brief removal of other reinforcers does not appear effective, he may increase the amount of the reinforcer which is withdrawn contingent on the inappropriate behavior. For instance, one might increase the token fine from 1 percent to 3 percent of a person's total tokens. (Moral limits are usually placed on increasing the intensity of social reprimands.) If such increases in the intensity of these punishment procedures are not effective in decreasing the behavior, noise, unpleasant tasting substances, slaps, or spanking may be required. (Again, this text recommends that other procedures such as time-out and overcorrection be tried first, before resorting to punishers such as these.) As a last resort, shock punishment may be necessary to reduce severe behavior problems. When electric shock is used, it is *not* recommended that the intensity of this punisher be gradually increased. (Commercially available inductoriums typically deliver a standard intensity of shock.)

After the most effective form and intensity of punishment is discovered, it should be used following each occurrence of the undesirable response. A therapist should not apply a mild punisher contingent on the first inappropriate behavior, and then present a more intense form of the punisher each time the individual engages in the inappropriate response. For instance, if he finds that withdrawing a client's food tray for one minute is the most effective consequence for food snatching, it should be removed for the full minute following each snatching response. It should not be withdrawn for fifteen seconds following the first snatch of the meal, thirty seconds following the second, and one minute following the third. This may sound fair, but will result in the person performing the undesirable behavior until the punishment becomes intense enough to be truly effective, and then the behavior will decrease. If the therapist wishes the behavior to be eliminated completely (or to a very low level) he should use the full, effective intensity of the punisher each time it is applied.

After the inappropriate behavior has been decreased, *perhaps* he can maintain that decrease with a less intense strength of the punisher. If the behavior begins to increase again, he can return to using the more intense punisher, and not employ the milder punisher again.

CONSISTENCY. A punisher should be presented following *each* occurrence of an inappropriate response. Unlike the case of positive reinforcement, intermittent use of punishment has no advantages. If punishment is used consistently, it will have to be used very infrequently, if at all (because the punished response will occur infrequently, if at all). It is sometimes recommended that the client receive one warning following an inappropriate behavior, and then the next occurrence of that behavior be punished. The use of *one* warning may be desirable in the early stages of treatment and is often combined with contingent education procedures to teach appropriate alternative behavior. With persons who can read or understand verbal instructions, a list of inappropriate behaviors and their consequences can be posted or read, e.g. at the start of each class or day in the cottage. Such statements of the rules can be useful, but are not necessary. Consistent punishment will work without prior explanation of the rules, and with individuals for whom such an explanation may have no meaning. Whether or not the rules are specified in this manner, a warning following an inappropriate behavior should only be used in the early stages of treatment. After that time, the client should be punished for each occurrence of the inappropriate behavior and should not be given further warnings. When using shock, no warning should be employed.

NUMBER OF PUNISHMENTS. Some punishers reduce the behavior completely after only one or two contingent presentations. For instance, electric shock has been shown to take effect that quickly. Other events such as reprimands or response cost may decrease an inappropriate behavior more gradually.

The period of time required to evaluate the effectiveness of a punisher partly depends upon the frequency with which the client engages in an inappropriate behavior. For instance, if aggression occurs several times a minute, the therapist can perhaps determine if a punisher decreases this behavior within ten minutes. On the other hand, if aggression typically occurs two or three times per day, several days may be required to evaluate if a punisher is decreasing the behavior.

POSITIVE REINFORCEMENT FOR THE PUNISHED RESPONSE. If an inappropriate behavior continues to be intermittently reinforced, punishment of any kind will be less effective. For this reason, it is *always* necessary to try to identify and then discontinue the positive reinforcer that is maintaining the undesirable behavior (the extinction procedure) even if punishment is also employed. Similarly, care must be taken to minimize positive reinforcement which may accompany punishment. Although it is recommended that some form of contingent education be used with response cost or social reprimands (not with the other types of punishment), this may consist of too much reinforcement. If the combination of contingent education and punishment is not effective in reducing a behavior problem (or if the problem is getting worse!) the therapist should discontinue contingent education and use punishment by itself. In this case, he does not do anything at the time of punishment except: (a) present the conditioned punisher such as "No" (once!), (b) then deliver the established punisher and, (c) turn and walk away with no further comment to the client.

POSITIVE REINFORCEMENT FOLLOWING PUNISHMENT. If a punisher is presented following an inappropriate behavior, and if punishment is then frequently followed by a positive reinforcer, the punishing event will become a signal that positive reinforcement may be forthcoming. In other words, presentation of the punisher will come to signal that reinforcement is on its way, and the inappropriate response will *not decrease*, and may *increase*. For instance, if the client has a tantrum, the therapist fines him a token, and soon after approaches and comforts him, makes up and is generally affectionate; having a tantrum may increase as that individual learns that punishment is usually followed by positive reinforcement. In this way, tantrums may be maintained by the eventual reinforcement the individual receives following punishment. Thus, it is generally wise to withhold any type of reinforcement for a few minutes following punishment. After this time has elapsed, the trainer should reinforce the client *as usual*, i.e. not making the requirements for reinforcement higher or lower than is normally the case. In summary, punishment should be followed with a short period of time in which no reinforcement is given. Then reinforcement should proceed as usual..

AVAILABILITY OF AN ALTERNATIVE RESPONSE. As stressed previously, any procedure for decreasing an undesirable response should accompany a program for increasing appropriate behavior. Further, punishment has been found to be more effective in reducing an undesirable behavior if more appropriate behavior is also reinforced. For instance, the therapist might design a treatment program which consists of punishment for aggression, *and* positive reinforcement for appropriate play and other desirable behavior. In this case, whenever the child aggresses, he is fined; whenever he plays in a desirable manner he receives attention and tokens. The reinforced response(s) can consist of any appropriate behavior or one that is incompatible with the punished response.

EFFECTIVENESS OF THE POSITIVE REINFORCER. Withdrawing a positive reinforcer contingent on a response (the response cost procedure) will only be effective in decreasing a behavior if the event that is taken away is truly reinforcing. The success of this procedure rests on the effectiveness of a positive reinforcer, e.g. the extent to which the individual is deprived of the reinforcer.

SIDE EFFECTS OF PUNISHMENT. A final consideration in employing a punishment procedure is whether or not it will result in undesirable side effects while producing a decrease in the target inappropriate response. There have been various suggestions that the following side effects may occur if punishment is employed: (1) other undesirable responses may increase (called *symptom substitution*), (2) the person who administers punishment and/or the situation in which the client is punished may become generally aversive, and the client may attempt to escape or avoid the person or situation, (3) the individual will generally become emotionally upset and fearful, (4) the client will become aggressive, particularly immediately after being punished, (5) the punished response will only decrease temporarily during the period in which punishment is used. It will increase again after the punishment procedure is discontinued, (6) the punished response will only decrease in the specific situation in which punishment is used.

There has been little experimental documentation of the first four proposed side effects. In fact, there is increasing research evidence which demonstrates that if other behaviors increase during the time in which an inappropriate response is decreased by punishment, these other behaviors will be *appropriate* ones. In short, the client is likely to begin engaging in desirable behaviors which can then be reinforced. This increase in appropriate responses includes behavior toward the person administering punishment and in those situations in which punishment is delivered. In those cases in which an undesirable behavior does increase when another inappropriate behavior is being decreased by punishment, that second behavior can also be eliminated by punishment or other procedures for decreasing behavior. Further research will expand and refine current information about both desirable and undesirable side effects of punishment. It is recommended, however, that potential undesirable side effects be carefully monitored, so that the program can be modified if these do emerge.

Data which show an increase in appropriate behavior during punishment have, of course, been collected under conditions in which the punishment procedure is run properly, following all the rules outlined on the preceding pages. If punishment is delayed following an inappropriate response (and consequently another, perhaps appropriate response is punished), if punishment is used inconsistently, or if the procedure is misused in any other way, any or all of the first four undesirable side effects may emerge.

The fifth proposed side effect, the temporary effects of punishment, has some research support. However, with a very intense punisher, e.g. intense electric shock, a small number of contingent presentations have been shown to decrease an inappropriate behavior for *very* long periods. With less intense punishers, the undesirable behavior may begin to reappear following discontinuation of punishment. However, if it is again punished, the behavior will again decrease. The same effect holds true for any procedure, whether it is designed to increase or decrease a behavior. For instance, if positive reinforcement is no longer presented for an appropriate response, or if an extinction procedure is not continued for an inappropriate response, the behavior may return to its previous level. In short, *any* procedure in behavior modification must usually be continued in some form if the improvement in behavior is expected to continue. In some cases, treatment such as positive reinforcement or punishment changes the client's behavior in such a way that improvement is maintained by "natural" contingencies. For instance, if a person has been spanked for crossing a street at any point other than a crosswalk, improvement may be maintained naturally after the individual receives a reprimand from a policeman for crossing inappropriately. In this case, one need not follow the person and be prepared to spank him, if a policeman's reprimand (a natural consequence) is an effective punisher for jaywalking. If such natural contingencies are not available, punishment must be employed *whenever* the client engages in the behavior. However, if punishment has been truly effective, the undesirable response will occur so infrequently that use of the procedure will rarely be necessary.

Similar points are relevant to the final, proposed side effect of punishment. Research has demonstrated that a behavior will only decrease in the situation in which punishment is used and/or only in the presence of those individuals who administer punishment. For instance, if aggression is punished in the classroom, but not in the individual's residence, aggression will decrease in the classroom, but will continue at its usual level in the cottage or home. Similarly, if only one staff member punishes an undesirable behavior, that response will be suppressed in the presence of that therapist, but will continue to be displayed when that person is absent. (This is an example of undesirable discrimination; see Chapter 9.) A similar, unfortunate effect is often seen with any procedure, whether it is designed to increase or decrease a behavior. If behavioral improvement is to be achieved throughout the day, in all situations and by all persons (staff and parents) with whom the person has contact, then the treatment procedure must be employed at all times, in all situations and by all persons. In short, punishment, as any other treatment procedure, only affects behavior in those situations in which it is used, and thus must be used in as many settings and by as many people as possible.

Determining Effectiveness of Punishment

The points described above pertain to both unconditioned and conditioned punishment. The following factors influencing the effectiveness of punishment relate specifically to conditioned punishers.

NUMBER OF PAIRINGS. A stimulus must be paired many times with an already established punisher before it becomes an effective conditioned punisher. Thus, it will take some time before the conditioned punisher can be used by itself, with only occasional re-pairing.

FREQUENCY OF RE-PAIRING. To retain its punishing power, the conditioned punisher must be intermittently re-paired with an established punisher. If behaviors which are followed by the conditioned punisher begin to increase, increasing the frequency of following a conditioned punisher with an established punisher may decrease the behavior again.

IMMEDIACY. When a stimulus is first being established as a conditioned punisher, it should be followed by the already effective punisher immediately. Although some delay can occur between these events after the stimulus becomes a conditioned punisher, it should remain as short as possible. For instance, if the therapist does not have the shock apparatus with him when an inappropriate response occurs, he should present the conditioned punisher, e.g. "No," and then *run* and get the inductorium and shock the client. If the delay is longer than perhaps one minute, he should probably not deliver the shock at all. If the inappropriate response does not continue to decline, or begins to increase, the delay between the conditioned punisher and the already effective punisher may be too long.

EFFECTIVENESS OF ESTABLISHED PUNISHER. The effectiveness of the conditioned punisher depends upon the effectiveness of the established punisher with which it is paired. For this reason, it *may* be best to test the effectiveness of a punisher *before* using it to establish a conditioned punisher.

THE SEQUENCE IN WHICH TO
TRY DECELERATING PROCEDURES

The previous sections describe a variety of procedures used to decrease behavior (decelerating procedures), and an approximate sequence in which they should be tried. This sequence reflects the author's interpretation of current moral and legal thinking concerning each procedure's relative degree of restrictiveness and severity. It should be stressed again that there is not universal agreement among either professionals or nonprofessionals as to the relative severity of each procedure.

The following list is a summary of the suggested sequence with which to try the various procedures for decreasing behavior problems. For instance, social reprimands and shock were described in the same section since they are both punishment procedures. However, the former is much less severe than the latter and should be used early in a treatment program designed to decrease behavior, e.g. before satiation, time-out, overcorrection, medication, or other forms of punishment are employed. Shock, on the other hand, is considered the most severe form of punishment and is recommended only as a last resort. The following list is intended to clarify confusion arising from such discrepancies by listing techniques in the order in which they should be used.

- Placement of the individual in a stimulating and enriching environment
- Extinction
- Differential reinforcement of incompatible behavior (DRI)
- Differential reinforcement of other behavior (DRO)
- Differential reinforcement of low rates (DRL)
- Placement of the individual in a new environment, distraction, attention to the victim of aggression, physical removal of the object or person toward whom the inappropriate behavior is directed, and pointed praise
- Contingent education
- Satiation
- Time-out in which the therapist turns away from the individual for a brief period of time
- Time-out within the same room in which the other clients are located
    a. Used with contingent education
    b. Used without contingent education
- Response cost punishment
    a. Used with contingent education
    b. Used without contingent education
- Overcorrection, either by restoring the environment to its previous state (usually brief), or by positive practice
- Time-out in an unlocked room, e.g. bedroom or hall, in which other individuals are *not* located
    a. Used with contingent education
    b. Used without contingent education
- Overcorrection in which the individual is required to restore the environment to a state better than it was previously (usually effortful and time consuming)
- Time-out in a locked room, e.g. bedroom or hall
- Time-out in a locked room specifically designed for that purpose, or restrained in a chair
- Medication
- Punishment in which a contingent aversive stimulus is used:
    a. With either an unpleasant tasting substance, spanking or noise

b. With electric shock

Each of the procedures presented above need not (indeed, should not!) be tried *by itself* before employing another procedure to decrease a behavior. For instance, it is customary and desirable to place a client with a behavior problem in a stimulating environment, discontinue reinforcement for the inappropriate behavior, and provide consistent reinforcement for appropriate behavior (DRI), as well as for *not* engaging in the undesirable behavior (DRO), *all at the same time.* If this combination of procedures does not prove effective, perhaps adding a combination of contingent education, response cost, and medication may reduce the inappropriate behavior. In general, for most clinical purposes, appropriate combinations of procedures can and should be tried.

As emphasized previously, several procedures should be included in *any* program to decrease behavior. These are: placing the individual in a stimulating, enriching environment; discontinuing as much reinforcement as possible for the inappropriate behavior; teaching and reinforcing appropriate behavior; and reinforcing the individual for not engaging in the inappropriate behavior. In short, these methods should be tried *first*, and if their combination is ineffective in reducing a behavior problem, they should be continued while other, more severe procedures are added.

Factors Affecting the Choice and Sequence of Punishment

The particular procedures which are employed, and the sequence in which they are tried must be determined for each individual case. Several factors contribute to the decision regarding *if* and *when* to try various techniques.

CHARACTERISTICS OF THE CLIENT. With an individual who totally lacks language and other social skills, contingent education *may* not be a reasonable procedure to attempt. On the other hand, shock punishment should rarely, if ever, be necessary for controlling a behavior problem in a mildly retarded individual. Further, if an individual is very large, uncooperative, and aggressive, it may not be possible to employ either a time-out procedure (it may be too dangerous to attempt to place the client in even a locked room) or overcorrection (it may not be possible to put him through the necessary behaviors).

SEVERITY OF BEHAVIOR PROBLEM. With inappropriate behavior that is not considered dangerous, time can be taken to try several of the less severe methods of decreasing behavior. Further, a mild procedure which reduces a behavior slowly and/or only partially may be acceptable in these cases. On the other hand, with behavior such as dangerous aggression or self-injury, one must quickly determine a procedure which will eliminate the behavior rapidly and completely. In this case, after placing the client in a stimulating environment and providing a consistent program of positive reinforcement, restrictive time-out, medication, or severe punishment may have to be employed immediately to effectively eliminate the behavior.

SITUATION IN WHICH PROCEDURE IS IMPLEMENTED. The procedures described in this chapter have all been thoroughly researched and documented effective in a variety of situations, and with a variety of individuals and behavior problems (unless specified otherwise). However, in most cases it is not possible to predict beforehand if a procedure will be successful with a particular individual displaying a particular behavior problem. As stressed previously, a procedure must be tried to determine its effectiveness in each case. Further, most techniques must be modified to fit a particular individual's problem and situation. (Typical modifications are described under each procedure.) An individual's problem and environment must be carefully evaluated when deciding which procedure to employ, or before concluding that a particular technique was ineffective. For instance, before attempting an extinction procedure, the therapist must ascertain whether lines of staff communication are adequate so that all will understand and consistently employ such a procedure. Similarly, when time-out is considered, he must judge whether or not the situation from which the client is removed is adequately reinforcing.

PRACTICALITY TO THERAPISTS. Some procedures require more time to employ than do others. For instance, initially DRO may require that a teacher remain in close proximity to a client and reinforce him every few seconds or minutes. Increasing the time between reinforcements is a gradual process and may take weeks. Thus, this procedure may require a great deal of teacher time to implement. Similarly, if the use of time-out requires that several teachers assist in placing a resistant student in the time-out room, this procedure may not be practical.

STAFF TRAINING AND SUPERVISION. No treatment program should be employed until staff are thoroughly trained in its procedures and effects. Some procedures appear to be more easily communicated than others, i.e. teachers may be able to employ certain procedures after less training and with less supervision than other methods of treatment. For instance, DRO seems to be a relatively difficult procedure to train teachers to use.

Training alone does not insure that the procedures are employed properly and consistently. In addition, the therapist will need to: continue supervision of their use, i.e. observe periodically and check on the records of the client's behavior, provide feedback to the staff about the proper and improper use of the procedures, and only involve in behavior modification programs persons who have demonstrated a willingness and competence to employ the prescribed procedures. (Some programs have arranged tangible reinforcers, e.g. money, trading stamps, or time off from work for appropriate staff behavior.) Some procedures require more supervision, feedback, and/or care in staff selection than do others. For instance, punishment with electric shock, although relatively easy to describe and implement, must be supervised closely because of its powerful effects when used or misused.

POTENTIAL FOR ABUSE. Even with well-trained and supervised staff, in some cases it may be decided to not employ certain procedures because of the danger of their misuse. Although *any* technique may be used improperly or for malevolent purposes, some are more susceptible to actual abuse than others. For instance, verbal reprimands may degenerate into screaming, abusive tirades. Spanking has the clear potential for physical mistreatment. As mentioned, shock may similarly be abused.

Overcorrection can become a wrestling match, dangerous to both client and therapist. When selecting a treatment procedure, one must weigh various techniques' potential for abuse against their possible therapeutic effectiveness. For instance, if overcorrection is judged likely to be effective with a particular behavior problem, and may prevent the use of more severe procedures, a decision may be made to employ that procedure despite its potential for misuse. Similarly, a decision may be made to employ shock punishment to quickly eliminate severe aggession which abused others and may result in danger to the aggressor through retaliation by other clients, or even staff.

PUBLIC AND ETHICAL ACCEPTABILITY. A decision regarding the use of any therapeutic procedure must be made in the context of society's moral and ethical standards. Professionals and nonprofessionals have a responsibility to decrease only those behaviors which are truly disruptive, dangerous, or otherwise deleterious to either the individual's well-being or those around him. Further, every precaution must be made to insure that the procedures used to decrease those behaviors are as benign and noncontroversial as possible, i.e. that the means justify the ends. Although the same issues apply to the selection and treatment of appropriate behavior, public and legal attention has been far more concerned with the use of aversive control on undesirable behavior. Currently, locked time-out, excessive medication, and electric shock have generated the most concern. Thus, these techniques may raise moral issues and have social repercussions which may dictate against their use in some facilities.

On the other hand, professionals and nonprofessionals *also* have a responsibility to provide effective therapy to their clients. In some situations, procedures such as locked time-out or shock punishment may be the only remaining alternatives in reducing a serious behavior problem. Thus, the therapist is faced with a dilemma between the ethical problem of deliberately withholding an effective treatment procedure on the one hand and possible public repercussions on the other. If a decision is made to proceed with treatment, several measures may prove helpful in avoiding adverse public reaction to the use of more controversial procedures. *First,* all staff employing the procedure should be thoroughly trained in its use, and supervised closely by competent professionals. They should also be familiar with the technique's rationale, use, and effects, in order to answer questions in a competent manner. *Second,* the administration should be fully informed of the details and general effects of the procedure, and be supportive of its use. *Third,* information regarding the technique should be given freely (but only by those competent to do so) and the procedure should be employed openly. *Fourth,* many facilities have found it prudent to obtain the guardian's (and sometimes the client's) permission before implementing certain programs such as shock and time-out.

NORMALCY. A procedure should be selected partly on the basis of its use in the natural community, such as the individual's own home. First, procedures which are commonly employed by society are less likely to concern the public. For instance, sending a misbehaving child to his room is quite conventional and not likely to cause public alarm, whereas restraining a child in a locked and barren time-out room may cause concern. Further, employing a procedure which is used by much of society increases the chances that inappropriate behavior which has been reduced by this technique in a special training facility will remain decreased when he enters the natural community. For instance, if a student has been reprimanded for spitting in school, his parents are likely to use a similar procedure for such behavior at home. Similarly, time-out in a bedroom and spanking are commonly used techniques in normal situations. If an undesirable behavior has been suppressed by one of these procedures, it is likely that parents and others will use the same or similar procedures, and thus the behavior problem is likely to remain decreased when the individual returns to the community. On the other hand, techniques such as satiation, DRO, and shock punishment are not likely to be used with inappropriate behavior which occurs in normal settings. It may be possible to specifically arrange for the use of these procedures in the client's natural community, or to maintain his improvement, i.e. keep the undesirable behavior at a low or zero level, by more normal procedures. However, when possible, it is desirable to first try procedures which are commonly available in society, to increase the chances that a behavior problem will remain suppressed naturally in the community.

DISRUPTION TO THE INDIVIDUAL'S OVERALL PROGRAM. A behavior problem should be treated with a procedure which interferes as little as possible with other aspects of a client's training program. For instance, when employing a DRO procedure, the therapist dispenses reinforcers after periods of time in which the individual has not emitted an undesirable behavior. If DRO reinforcement is frequent, the person may become satiated with the reinforcer, which cannot then be used to strengthen appropriate behavior (at least temporarily). Similarly, long periods of isolated time-out deprive the client of participating in activities which should be important educational experiences for him. Although disruptive techniques may be necessary, an attempt should be made to select one which interferes as little as possible with other aspects of a client's program.

REFERENCES

Ayllon, T.: Intensive treatment of psychotic behavior by stimulus satiation and food reinforcement. *Behavior Research and Therapy, 1*:53-61, 1963.

Azrin, N. H. and Foxx, R. M.: A rapid method of toilet training the institutionalized retarded. *Journal of Applied Behavior Analysis, 4*:89-99, 1971.

Azrin, N. H. and Nunn, R. G.: Habit-reversal: A method of eliminating nervous habits and tics. *Behavior Research and Therapy, 11*:619-628, 1973.

Epstein, L. H., Doke, L. A. Sajwaj, T. E., Sorrell, S., and Rimmer, B.: Generality and side effects of overcorrection. *Journal of Applied Behavior Analysis, 7*:385-390, 1974.

Foxx, R. M. and Azrin, N. H.: Restitution: A method of eliminating aggressive-disruptive behavior of retarded and brain damaged patients. *Behavior Research and Therapy, 10*:15-27, 1972.

Foxx, R. M. and Azrin, N. H.: The elimination of autistic self-stimulatory behavior by overcorrection. *Journal of Applied Behavior Analysis, 6*:1

14, 1973.

May, J. G., Risley, T. R., Twardosz, S., Friedman, P., Bijou, S., Wexler, D., et al.: Guidelines for the use of behavioral procedures in state programs for the retarded persons. *MR Research Monograph*, Vol. 1, No. 1, National Association of Retarded Citizens, 1975.

Phillips, E. L., Phillips, E. A., Fixen, D. L., and Wolf, M. M.: *The Teaching Family Handbook*, University of Kansas Printing Service, 1974 (revised).

Sajwaj, T., Libet, J. and Agras, S.: Lemon-juice therapy: The control of life-threatening rumination in a six-month-old infant. *Journal of Applied Behavior Analysis*, 7:557-563, 1974.

Webster, D. R. and Azrin, N. H.: Required relaxation: A method of inhibiting agitative-disruptive behavior of retardates. *Behavior Research and Therapy*, 11:67-78, 1973.

Chapter 8

TOKEN SYSTEMS

TOKEN programs are based upon the principles and procedures of positive reinforcement which have been described previously. Other techniques, such as response cost, punishment, and contingent education, are also employed in token systems. Therefore, the following discussion of token programs is based upon the assumption that the student has read and understands these concepts which are incorporated into a token economy.

Token reinforcement systems have been used successfully with a variety of populations, e.g. public school students (Wolf, Giles, and Hall, 1968; O'Leary, Becker, Evans, and Saudargas, 1969), psychotic adults (Ayllon and Azrin, 1965), delinquents (Phillips, 1968; Burchard and Tyler, 1965), and retardates (Zimmerman, Zimmerman, and Russell, 1969; Hunt, Fitzhugh, and Fitzhugh, 1968).

Token economies are intended as a temporary, therapeutic program to improve the behavior of individuals or groups. They are not designed to be continued indefinitely, but to improve behavior and then be phased out, maintaining improvement in the individual's natural environment.

Token Reinforcement

Tokens take many forms, e.g. plastic chips, paper slips, marks in a book, or coins. In general, any type of item which has the following characteristics can be used as tokens: (1) cannot be duplicated or obtained in an unauthorized way, (2) lightweight, (3) durable, (4) small enough to allow therapists to carry many, (5) easily kept and banked by the individual, and (6) easily given and taken away.

Tokens are not natural, unconditioned reinforcers. They must be established as a conditioned reinforcer by being paired

182

with an already effective reinforcer. When an appropriate response occurs, the client is praised and handed the token immediately; then the token is reclaimed and an already effective reinforcer is given (usually an unconditioned reinforcer such as food or liquid). Notice this sequence:

- The appropriate behavior occurs.
- The client is handed a token (always accompanied by social praise, e.g. "That is the correct answer, here's your token!")
- The token is immediately taken back.
- The person is then handed his already effective reinforcer (called a *backup reinforcer*).

This process is repeated over and over again following one or a variety of appropriate behaviors. Generally, these appropriate behaviors are ones the client has learned previously and are easily performed, e.g. sitting in a chair when told to, opening and closing doors, and looking at the therapist on command. One should not attempt to teach a new response (one that the client has not performed previously) while establishing tokens as reinforcers.

One must watch for signs that the individual is beginning to learn the exchange procedure, e.g. he quickly hands the therapist the token (instead of the therapist taking it from him) and then reaches or holds out his hand to receive the "goody" (backup reinforcer). When these behaviors occur consistently, the therapist should begin to gradually lengthen the time between giving the client the token and redeeming it for an already effective reinforcer. The procedure is as follows: present a token following an appropriate behavior, but do not trade it; wait for a second appropriate behavior (or prompt one, e.g. ask him to sit down and then gently press him into a chair); pay him a second token and then immediately redeem both for a backup reinforcer. One should continue requiring the client to earn two tokens before trading until he again shows signs of learning this arrangement. He will generally stop trying to trade the first one until he receives the second, and upon receiving the second, he will hand the therapist his tokens and reach for his reinforcer. Next, the therapist begins introducing a delay between receiving the second token and redeeming both. As before, during the delay he presents a third token for an appropriate behavior and then trades all three for a reinforcer. In this way, he gradually lengthens the time between receiving tokens and redeeming them. It cannot be overemphasized that this delay must be increased *gradually*. The individual's behavior must be the therapist's guide. If he ceases to perform appropriate behaviors for which tokens are presented, the delay between receiving and trading tokens should be *shortened*. On the other hand, the delay should be increased as fast as possible without disrupting his behavior. During this time, the therapist may also begin to present a different number of tokens for different behaviors. For instance, he may give a person two or three tokens for a behavior judged to be more difficult or more desirable, while presenting one token for a less appropriate behavior.

The process of establishing tokens as effective reinforcers can be aided greatly by the use of verbal instructions. If the therapist even suspects that the client (or clients) may respond to instructions, then they should be used in combination with the procedures described. For instance, when initially pairing the token with a reinforcer, the therapist might say: "When you earn a token like this (hand him a token), you can trade it for a piece of candy (show him how the token is traded)." Later, when a delay is gradually being introduced between giving the token and redeeming it, the therapist can tell him, "Now you must earn two tokens, this one and one other to get the piece of candy," or "You can trade your tokens in just a minute." The most important aspect is the pairing procedure (trading) and the gradual increase in the delay between receiving the token and trading it. Instructions are only supplementary and should not be relied on too heavily. In fact, instructions and verbal prompting should be faded out as quickly as possible, and only used when rules are changed, e.g. when new appropriate behaviors are added to the list or when backup prices are changed.

Clients may be trained individually or in groups. Of course, the fewer the number of individuals trained simultaneously in the use of tokens, the more immediately the therapist is likely to reinforce each appropriate behavior, and the more appropriate behavior he is likely to see. For instance, while he is trading tokens with one, another may be emitting a desirable behavior that should be reinforced. On the other hand, clients may benefit by observing others earning and trading tokens. When a token program is being implemented with a group of clients, it may be most efficient to attempt training them together first. For instance, the therapist can tell everyone to sit down and when they do, praise them and move from one to another presenting and trading tokens. Similarly, he can move among them in a free-play situation, praising, presenting, and trading tokens, making sure to reinforce each an approximately equal number of times. In this process, he may notice one or more individuals who are not catching on to the token system and provide them with individual instruction.

An important feature of token systems is the variety of backup reinforcers available. Backup reinforcers are those already effective reinforcers with which the token is paired, i.e. items and activities which are purchased by the tokens. Although these need not be expensive, they should be very desirable and varied as often as one's budget and imagination allow. Further, as wide a variety of backups should be available simultaneously as is possible. The backups might include:

1. edibles (candy, cereal, fruit, and soda)
2. toys (balloons, games, bubble soap, cards, and crayons)
3. school and play equipment (pencils, paper, books, clay, and scissors)
4. personal items (cosmetics, clothes, sunglasses, and jewelry)
5. other activities and privileges (tickets providing access to reading materials, movies, the playground, bus rides, running errands, and helping the teachers).

When selecting backups, be sure to take advantage of nonessential materials and activities which are normally available *free*, e.g. nightly snacks, drinking through a straw, and recess.

Although some backups can be made available for purchase by all clients in the program, others can be made available only to a particular client. For instance, an individual might purchase the opportunity to play with a game his parents have provided, or that he had purchased with his tokens at a previous time.

Guidelines for Using a Token System

In general, when establishing and running a token system, the following procedures should be followed.

Start by redeeming tokens immediately, then gradually increase the number of tokens earned before trading (which results in a gradual increase in the time between receiving and redeeming the tokens).

After such training, the clients should earn tokens throughout at least a one-hour period, at which time the token store may open (juice time occur, or recess scheduled, etc.) and all can redeem some of their tokens. If the therapist must trade the tokens more than once an hour to increase and maintain an appropriate behavior, few of the advantages of the token system (described below) will be achieved. On the other hand, the maximum delay between receiving and redeeming the tokens must be adjusted to each client. In some cases, low frequency behaviors may be increased and maintained at a high level by tokens which are redeemed after a week or two. In other cases, this delay would result in tokens becoming ineffective. The therapist must *test* various delays and see what works! Usually, a token system features a variety of delays, so that the person redeems some tokens soon after receiving them, others he spends on backups occurring in the future, e.g. a movie in two days.

When a client keeps tokens to spend at future dates, generally a banking system must be implemented. This helps in preventing an individual from losing his tokens, and can provide training in the usual banking procedures that exist in the community, e.g. writing checks, and making deposits and withdrawals. Despite the advantages of such training, clients generally should not be allowed to accumulate a great many tokens in a bank, unless they will be required for a big event, such as a trip to the Ice Capades. If a large accumulation does occur, clients will not have to behave appropriately for long periods, during which they can buy all the desired backups with tokens earned in the past. A possible solution involves requiring that many backups, e.g. daily activities, be purchased only with tokens earned that same day, and allowing the clients to bank (save) only a certain amount daily for future events. Another remedy may consist of restricting access to banked tokens by requiring that a certain number of newly earned tokens be on hand before a withdrawal can be made. As an alternative, the therapist might use different kinds of tokens, some of which can only be spent on future events such as movies, and others which are spent on daily needs, e.g. cigarettes. Regardless of which of these or other solutions are adopted, many events which require tokens should be scheduled each day. Further, these backup reinforcers should be priced high enough to require clients to continue earning tokens.

At first, backups should be priced low so that the clients can easily come in contact with the already effective reinforcers. Then gradually the number of tokens needed can be increased to buy each backup, until it reaches a *relatively* fixed value.

After tokens have been initially established as reinforcers, there should be a variety of prices corresponding with the desirability of the item, i.e. the more popular the item, the more expensive it will be. The therapist should make sure there are *at least* one or two items that cost a minimum (usually one token). Notice that token prices have little relation to the actual retail price of an item. For instance, even though an apple may cost ten cents in the grocery store, and a candy bar sells for five cents, the clients might be charged more tokens for the candy bar than for the apple (since candy is often preferred to fruit).

The therapist must be sure that prices are set high enough so that the clients must consistently engage in appropriate behavior for which tokens are earned, in order to buy the backups. On the other hand, prices should be low enough so that it is possible to earn desired backups if a person behaves in appropriate ways.

There should usually be a standard set of prices that apply to all on the token program, e.g. if a toy car is priced at ten tokens, it should cost any client that amount (individualizing the program is discussed below).

If the therapist wants clients to purchase a backup, e.g. deodorant, or a trip to a library which is considered to be educational, he reduces the price (has a "sale" on that item), or pays them to buy the item, e.g. charges them one token for the trip, and pays them ten tokens for participating. Gradually, as the item becomes more reinforcing, he reduces the amount he pays a student for purchasing it (to zero). If the backup never does acquire reinforcing value and yet the therapist feels the child should continue to buy it, he continues to pay the child for it. (Meanwhile, if others will buy the same item that this client is being paid to buy, the therapist charges them for it.)

At first, the therapist may pay tokens for behaviors that are easy for the individual to perform, and ones that are only approximations to desirable behavior. Then gradually he raises the standards for reinforcement, i.e. gives fewer or no tokens for behaviors that are less desirable or less similar to desirable behavior. However, as stated previously, he does not try to shape (teach) new behaviors during the time that tokens are being established as conditioned reinforcers.

Usually, there are a number of standard behaviors for which everyone is paid equally, e.g. the same number of tokens is paid to whomever washes his hands. Often, these behaviors which will be rewarded, and the number of tokens earned for each is posted for the teachers and clients.

•Washing hands	— five tokens
•Sitting down when told to	— one token
•Saying "thank you" when given something	— one token
•Returning tray to counter	— three tokens

If the clients have trouble reading the list, pictures depicting the various behaviors can be displayed. Occasional verbal instructions can also be useful, e.g. "If you put your doll away when I tell you to, you will earn three tokens."

The standard list of appropriate behaviors and the tokens received for each should be modified if necessary for each individual. For instance, the therapist might establish ten tokens as the standard price for completing two arithmetic problems; however, different students might receive different amounts of tokens for completing these ten problems. If one typically only completed seven or eight problems, he might receive fifteen tokens for his improvement. If a second student has been doing ten problems for some time, he might receive the standard ten. These adjustments in the number of tokens given allow teachers to reinforce *improvement* in learning and performing appropriate behavior.

An effective token system should balance the number of tokens given against the price of purchasing backups. If many tokens are given for various appropriate behaviors, and the price of backups is low in comparison, the clients will not have to engage in much appropriate behavior to buy all the backup reinforcers they want. This unbalanced system will result in a client behaving appropriately just long enough to earn enough tokens to buy the desired backups, and then ceasing. On the other hand, appropriate behavior will also decline if the price of backups is so high that regardless of how well he behaves, the individual is rarely able to earn enough tokens to buy the things he wants.

The proper balance between token payment and prices will result in the following: if a client (clients) engages in all or most of the behavior that has been specified as appropriate, he can buy the backups that are reinforcing to him. How much appropriate behavior is required for reinforcement (and how much inappropriate behavior is tolerated without substantial loss of "buying power") is a moral as well as a therapeutic decision. The objectives of teaching the individuals to behave appropriately should not lead to arranging a set of rules that even an angel could not follow.

Fining

As stressed previously, many behavior problems may be reduced simply by reinforcing appropriate alternative behavior. However, it is likely that at least some undesirable behavior will persist even when individuals are consistently being reinforced for responding appropriately. Therefore, token reinforcement programs often employ a "fining" contingency for misbehavior. Fining (taking tokens away) should only be instituted after the token system is reasonably well established. The students should demonstrate that they understand the system by trading skillfully, holding onto their tokens until redemption time, and verbalizing accurate statements about the tokens and how they are spent (if applicable). More importantly, they should be consistently performing responses for which tokens are given.

Before resorting to fines for misbehavior, several other procedures should be considered. Techniques such as extinction, DRO, DRI, and pointed praise may be effective in reducing a behavior problem and are usually considered less severe than fining. If these are ineffective or impractical, a fining consequence must be used.

In general, fining consists of withdrawing tokens immediately following an inappropriate behavior. Fining is an example of a response cost punishment procedure, i.e. removal of a positive reinforcer contingent upon a response. When an unacceptable behavior occurs, the therapist should immediately present a verbal signal that tokens will be taken. This signal should indicate who will be fined; a description of the misbehavior; appropriate, alternative behavior; and the amount of the fine, for instance, "John, a ten token fine for yelling, you should talk quietly in class." Such a statement should be given in an unemotional tone of voice, yet loud enough for the misbehaving student to hear. The teacher should then immediately remove the specified number of tokens from the student, e.g. cross out a number received in a token book or take plastic chips from the student's token bag.

The amount of the fine should be kept relatively small for each misbehavior. It may be neither fair nor effective to revoke a large number of tokens for a single inappropriate action. On the other hand, the fine should be large enough to truly "cost" the client something. Further, the amount of the fine is often adjusted to the seriousness of the misbehavior. Fifteen tokens might be revoked for hitting someone, five removed for tearing a book. (These and other issues are more fully discussed later in this chapter in the section entitled, "Factors influencing the effectiveness of a token program.")

Whenever possible, a fine should be accompanied by contingent education. For instance, immediately after being fined, the client might receive training in appropriate alternative behavior through reasoning, verbal instructions, and modeling. He could then earn back a portion of the fine for practicing appropriate behavior. If the client cooperates in the contingent education procedure, he receives tokens and then returns to the regular activities. If he refuses to attend to or practice appropriate behavior, he is allowed to rejoin the activities, but does not earn back a portion of the fine. If he is aggressive, argumentative, or displays other more severe inappropriate behavior during contingent education, he may be fined for these behaviors. Contingent education should *then* be applied to learning how to accept a fine. If he participates in this training, a portion of the second fine should be returned to him. Next, the student should be given one more opportunity to practice appropriate behavior that is opposite from the undesirable response which resulted in the fine in the first place. He may re-earn a portion of that first fine if he cooperates, but whether or not he does so, the contingent education episode is then terminated.

When fines are followed by contingent education, such a combination is sometimes called *educational fines*. When a decision is made to use a fining procedure for a particular behavior problem, educational fines should be tried first. However, if the individual consistently refuses to either participate in contingent education, or is aggressive or otherwise abusive, the contingent education component of the fining procedure should be discontinued. Similarly, if the behavior problem is not decreasing, it may be due to the positive reinforcement the student receives from the teacher's attention which necessarily accompanies contingent education. If this is the case, contingent education should be stopped, and fining used by itself. In these cases, immediately following the inappropriate behavior, the therapist should identify the misbehaving student by name, and briefly describe the inappropriate behavior, its acceptable alternative, and the amount of the fine. He should remove the specified number of tokens and then walk away with no further comment. For individuals who continue to exhibit highly dangerous or disruptive behaviors after being fined, a time-out or required relaxation contingency may need to be arranged (either following or replacing the fine).

Evaluating the Token Program

How will the therapist know if token reinforcement is effective? As mentioned previously, the client should show consistent trade behaviors, e.g. handing the therapist the token when trading. When a verbal individual can accurately describe the token arrangement, e.g. "I get a token and trade it for my candy," this is generally considered a good sign that the client is learning the token system. However, the only certain indication of token effectiveness is whether their contingent use can change target behaviors, that is, if contingent token presentation can increase low frequency behaviors or maintain an increased behavior. If it cannot increase behavior, it has *not* become a positive reinforcer (or something else is wrong). Similarly, the effectiveness of fining is evaluated by whether or not this procedure decreases the *future* occurrence of inappropriate behavior. Effectiveness is *not* judged by whether the client stops the inappropriate behavior immediately after his token(s) has been removed, nor whether the person acts as though token removal is unpleasant, e.g. cries. *Decreasing the future occurrence* means that the individual *starts* the inappropriate behavior less frequently.

Collection of data is a very important tool in evaluating the effectiveness of a token program. The therapist may casually notice ways in which the system can be made more efficient and convenient for teachers, general loopholes, and inequities in token delivery, fining, etc. However, in order to precisely evaluate the effects of the token system on the behavior of the students, the therapist should directly observe and record various target behaviors by one of the methods presented in Chapter 3. As always, the target behaviors that are recorded are those which all decide are important to increase or decrease. In a classroom for instance, study behavior (looking at books and answering arithmetic problems) and disruptive behavior (making noise) are target behaviors that would probably be measured to assess the effects of giving and revoking tokens. In a cottage, performing self-help behaviors, following instructions, and aggression are examples of behaviors that might be observed to evaluate if giving and taking tokens affect their level of occurrence.

Factors Influencing the Effectiveness of a Token Program

If data and informal observations indicate that the token system is not increasing and maintaining appropriate behavior and/or not reducing undesirable responding, several features of the program should be examined.

Are all (or most) appropriate behaviors being reinforced? If the list of behaviors for which tokens are earned omits many desirable behaviors, or only includes those that the "best" clients can perform, many students will rarely earn tokens even though they behave appropriately. As stressed previously, even though a specified list of appropriate behaviors may be posted, the token program must be individualized and flexible so that all are reinforced for approximations and improvements toward performance of target behavior.

Are all (or most) inappropriate behaviors being consequated (either with fines or some other procedure designed to decrease their occurrence)? Although a standard list of misbehaviors which will result in fines may be posted, the fining program must remain flexible and individualized, just as with token reinforcement. For instance, a student who had been taught table manners might be fined for violations of proper etiquette, whereas a client who has received no such instruction would not.

Were the tokens immediately traded for effective reinforcers a sufficient number of times before the therapist began to introduce a delay between earning and trading? The effectiveness of tokens rests upon the number of times they have been paired with backup reinforcers. If delays between receiving and trading tokens have been increased too rapidly, the therapist should back up to shorter delays or immediate trading for a time. Even though the tokens may have been traded immediately a sufficient number of times, and the delays were increased gradually, the present delay between receiving and redeeming tokens may be too long.

Is the token consequence immediate? Since the time involved in even walking across a room may to a client be too long of a delay, the therapist must *always* use a verbal statement to bridge the delay between the occurrence of a behavior and the token consequence. For instance, immediately following an appropriate behavior, the therapist might say: "Mary, you sat down so nicely when I asked you to, have two tokens!" and then immediately walk to the child and give her the tokens. Similarly, immediately after an unacceptable behavior occurs, the teacher might say: "Martha, you are not to run in the hall. I am going to take five tokens for that. In the future, please walk." The therapist should then immediately approach the student and take the tokens.

Are the backups truly reinforcing? Tokens are only as effective as the backups for which they are traded. The array should include *at least* one or two items for which each client will work. These must be changed frequently to reduce the chances of satiation.

Has each client come into contact with all of the backups available? The therapist should insure that clients contact all of the backups in the beginning and periodically throughout the program. One way of accomplishing this is to display the backups conspicuously at the time that the desired behaviors are to be emitted. For instance, instead of placing the store of backups down the hall from his classroom, or behind solid doors, he could display at least a sample of the items within the class, but out of the reach of the students, and call the students' attention to these items periodically.

A second procedure, called "reinforcer sampling" (Ayllon and Azrin, 1968), involves requiring all clients in the token program to engage in the event for a short duration each time it is available. For instance, when a walk is scheduled, everyone is required to assemble outside, where they can contact (see and hear) the stimuli comprising a walk. Then, the therapist asks who wants to buy the event and returns those who do not to the cottage or classroom. Similarly, all clients are taken to the movie, and in the lobby or theatre, the therapist collects the tokens of those wishing to stay; he returns the rest of the clients. Of course, the free sample of the event should be brief, so that they cannot satiate on the event without having to purchase the rest. Reinforcer sampling is probably most useful when a backup reinforcer is available infrequently, e.g. once a week or less. Reinforcer sampling increases the participation both by clients who regularly buy the backup activity, and those who do not. The procedure seems to not only familiarize the individuals with the event, but also triggers participation in it.

Is there a balance between tokens paid, tokens revoked, and the price of backups? If clients can engage in little appropriate behavior while still buying many of the desired backups, the prices are too low relative to the amount paid. The therapist should then reduce the number given and/or increase prices. On the other hand, if clients engage in appropriate behavior, but cannot buy at least some backups, they will stop working for the tokens. In this case, the therapist should either increase the number of tokens given, and/or reduce the price of backups.

The therapist must similarly adjust the size of fines. Increasing the amount of a fine in comparison to the overall number of tokens received for appropriate behavior may be effective in reducing inappropriate behavior. For instance, if a fine which subtracts one percent of an individual's tokens is ineffective, perhaps increasing each fine to three percent of the student's tokens will decrease a behavior problem. In general, each fine should be large enough to make a difference in the individual's buying power. On the other hand, if one inappropriate behavior results in the loss of so many tokens that the student cannot possibly earn even small backups for lengthy periods of time (regardless of how appropriately he behaves following the undesirable behavior), he may well continue to behave inappropriately. The system should be arranged so that tokens earned for appropriate behavior can *always* buy backups which are sufficiently reinforcing to maintain the appropriate behavior *whenever* it occurs.

Has the present version of the token system been operating long enough to evaluate its effects? It takes many pairings (tradings) for tokens to become conditioned reinforcers, and it requires time for reinforcement to strengthen behavior. The number of days that are required to evaluate the system's effectiveness depends on how many hours per day the clients live within it. If they are on a token program for twenty-four hours per day, five to fifteen days may be needed before assessing whether or not the system needs to be changed. If they participate one hour per day, a longer period may be needed. On the other hand, some problems with the procedure can be identified immediately. For instance, if it is clear that a student can behave appropriately only in the last ten minutes before recess, and earn enough tokens to purchase access to the playground, the therapist should immediately increase the price of recess and/or space out the presentation of tokens.

Can the students obtain tokens in unauthorized ways? For instance, if an individual can obtain tokens by stealing from others, one of several procedures can be tried:

1. Give each client a distinctive type of token. Of course, this is not always practical.
2. When a client receives a token, secure it firmly on his person, e.g. pin a ring on his clothing on which tokens are placed so that putting tokens on and taking them off involves some effort. Although this is likely to dissuade the token snatcher, it also requires more teacher time to reinforce appropriate behavior, and increases the chances that the student will receive attention when a token is removed for inappropriate behavior.
3. Keep records of how many tokens have been earned by

each student. This procedure is also time-consuming for teachers, and may dissuade them from using tokens.

4. Have each student carry a book in which token delivery and fines are noted. To prevent the student from giving himself tokens, a nonduplicable mark should be made, e.g. a stamp of the teacher's initials which she carries in her pocket. (Stealing should result in a fine.)

Is inappropriate behavior being reinforced? As stressed previously, it is important to minimize reinforcement during fining and contingent education. If a behavior problem is not decreasing, first discontinue the use of contingent education, i.e. employ fining by itself before resorting to more severe procedures such as time-out.

Summary

Establishing an effective, balanced token system is often a matter of trial and error. The therapist can begin with a program that at least "looks good on paper." Specifically, he arranges a list of appropriate behaviors and the number of tokens that will be given for each. At the same time, he lists inappropriate behaviors and specifies the number of tokens that will be withdrawn for each. Further, he lists and displays as wide an array of backup reinforcers as his imagination and budget will allow, and establishes an approximate price for each (according to the guidelines outlined previously). Next, he *tries the program.* First, he establishes tokens as reinforcers. Then, he presents tokens for the behaviors specified as appropriate, revokes tokens for inappropriate behavior, and provides backups to trade. If problems arise, e.g. if clients behave appropriately but do not contact backups, or they buy most of the backups they want and still behave inappropriately, he modifies the system according to the guidelines presented previously.

After the Token System Is Established

After the token reinforcement and fining program is running smoothly, it can be employed to teach an unlimited variety of new behaviors, e.g. academic, social, vocational and self-help skills that the student(s) has not displayed previously. Of course, all of the techniques such as shaping, prompting and fading which were described in Chapter 6 should be employed in conjunction with token reinforcement.

After appropriate behaviors are well established by reinforcing them each time they occur, they should be reinforced on an *intermittent schedule.* For instance, when a client is told to sit down at a table, instead of giving him a token each time he sits, the therapist begins to reinforce him every other time. If his behavior is not disrupted by this change (i.e. if he does not cease sitting down when instructed to do so), the therapist might reinforce him every third time he obeys the command, and arrange reinforcement so that the individual cannot predict when he might earn a token for sitting. In other words, the client can be reinforced on an *average* of every third response so he will be unable to predict which time his sitting will pay off. The therapist continues to reduce the frequency of reinforcement in a *gradual* manner. If performance of the desirable behavior is disrupted, he backs up and reinforces the response more frequently. (These issues are discussed more fully in Chapter 6 under the section entitled "Intermittent Schedules of Reinforcement".) The ultimate objective is to reinforce behavior on a schedule which a client is likely to encounter in the natural community. For instance, in the "real world" paychecks are usually issued every one to two weeks, i.e. on a very intermittent schedule. Further, some behaviors such as toothbrushing are *never* reinforced with tangible reinforcement. In these cases, token reinforcement should be gradually reduced until it is never given and more natural reinforcers (such as praise) should be substituted.

Similarly, as new behaviors are taught and the clients gain more and more experience with the token economy, it may be wise to incorporate longer delays between earning and spending tokens. In the natural community, there is often a delay between earning and spending money (trading it for backup reinforcers). Although it was noted previously that most token economics feature a variety of different delays, i.e.

some tokens are redeemed immediately, others are spent later, it is important to arrange delays which closely resemble those in the real world.

In general, a token economy is established as a temporary therapeutic program to teach appropriate behavior and decrease undesirable responding. It is clearly best to begin with a token system which is as similar as possible to conditions which will exist in the community in which the student will eventually live. When more artificial procedures must initially be instituted to establish appropriate responding and eliminate behavior problems, every effort should be made to modify the program so that it will increasingly resemble the most natural, normal environment possible. In summary, these alterations consist of:

1. the use of intermittent token reinforcement for behaviors which normally earn money, e.g. vocational skills.
2. intermittent natural reinforcement for behaviors which do not typically receive money. Natural reinforcers are events which *typically* occur following the behavior. For instance, individuals are sometimes praised for good grooming, students who finish their assignments first are often allowed to help the teacher, and those who demonstrate competence in a sport are usually appointed team captain.
3. incorporation of delays between appropriate behavior and earning reinforcement, and delays between earning tokens and redeeming them for backup reinforcers.

These changes need to be instituted *gradually*, to insure that behavioral improvements are maintained.* The extent to which these alterations can be achieved depends upon the skills of teachers and the capabilities of the students. For instance, some retarded individuals may not be able to tolerate infrequent or delayed reinforcement, or the natural consequences for appropriate behavior may not function as a reinforcer. In such cases, the student will have to remain on a more structured token

---

*For a more thorough description of maintenance, see Chapter 11.

regime. Nevertheless, efforts should be made to determine the *most* natural system that teaches and maintains appropriate behavior in each individual.

Advantages and Disadvantages of Token Systems

Token systems have several advantages which make them extremely useful for groups in settings such as classrooms, cottages, and group homes.

Tokens can be easily dispensed immediately and on any schedule. They can be delivered quickly without causing a prolonged interruption in the client's activity (as would be the case if, for instance, the individual had to stop and consume a primary reinforcer). They can be made easy to carry by the therapist and client, and are not messy to handle and deliver.

A single potent backup reinforcer can be used to increase and maintain a great deal of appropriate behavior. With tokens, one backup, e.g. a trip to the zoo, can be transformed into *many* reinforcers.

Token systems provide for convenient alteration in the amount of reinforcement (number of tokens) in comparison to the amount of the behavior. By shifting the number of tokens earned for different behaviors and the number of tokens required for different backup reinforcers, the system can be made very sensitive to changes in the students' behavior.

When dealing with a group, tokens can overcome much of the variability in what individuals find reinforcing. With a sufficient number and variety of backups, it is more probable that there is at least one potent reinforcer for every client. Further, since an individual varies from time to time in what is reinforcing to him, tokens eliminate the necessity of knowing exactly what reinforcer is effective with the client at the moment each appropriate response occurs. In short, the therapist can give a client tokens without knowing what he will later buy with those tokens.

Token systems can be made highly similar to the token program operating in the community, i.e. our monetary system. It can provide training in the behaviors necessary to participate in that monetary system, i.e. earning, spending, and saving.

On the other hand, the advantages of token systems must be qualified by several considerations. Token systems require planning and time to establish and maintain. Therapists must first be thoroughly trained, a general token system must be outlined, and then tokens must be established as reinforcers for the student. Once established, the effects of the token program should be carefully monitored. Adequate monitoring generally requires keeping data on whether appropriate behavior is increased and maintained, and whether inappropriate behavior is reduced to low levels. On the basis of these data, teachers should modify the system to make it more effective in obtaining the desired results. However, the time required to establish and maintain an adequate token system is usually inconsequential compared to the benefits which will accrue from it.

A token system is no better than its backups. If these do not include a sufficient variety and number of potent reinforcers, then few advantages of the token system will be realized.

Token systems may require *some* money. However, it is not true that the more money spent on backups, the more effective the token program. Often, very inexpensive items are extremely reinforcing, whereas more costly backups may be ignored by students. Further, the array of backups should include many materials and activities that would otherwise have been given free, e.g. juice at snack time, recess, and puzzles.

REFERENCES

Ayllon, T. and Azrin, N. H.: The measurement and reinforcement of behavior of psychotics. *Journal of the Experimental Analysis of Behavior, 8*:357-383, 1965.

Ayllon, T. and Azrin, N. H.: *The token economy: a motivational system for therapy and rehabilitation.* New York, Appleton, Crofts, 1968a.

Ayllon, T. and Azrin, N. H.: Reinforcer sampling: a technique for increasing the behavior of mental patients. *Journal of Applied Behavior Analysis, 1*:13-20, 1968b.

Burchard, J. D. and Tyler, V. O.: The modification of delinquent behavior through operant conditioning. *Behavior Research and Therapy, 12*:245-250, 1965.

Hunt, J. G., Fitzhugh, L. C., and Fitzhugh, K. B.: Teaching "exitward" patients appropriate personal appearance by using reinforcement techniques. *American Journal of Mental Deficiency, 73*:41-45, 1968.

Kazdin, A. E. and Bootzin, R. P.: The token economy: an evaluative review. *Journal of Applied Behavior Analysis, 5*:343-372, 1972.

O'Leary, K. D., Becker, W. C., Evans, M. B. and Saudargas, R. A.: A token reinforcement program in a public school: A replication and systematic analysis. *Journal of Applied Behavior Analysis, 2*:2-13, 1969.

Phillips, E. L.: Achievement place: token reinforcement procedures in a home-style rehabilitation setting for 'predelinquent' boys. *Journal of Applied Behavior Analysis, 1*:213-223, 1968.

Wolf, M. M., Giles, D., and Hall, R. V.: Experiments with token reinforcement in a remedial classroom. *Behavior Research and Therapy, 6*:51-64, 1968.

Zimmerman, E. H., Zimmerman, J., and Russell, C. D.: Differential effects of token reinforcement on instruction-following behavior in retarded students instructed as a group. *Journal of Applied Behavior Analysis, 2*:101-112, 1969.

Chapter 9

SELECTING AND APPLYING A TREATMENT PROCEDURE: ESTABLISHING STIMULUS CONTROL

THE previous two chapters have described methods of increasing appropriate behavior and decreasing undesirable behavior. In some cases, a target behavior is appropriate in all situations, and thus the objective is to increase it in as many situations as possible. For instance, using correct grammar is a behavior that is desirable in any setting, e.g. the classroom, home, and playground. Other behaviors are *in*appropriate in all situations, for example self-injury is never acceptable. On the other hand, many target behaviors are desirable in certain situations and undesirable in others. For instance, whispering is only necessary in places such as classrooms and the library, whereas it is inappropriate when cheerleading. Similarly, undressing is desirable before showering and bedtime, but usually unacceptable in parks and other public places.

With any behavior change, it must be decided in which situations a response should occur and in which situations a behavior should not occur. Thus, the training objective is not just to increase or decrease a behavior, but to do so in certain situations. Technically, this is called *bringing the behavior under proper stimulus control*.

A situation, i.e. stimuli which comprise a total situation, can come to reliably induce a target behavior if that target behavior has been consistently reinforced in that situation. For instance, if a student has been reinforced for whispering in class, he will immediately lower his voice upon entering the classroom. In this case, the stimuli comprising a classroom serves as a signal, telling the student that whispering will be reinforced. Similarly, if a particular therapist has consistently reinforced a child for playing with toys, such behavior will typically occur in that teacher's presence, and may cease when the teacher leaves the room. Further, a situation can reliably signal the *non*occurrence of a behavior, if that behavior has been decreased in that situation by some procedure. For instance, if an aggressive student has been consistently punished for such behavior by a particular teacher, he will probably not display aggression when that teacher is present, but may continue to be aggressive in her absence. Similarly, if tantrums have been ignored at home, the individual will not engage in the behavior in that setting, but may have tantrums in other situations, i.e. those in which he has received attention for such behavior.

In general, if a behavior has been reinforced (or increased by some other method) in a particular situation, it is likely to occur in that situation. If a response has been punished (or decreased by another procedure) in a specific situation, that behavior is likely to not occur in that situation. In other words, if in a specific setting a particular procedure, e.g. reinforcement or punishment, is used consistently with a particular behavior, that situation will become associated with that procedure. The stimuli comprising the situation will signal the client as to what consequence will be available for a particular behavior. For instance, after whispering has been reinforced in the classroom, it is as though the stimuli comprising the classroom say to the student, "If you whisper in here, you'll earn a token!" The sight of a person who has punished aggression signals to the child, "Remember, she'll spank you if you hit someone, so don't do it!" Thus, the child will begin to respond differently in different situations, depending upon what consequences each situation is associated with.

Each situation is composed of many stimuli (environmental events). For instance, a classroom situation is composed of such stimuli as desks, blackboards, other students, the teacher, and verbal instructions ("Get your math books out"). A bedtime situation is composed of distinctive stimuli, too. These may include verbal instructions ("Susie, it's time for bed"), being read a story, darkness, and the individual's own yawns.

Each stimulus which comprises a situation may become a *discriminative stimulus* (S^D). A discriminative stimulus is a stimulus which is associated with a particular procedure for a particular response, and which signals the occurrence or non-occurrence of that response. This definition of an S^D includes the following points.

A discriminative stimulus occurs before the response and may continue to be present throughout performance of the response and delivery of the consequence. For instance, the discriminative stimulus "John, come here" occurs before the response of walking to the therapist. Other discriminative stimuli, for instance the presence of the therapist holding the reinforcer, occur not only before the response, but also during the response and delivery of the consequence as well. Similarly, the discriminative stimulus "Settle down" occurs before the response of speaking quietly; the discriminative stimuli of the classroom, e.g. the sight of other students studying at their desks and the presence of the teacher, occur before and during the response. In short, since S^D's occur before the behavior, they are called *antecedent stimuli*. They are contrasted with stimuli which occur following a behavior, which are termed *consequent stimuli*. Most of the procedures described previously to increase or decrease behavior employ consequent stimuli. That is, when a behavior occurs, it is followed by some consequence, e.g. positive reinforcement, contingent education, time-out, or punishment.

The presence of the S^D is associated with a particular consequence (procedure) for a particular response. After several occasions in which a procedure is used with a behavior in a specific situation, the stimuli comprising that situation will become associated with that procedure. Thus, the presence of those stimuli will signal that if a particular behavior occurs, a specific procedure will be used.

A number of separate terms have been used to refer to antecedent stimuli associated with particular procedures. For example, S^D has frequently been used to refer only to an antecedent stimuli associated with positive reinforcement. Similarly, $S^{D\Delta}$ (occasionally written S-delta) is used to refer to an antecedent stimulus associated with extinction. The term *warning stimulus* has been used to designate an antecedent stimulus associated with negative reinforcement.

For the purpose of clarity and simplicity in this text, this author has chosen to use the term S^D in a broader sense and to define it to include any antecedent stimulus which is associated with a particular procedure and which controls the occurrence or nonoccurrence of a particular response. Further, she will use the symbol S^{D-} to designate a discriminative stimulus which is associated with a procedure to decrease a response, and controls the nonoccurrence of that response. Thus, an S^{D-} is associated with any procedure which decreases a response, e.g. extinction, DRO, time-out, punishment, contingent education, or DRI. The symbol S^{D+} will be used to indicate an S^D which is associated with a procedure to increase a response, and which controls a relatively high occurrence of that behavior. Thus, an S^{D+} is associated with any procedure which increases a behavior, for example, positive reinforcement, negative reinforcement, or discontinuing a procedure which is suppressing a behavior.*

In summary, if a response occurs during or after the presentation of an S^{D+} for that behavior, it will be reinforced. For instance, if the client sits down after being presented with the verbal S^{D+} "Sit down," he is reinforced. However, he is not reinforced for sitting if the S^{D+} has not been presented. If a response occurs after or during presentation of an S^{D-} associated with time-out for that behavior, it will be followed by time-out. For instance, if an individual yells during naptime, he is timed out; if he yells at other times, he is not.

After several occasions in which a response is followed by a particular consequence in the presence of a stimulus, the stimulus will begin to *signal* or *control* the occurrence or nonoccurrence of the response. That is, a response which has been reinforced in the past when a particular S^{D+} has been presented, will be very likely to occur whenever that S^{D+} is present. A response which was, for instance, punished or timed out whenever a particular S^{D-} was present will be very unlikely

---

*It is important to remember that the terms S^{D-} and S^{D+} are not used in *any* other textbook. The author has employed them here in an attempt to avoid the confusion which she feels exists with the more conventional terms.

to occur when that S^{D-} is presented. For instance, after repeated occasions in which the stimulus "Come here" is associated with reinforcement for walking to the therapist, the client will consistently and promptly come to him when that S^{D+} is presented, but not necessarily approach the therapist at other times. Similarly, if the therapist's presence is consistently associated with punishment for aggression, the client will not aggress when he is present, but only in his absence. An antecedent stimulus cannot be called an S^D unless it controls the occurrence or nonoccurrence of the target response (whichever is appropriate to the consequence associated with the S^D). Before it has such control, the stimulus is called an *antecedent neutral stimulus* because, although it does occur before the response, it does not have any special effect on that behavior (or its effect is not known). Various words are used to describe the fact that the response begins to occur at a frequency appropriate to the consequence associated with the S^D, i.e. at a high rate in the presence of an S^{D+}; at a low (or zero) rate in the presence of an S^{D-}: The S^D *controls, signals,* and *sets the occasion for* the occurrence or nonoccurrence of the response.

In summary, an S^D provides the individual with information about a consequence for a particular response. After consistent association with a consequence, it tells the client that if a certain response occurs, it will be followed by a specific consequence. Thus, a response will be very likely to occur in the presence of an S^{D+} associated with positive reinforcement for that response; a behavior will be very unlikely to occur in the presence of an S^{D-} associated, for instance, with extinction or time-out for that response.

When a behavior occurs in the presence of an S^{D+} and/or does not occur in the presence of an S^{D-}, it is said to be under proper *stimulus control*. Stated simply, proper stimulus control has been achieved when the behavior occurs in the appropriate situations and/or does not occur in inappropriate situations. As stressed previously, bringing a behavior under proper stimulus control is an important part of any treatment program. It is not sufficient to aim for increasing or decreasing a target behavior; the therapist must also be concerned about the situations in which the behavior should or should not occur.

Bringing a behavior under proper stimulus control consists of *discrimination* training and/or *generalization* training.

DISCRIMINATION TRAINING

When a client performs a response in the presence of an S^{D+}, but does not perform it in the presence of the S^{D-} he is said to be making a *discrimination*. For instance, if Johnny yells on the playground, but does not yell in the classroom, he is making the proper discrimination between the S^{D+} of the playground and the S^{D-} of the classroom. Similarly, if Mary undresses at bedtime, but does not undress at other times, she is making a discrimination between the S^{D+} for undressing (bedtime), and the S^{D-} for undressing (the presence of any stimuli other than those comprising bedtime).

To teach a discrimination, the therapist simply presents the S^{D+} and reinforces the response in its presence, and occasionally presents the S^{D-} and employs a procedure such as extinction or time-out to decrease the response in its presence. A more detailed description of the discrimination training procedure follows.

First, the therapist selects the stimuli that he wants to become S^{D+}'s and S^{D-}'s. In other words, he decides in which situations the response should and should not occur. Discrimination training is typically considered relevant when there is a definite situation(s) in which a response should occur and a specific situation(s) in which the response should not occur. However, sometimes he will only need to specify the situation in which an appropriate response should occur or an undesirable response should not occur, and not identify any other situation. For instance, if he wants an individual to swallow when he puts a pill in his mouth, but is not concerned about modifying the behavior in other situations, then he only needs to select one S^{D+} (placing a pill on his tongue and saying "Swallow"). In this case, he needs not specify an S^{D-}. Similarly, if he wants to decrease running only in the school building, but does not care if the student runs at any other time, then he only specifies the S^{D-} (the school building).

Often the appropriate and inappropriate situations are self-evident. For instance, it is clear under what circumstances undressing should occur, and when it should not. However, when identifying S^{D+}'s and S^{D-}'s, certain guidelines should be followed. First, the therapist should be sure the client is capable of perceiving the stimuli. For instance, if he wants to train the discrimination of going to the dining room when a dinner bell rings, the dinner bell should be loud enough to be heard wherever the client might be in the building and should sound long enough to be clearly perceived. Similarly, it may be best to teach a child to go to bed when told to rather than when it is 8:30. The latter cue may be difficult to perceive (and, of course, requires that he tell time). A second consideration when selecting an S^D is how likely it is that the cue will be used by others with whom the client will interact in the future. For instance, getting out of bed in the morning would most certainly be an appropriate S^{D+} for getting dressed in a client's own home or in any other living situation. Similarly, the verbal cue "Quiet down" would probably be used by teachers in virtually any public school classroom, and thus would be useful to train as an S^{D-} for yelling.

In summary, situations should be selected which will become S^{D+}'s for the occurrence of the target response and/or select the situations which are to become S^{D-}'s for the nonoccurrence of the target response (those situations in which the response should not occur). For instance, the therapist may specify that the client should undress at bedtime, before showering, and when asked to by the therapist. He may also specify that the S^{D-} is any time or place other than in the presence of these S^{D+}'s. Similarly, it may be determined that a student should speak in class when called on or during group discussions and free play. In this case, all situations other than these S^{D+}'s will constitute the S^{D-}'s.

After selecting S^{D+}'s and S^{D-}'s, discrimination training may begin. The therapist simply presents the stimulus which he wants to become the S^{D+}, and when the appropriate response occurs, he reinforces it. If it does not occur in the presence of the S^{D+}, shaping and/or prompting and fading may be necessary. Next, he presents the stimuli making up the inappropriate situation, and when the target response occurs, uses some procedure for decreasing the behavior, e.g. extinction or time-out. He continues this, sometimes presenting the S^{D+} and always reinforcing the response in its presence, and sometimes presenting the S^{D-} and always using a procedure for decreasing the behavior in its presence. The response will gradually begin to occur consistently in one situation (the S^{D+}), and not in the other (S^{D-}). For instance, occasionally he presents the verbal stimulus "Undress" and if the client performs the response in its presence, delivers a positive reinforcer. If the response occurs in the presence of any other stimulus, e.g. at school, he uses time-out. Similarly, if a client is to be trained to cross a street when a traffic light is green and not to cross when it is red, he presents the green light and reinforces crossing. He occasionally illuminates the red light and reinforces not crossing (the DRO procedure), times the individual out for attempts to cross, or employs some other procedure for decreasing street crossing in the presence of the red light.

These are examples of *sequential discrimination* training, in which the S^D is presented alone. In the example above, sometimes the green light was presented, and sometimes the red light was illuminated; they were never presented at the same time. For some discrimination problems, *simultaneous discrimination* training makes more sense. For example, if a student is being taught to identify his name (by pointing to it when told to), the skill will be much more relevant if he can select his name from other students' names. It is of little use to teach a student to point to his name when his is the only name displayed. The same is true when training individuals to identify words, pictures, and colors and to make many other discriminations as well. In these cases, the therapist presents both the S^{D+} and the S^{D-} at the same time. For instance, he displays several names to the student (one of which is his own) and tells the child to point to his name. The card bearing his own name is the S^{D+} (the stimulus in the presence of which a pointing response will be reinforced) and the other names are S^{D-}'s (stimuli in the presence of which a pointing response will be, for instance, extinguished). After the student responds, the therapist again presents the S^{D+} and the S^{D-}'s simultaneously, i.e. collects the name cards, then presents them again, but in different positions.

As mentioned previously, in some cases the objective is to *either* increase a response in the presence of an S^{D+} *or* to decrease a behavior in a particular situation (S^{D-}). When this is the case, the therapist repeatedly presents the relevant stimulus situation. For instance, if the therapist wants an individual to swallow when a pill is placed on his tongue, he presents that stimulus over and over, each time reinforcing the response if it occurs in that situation. No procedure is employed to alter swallowing in any other situation. Gradually, she will always swallow when given a pill, but may or may not at other times.

Discrimination training may be conducted either *after* the behavior has been modified in one situation or *at the same time* the behavior is initially being changed. In the former case, for instance, a client may first be trained to undress during special training sessions, and *then* taught when and where to undress in the usual cottage routine. In this example, first the target behavior was trained, and then the proper discriminations were established. Similarly, a student may first learn to say his name, and next be taught the appropriate circumstances under which to say it. This two-stage approach may facilitate training by requiring him or her to learn only one thing at a time, i.e. first to perform the response in special sessions, and *then* in what situations the behavior should and should not occur.

On the other hand, in some cases it may be best (or necessary) to begin discrimination training *before* the behavior change is well established. However, if an appropriate target response does not occur consistently, it will not be likely to occur in the presence of the S^{D+}. Thus, the response will rarely, if ever, be reinforced and therefore will not increase in strength in the presence of the S^{D+}. In cases where the behavior is being trained at the same time it is being brought under discriminative control, shaping and/or prompting and fading may be necessary. For example, if a student is being taught to identify his name, i.e. point to it, and not to other names, when instructed: "Point to your name", the target behavior of selecting his own name is being taught at the same time he is being trained to discriminate between his own and other names. If shaping is used, the teacher presents the stimuli (names) and reinforces an approximation to pointing to the correct name. After delivering the reinforcer, he presents the stimuli again, and again reinforces approximations to appropriate responding. If at any time the student points to an S^{D-} (another name), he uses some procedure to decrease the response to this stimulus, e.g. correction, extinction, or response cost. He continues shaping in the presence of the S^{D+} until the client correctly and consistently points to his name and not to other names.

Prompting and fading may also be employed when training a new behavior while at the same time bringing it under the proper discriminative control. With this procedure, the therapist begins discrimination training with a prompt that is effective in getting the target response to occur. He presents this prompt at the same time that he presents the stimulus that he wants to become an S^{D+}. The response is reinforced each time it occurs following the presentation of these *two* events (the prompt and the other stimulus). Then gradually the prompt is reduced ("faded out") at a rate that does not disrupt the target response, i.e. so that the target response continues to be performed following presentation of the stimulus which is becoming an S^{D+}. If at any point during fading the response ceases to occur, the therapist should back up to a previous fading step with a larger prompt, and, after responding is reestablished, begin fading again at a slower rate. Of course, throughout this process, occasionally he presents the S^{D-}, and employs some procedure to decrease the behavior in its presence. After such discrimination training, the prompt should be eliminated entirely, and only the S^{D+} should be necessary to occasion the target response.*

After establishing the proper discriminations by CRF, an

---

*A more thorough description of shaping, prompting, and fading is found in Chapter 6 in the discussion of increasing behavior by positive reinforcement.

intermittent schedule of reinforcement is gradually introduced. The target response is occasionally reinforced in the appropriate situation (S^{D+}), for instance on a variable interval or variable ratio schedule (see in Chapter 6, the discussion of intermittent schedules of reinforcement for more detail). Whatever consequence was employed to decrease the response in the presence of the S^{D-} should continue to be used each time the behavior occurs in the inappropriate situation(s). This is true, for instance, when using time-out, punishment extinction, and contingent education. When using procedures which rely on positive reinforcement of other behaviors to decrease an inappropriate response (DRO and DRI), reinforcement should gradually be made more and more intermittent.

GENERALIZATION TRAINING

The section on discrimination discussed the fact that when a reinforcer follows a response, that response increases in strength only in the presence of stimuli associated with that reinforcement, and that a response decreases only in the presence of stimuli associated with a procedure for decreasing the response.

Many stimuli are *similar* to the S^D's which control a target response, and they are also likely to signal the same occurrence or nonoccurrence of the target response as the original S^D. For instance, if the ringing of a particular dinner bell has been established as an S^{D+} for going to the dining room, i.e. the response of going to the dining room was reinforced by receiving a food tray when the dinner bell was ringing, it is very likely that other bells which make a sound similar to the one used as the dinner bell will also occasion the target response. For instance, the client may run to the dining room at the sounding of a doorbell, which is similar but different from the usual dinner bell. However, some other stimuli are so different from the original S^D that they will not signal the target response. For example, if a fire alarm or fog horn is sounded, the client will probably not go to the dining room. This is an example of *generalization*. The principle of generalization states: a target response will increase in strength, not only in the presence of the S^{D+} which signals reinforcement, but also in the presence of stimuli which are similar to, but different from this S^{D+}, even though the individual has never before been reinforced in the presence of these stimuli. Similarly, a target response will decrease in strength, not only in the presence of an S^{D-} which signals a consequence for decreasing a behavior, but also in the presence of stimuli which are similar to, but different from this S^{D-}, even though the client has never before received that consequence in the presence of these stimuli.

The likelihood that a target response will or will not occur following presentation of each new stimulus situation depends on how similar that stimulus is to the original S^D, i.e. the one which was originally associated with a consequence for a particular response. The more similar the stimulus is to an S^{D+} signaling reinforcement, the more likely it will be to promptly and dependably occasion the target response, even though the response has not been reinforced in the presence of this different (though similar) stimulus. On the other hand, the less similar the stimulus is to the S^{D+}, the less likely it will be to cue the target response. The same relation holds true for S^{D-}'s: the more similar the stimulus is to an S^{D-} signaling, for instance, punishment, the more likely it is to control the nonoccurrence of the target response. The less similar, the less likely. Technically, this is called a *generalization gradient*.

Assume for instance that one has trained an individual to put on his shirt in the bedroom when the cue, "Put on your shirt," is presented. Specifically, the S^{D+}'s of the therapist's presence, the bedroom, the shirt on the bed, and the verbal cue have come to signal that the target response of putting on a shirt will be reinforced. If another person (one who has never yet reinforced the client for putting on his shirt) replaces the therapist but every other S^D is the same (he presents the same verbal cue, in the same bedroom, with the shirt lying in its usual place), the client may perform the response. If he does, it is said that the behavior is generalizing across therapists. That is, this new situation is similar enough to the original S^{D+} that it also signals the target response. If the individual does not perform the response in the presence of the new person, he is discriminating between therapists (is making a discrimination). The therapist's presence is an S^{D+}, the new person's is not. In this case, the new stimulus is not similar enough to the S^{D+} (the therapist) to signal the response. Similarly, if the therapist keeps all the S^{D}'s the same (his own presence, the shirt lying on the bed and the verbal cue) but changes the *room* in which the S^{D}'s are presented, e.g. instead of the cottage bedroom in which the client has been reinforced for putting on his shirt, he presents all other S^{D}'s in the individual's bedroom at home; he may observe that the client does perform the target response. If he does, he is generalizing across bedrooms, i.e. this new situation is similar enough to the original S^{D+} to occasion putting on his shirt. If he does not, he is discriminating between bedrooms; the new stimulus is too different from the original S^{D+} to occasion the target response.

Discrimination and generalization are opposite processes that go hand in hand. If a client does not emit a target response in the presence of a stimulus which is different from the original S^{D+}, he is making a discrimination. If he does perform the target response in the presence of the stimulus which is different from the original S^{D+}, even though he has not yet been reinforced for that response in its presence, he is generalizing. Similary, if an individual displays an inappropriate response in the presence of a stimulus that is different from the S^{D-} which controls the nonoccurrence of that behavior, he is making a discrimination. If he does *not* perform a target response in the presence of a stimulus which is different from the original S^{D-} controlling its nonoccurrence, even though no procedure to decrease the behavior has been applied in the presence of this new S^{D-}, he is generalizing.

When modifying a response, usually *both* discrimination and generalization training are relevant. For instance, a child should usually dress only when told to, and/or at the appropriate time and place, e.g. after getting out of bed in the morning, after a nap, and in the bedroom. In other words, the therapist has specified that he should perform the response in the presence of these S^{D+}'s and not in the presence of other stimuli (S^{D-}'s). In addition to these discriminations, the response should generalize across a number of stimuli. For instance, he should dress regardless of who presents the verbal cue (a teacher or a parent) and in any bedroom in which he has slept (at camp, home or on a trip) and regardless of the type of clothing lying on the bed.

As indicated, the more similar the new situation is to the original S^D, the more likely it will be to have a similar effect on the target behavior. This effect occurs naturally, i.e. without any training (except in the presence of the original S^D). However, generalization training is required to: (1) *maintain* generalization of a response to stimuli which are similar to the original S^D, and/or (2) *establish* a generalization to stimuli which are not similar to the original S^D, but which the therapist wants to signal either the occurrence or nonoccurrence of the response.

Before training a generalization, the therapist first selects the situation(s) in which the behavior should ultimately occur or not occur, i.e. specifies the stimuli across which the occurrance or nonoccurrance of the response is to generalize. In general, behavioral improvements should be generalized to the individual's usual routine in the environment in which he currently functions, and to situations typical of those in which he will ultimately live, e.g. his natural home and a public school classroom. Next, he presents each of these situations. For instance, when training toothbrushing in a residential facility, one would probably want the behavior to occur in the client's bathroom in the cottage and in his own home. In this case, the therapist presents the verbal cue "Brush your teeth" in the client's bathroom in the cottage with all the usual distractions such as others brushing their teeth. In addition, the client's parents will present the verbal cue at home. Similarly, with aggression, one would probably want the behavior to *not* occur regardless of which clients were in the room, and which adult was supervising them. In this case, a variety of different clients and adults are placed in the room with him. When each new situation is presented, some procedure is employed to modify the response in the presence of the new S^D. In the case of an appropriate response, if the response occurs in the new situation, it is reinforced. On the other hand, if the behavior does not occur in that appropriate situation, the therapist may have to employ either shaping, and/or prompting and fading to establish it. Similarly, some procedure is employed to decrease an undesirable behavior in each new situation.

The therapist continues to present new situations and, in the presence of each, employs whatever consequence is appropriate to increase or decrease a target behavior and/or maintain the behavioral improvement. It should be emphasized that even if a response appears to be appropriately generalized (occurs in the presence of stimuli similar to an S^{D+} or does not occur in the presence of stimuli similar to an S^{D-}), the consequence which increased or decreased the response must continue to be available, not only in the presence of the original S^D, but in the presence of the new S^D's as well, if the improvement is to be maintained in these situations. For instance, if one finds that the client will dress, not only when the original therapist presents the verbal cue "Get dressed," but also when new therapists present the same cue, these other adults must *also* reinforce dressing if the generalization is to be maintained. The same holds true for an S^{D-} associated with a procedure which decreases a behavior. For instance, if one finds that the client has ceased breaking toys, not only in the presence of a therapist who originally timed out the response, but also with other new therapists, then these other adults must be prepared to follow the inappropriate response (if it should occur) with time-out if the generalization is to be maintained.

During the process of establishing and/or maintaining proper generalization, discrimination training may also be conducted. For example, while the skill of undressing is being generalized to a variety of S^{D+}'s (bedrooms, therapists, and different times of day such as night, naptime, and before showering), the individual may also be taught when and where such behavior is inappropriate. Occasionally he may be placed in situations, such as playgrounds and classrooms, which should signal the nonoccurrence of the behavior, and if the behavior occurs apply some procedure to decrease it in such settings. Thus, as the behavior is generalized to all appropriate situations, the client is also taught to discriminate between these situations and those in which the response should not occur.

In summary, after specifying which stimuli should occasion the target response (the range of stimuli across which the behavior should generalize), the therapist begins presenting one stimulus at a time. After a stimulus is presented, he allows enough time for the response to occur. In the case of an appropriate behavior, if it does occur, he reinforces it. If it does not occur, he either shapes it, or prompts it and then fades that prompt out. Of course, one must reinforce the behavior in the presence of each S^{D+} on many different occasions to firmly establish the generalization. During this process, if there are situations which the therapist wants to signal the nonoccurrence of the response, he occasionally presents those, and if the response occurs he employs some procedure for decreasing the target response in those situations. In this way, discrimination and generalization training may be conducted at the same time. Of course, this discrimination training is not necessary if the response is appropriate or inappropriate in all situations, e.g. good grammar or self-destruction. In the case of an inappropriate behavior, if it does *not* occur in the presence of each new situation, the therapist need not do anything (unless he is using, for instance, a DRO procedure to maintain the decreased behavior at a low level, in which case he should present a positive reinforcer following a period in which the inappropriate behavior does not occur). If the undesirable behavior *does* occur, whatever consequence was used in the presence of the original S^{D-} should be used, e.g. extinction, punishment, or time-out.

After establishing the proper generalizations by CRF, an intermittent schedule of reinforcement is usually introduced. The target response is occasionally reinforced in all appropriate situations, for instance, on a VI or VR schedule (see Chapter 6 for more details). In the case of an inappropriate behavior, a generalization is maintained by applying whatever consequence decreased the behavior originally each time the behavior occurs in any inappropriate situation. This is true, for instance, when using time-out, punishment extinction, and contingent education. When using procedures which rely on positive reinforcement of other behavior to decrease an inappropriate response (DRO and DRI), reinforcement should gradually be made more and more intermittent.

CONCEPTS: AN EXAMPLE OF STIMULUS CONTROL

The teaching of concepts provides an example of establishing stimulus control and is critical in many training areas. A concept is a class or set of stimuli which share one or more common characteristics. The concept of "red," for instance, includes all objects which have one stimulus in common: the color red. Similarly, the concept "cat" includes all animals with certain distinctive features, e.g. pointed ears, a particular shape of head and eyes, etc. Teaching a concept involves teaching stimulus control. A student is trained to generalize across instances of a concept, and to discriminate between instances of a concept and other stimuli (noninstances). For instance, when learning the concept "red," the student must be taught to identify the color regardless of which object is red (generalizing across instances of a concept) and must also learn to discriminate between red and other colors (noninstances).

A concept such as "cat" is trained by presenting many instances of the concept, and each time reinforcing the student for either saying the word or otherwise indicating "cat" in the presence of these stimuli. A variety of types, colors, sizes, and postures of cats should be shown to fully generalize the response of "Cat" to many instances of the concept. This also entails teaching a discrimination. The student is taught to discriminate between the critical features which define a cat, e.g. short pointed ears, and other characteristics such as color which are *not* relevant to the concept "cat." Examples of the "nonconcept" such as dogs, horses, cows, and mice are also presented, and the response of "Cat" should be decreased in the presence of these stimuli by some procedure. After repeatedly reinforcing the response of "Cat" in the presence of a wide variety of examples of cats and *not* reinforcing that response (or using some other procedure to decrease the behavior) in the presence of a wide variety of examples of "noncats," the student should acquire the concept of "cat." In a similar manner, other concepts such as letters, numbers, shapes, and colors may be trained.*

UNDESIRABLE STIMULUS CONTROL

The previous sections have described methods of *training* discriminations and generalizations, i.e. bringing behavior under *proper* stimulus control. However, in some cases a student's problem is that his behavior is under *improper* stimulus control. For instance a student may work diligently in class, but only when the teacher is present. In this case, studying behavior is inappropriately discriminated. The objective is thus to generalize studying to situations in which the teacher is absent. This may be accomplished by the same procedures used to train a new generalization. For instance, the teacher may leave the room (that is, present the situation which is to become an S^{D+} for studying) and when the student attends to his assignment properly, she may re-enter the classroom and reinforce him. (Alternatively, the assignment may be arranged such that the student's written answers may be checked when the teacher returns, and if a specified number are completed and correct, he or she is then reinforced.) In this way, an improper discrimination may be eliminated, i.e. the behavior may be appropriately generalized to situations which previously did not signal its occurrence. Similarly, one who has toilet trained an individual may find that the child will use the toilet when his teacher is present, but not in his absence. Again the problem involves an inappropriate discrimination. Other adults must reinforce appropriate toileting if their presence is to become an S^{D+} for the target behavior.

On the other hand, a behavior may be improperly generalized, in which case discrimination training is required. An individual who calls all adult males "Daddy" exemplifies such a problem. The response must be reinforced in the presence of

---

*For more information on teaching concepts, see *Teaching: A Course in Applied Psychology* by Becker, Engelmann and Thomas, (Science Research Associates, Inc., 1971).

his or her own father (S^{D+}) and decreased by some procedure in the presence of others (S^{D-}'s). Similarly, a student who identifies all animals as horses must be taught to discriminate between those stimuli which comprise a horse and those stimuli which characterize other animals.

In general, errors in stimulus control may be remedied by the same procedure used to establish any proper discrimination and generalization. Of course, when possible it is best to avoid the development of improper stimulus control in the first place. Often this involves training appropriate discriminations and generalizations *at the same time* the behavior is initially being modified. For instance, while toilet training a student, it is advisable to employ many different persons in the training so that undesirable discriminations will not be established. On the other hand, it is not always possible to establish stimulus control at the same time the behavior is initially being increased or decreased. For instance, although toothbrushing must ultimately occur in the child's own bathroom with several individuals and many other distractions present, it is sometimes found that early in training a client is very distractable and difficult to train in the usual toothbrushing environment, or that other individuals distract the therapist, e.g. try to snatch food used as his reinforcer. In such cases, it may be expedient to begin training in a more controlled situation. After training has progressed to the point where the client brushes his teeth in that setting, the skill may be generalized to the more natural situation in which it must typically occur. In general, however, the more similar the original training situation is to the one in which the behavior is eventually to occur, the easier is the process of establishing proper stimulus control.

FACTORS AFFECTING STIMULUS CONTROL TRAINING

There are a number of factors which influence the effectiveness of both discrimination and generalization training. If training is not proceeding satisfactorily, a number of factors should be checked.

The Appropriateness of the S^D

The situation which, after training, will control the target response must be appropriate to the physical capabilities of the client. Obviously, one cannot train a blind individual to perform a response in the presence of a visual S^D. Similarly, the S^D must be distinctive enough so that the client can easily perceive it. If discrimination or generalization training is not progressing properly, the S^D's should be made more distinctive, i.e. more easily detected by the individual. In the case of discrimination training, the difference between the S^{D+} and the S^{D-} may be exaggerated. For instance, if the therapist wants a student to get out an arithmetic book when told to, but the student continues to get out other books when instructed "Get out your arithmetic book," he might stress the word "arithmetic" and hold up a sample of the appropriate book. In this way, the therapist may make the S^{D+} more discernible and distinctive from other cues, and thus speed discrimination training.

Effectiveness of the Procedure Used to Increase the Response

When reinforcement is used, the success of discrimination and generalization training depends on, for instance, the potency of the reinforcer which follows the target response. All of the factors influencing the effectiveness of reinforcement are therefore relevant to the successful establishment of stimulus control. Further, it may be necessary to employ shaping and/or prompting and fading to establish the response in the presence of each appropriate situation.

Effectiveness of the Procedures for Decreasing the Response

Just as when using reinforcement, the therapist must insure that the reinforcer is a potent one, he must also insure that the procedure for decreasing the behavior in the presence of the S^{D-} is truly effective in decreasing the response. For instance, if he is using extinction by withholding attention following an undesirable response, he should not comment on, look at, touch, reprimand, or in any way attend to the client when he performs the response in the wrong situation.

Number of Times the Response Is Followed by the Appropriate Consequence

Since most learning is gradual, the therapist will probably have to reinforce the response many times in the presence of each S^{D+}, and frequently apply some procedure(s) for decreasing the behavior in the presence of the S^{D-}, before stimulus control will be established.

Chapter 10

TEACHING COMPLEX BEHAVIOR: CHAINING

PREVIOUS sections on teaching appropriate behavior and bringing that response under proper stimulus control have been primarily concerned with single responses, such as saying "Thank you" or pointing to one's own name. However, many appropriate target behaviors actually consist of groups of individual responses, or are composed of several parts. For instance, dressing involves putting on each of several items of clothing, e.g. underwear, pants, shirt, socks, and shoes. Further, putting on each piece of clothing actually consists of many different steps or separate behaviors. Putting on underpants includes: grasping the pants by the waistband, putting the left foot in the left leg hole, putting the right foot in the right leg hole, and pulling up the pants to the waist. Thus, what may appear to be a single, simple behavior is actually a *chain* of behaviors, i.e. a sequence of behavioral parts which comprise a complex response.

In many cases, a behavior can be more easily trained by breaking it into parts and teaching each part separately, rather than attempting to train the entire behavioral chain at once. The procedure of breaking a behavior into parts, teaching each separately, and combining these parts into their proper sequence is called *chaining*. Chaining combines the usual procedures for teaching and/or maintaining behavior with the methods for establishing stimulus control.

Chaining is particularly useful if: (1) the client has severe behavioral deficits, (2) he can already perform some of the parts of the chain, but does so in the wrong order or skips parts, for example, rinses his mouth before he brushes his teeth or does not wash his legs when showering, or (3) the skill includes several parts and is complex, e.g. getting ready for school in the

224

morning.

To test whether or not chaining is necessary, the therapist may try training the entire behavior without breaking it down into parts, using the procedures described in Chapter 6: he waits for the entire response to occur and when (if) it does, he reinforces it; shapes and/or prompts it; negatively reinforces it (with either the escape or avoidance procedure); or discontinues a procedure which is suppressing the behavior. For instance, in the case of putting on pants, the therapist may hand the individual his pants and tell him to put them on. If he puts them on, he is reinforced. If he repeatedly does not respond appropriately, the therapist could begin to shape closer and closer approximations to the behavior, e.g reinforce the client for grasping the pants and attempting to put them on, or putting them on even improperly, and then steadily reinforce closer and closer approximations until he finally reinforces the child only for performing the entire skill appropriately.

Prompting may also be useful. Initially, the therapist should model the behavior for the individual, provide physical assistance, or prompt correct responding in some other way. Next, he fades these prompts out, while reinforcing continued correct performance of the skill. In rare cases negative reinforcement may be used, in which, for instance the client may avoid a verbal reprimand by putting his pants on.

If the therapist notices a factor which he thinks might be suppressing the desirable behavior, e.g. other individuals distracting the client, the therapist could take steps to stop these interferences. These procedures, or a combination of them, may be adequate to increase an appropriate behavior in its entirety. However, if these are not successful (after being given enough time to work) the chaining procedure may be necessary.

A chain is a sequence of stimuli and responses which occur in the following pattern:

Positive
Stimulus→Response→Stimulus→Response→Reinforcer

For example, operating a vending machine consists of such a chain. First a stimulus occurs such as the internal cues of one's own hunger, or the sight of a candy machine. This stimulus signals the occurrence of the response of depositing a coin in the machine. That response is followed by stimuli indicating that the coin has been received, such as the "clink" of the money or the illumination of a "Make selection" sign. This stimulus in turn controls the response of depressing the button associated with the desired food. That response is followed by positive reinforcement, i.e. candy.

Several important aspects of the definition of a chain should be noted:

1. A chain is composed of two or more behaviors (each behavior in a chain is called a component).

2. These behaviors are arranged in a series, one after the other.

3. One stimulus (S^D) signals the occurrence of the first component of the chain.

4. The first behavior in the chain is followed by a stimulus which controls the occurrence of the second behavior in the chain, which occasions the third behavior in the chain, etc. Each stimulus which occurs within the chain has two effects: it serves as an S^D for the occurrence of the next response, and it reinforces the preceding response. In the case of operating a vending machine, the "clink" of the coin controlled the response of pressing the candy selection button, *and* it reinforced the response of inserting the coin. Thus, each stimulus in a chain is *both* an S^D and a conditioned positive reinforcer. (Of course, this is not true of the *first* stimulus in a chain, which only signals the occurrence of the first chain response. It does not follow, and thus does not reinforce, a previous response.) Sometimes the S^D for each behavior consists of stimuli presented by another person or object, e.g. the "clink" of a coin or a parent saying "Now pick up your books for school." Often, however, the S^D for one behavioral component consists of the preceding behavior in the chain. For example, when putting on a T-shirt the behavior of pulling the shirt over the head is an S^D for putting one arm in a sleeve. That behavior in turn controls putting the second arm in the other sleeve, which then signals the behavior of pulling the shirt down to the waist.

Similarly, when completing an arithmetic assignment, the behavior of finishing the last problem is an S^D for handing the assignment to the teacher.

5. Following the last component of the chain, a positive reinforcer (usually an unconditioned reinforcer such as food) is delivered. The presentation of this unconditioned positive reinforcer at the end of the chain explains why stimuli occurring within a chain become conditioned reinforcers. By occurring sometime before an already effective reinforcer, these stimuli become associated with that reinforcement and gradually acquire reinforcing power of their own.

More specifically, if a stimulus is an S^D for a response that is reinforced, that stimulus is likely to also be a conditioned reinforcer. For instance, as the stimulus "Come to me" becomes an S^D for the individual's approach (because her compliance with that instruction is reinforced), the words "Come to me" will also become a conditioned reinforcer. That is, that stimulus can be used by itself and contingently (immediately following a behavior) to increase and/or maintain other behavior. Of course, "Come to me" must continue (at least occasionally) to signal that the approach response will be reinforced with an unconditioned reinforcer, if it is to remain effective as an S^D and conditioned reinforcer. Thus, a conditioned reinforcer can be established either by being paired with an already effective reinforcer *or* by being *made into an* S^D for a response which is followed by an already-effective reinforcer.

In summary, a chain consists of an alternating series of stimuli and responses, and reinforcement for completion of the final response.

In preparation for training a chain, the therapist first divides the behavior into simple parts. For instance, handwashing may be broken down into the following components:
- turning on the water faucet
- wetting hands
- soaping hands
- rinsing hands
- drying hands

Similarly, putting in a piece of a puzzle can be considered one behavioral part of assembling a puzzle. The following behaviors might serve as parts of the chain in getting ready for school: getting out of bed, taking a shower, dressing, eating breakfast, collecting books, and walking to the bus.

There are no fixed rules as to how such division should be done, and often the behavioral parts must be altered during training (made larger or smaller). Nevertheless, the therapist begins by separating the behavior into segments which he believes will be a manageable size to train.

Next, training can begin. In general, one behavioral part will be trained at a time, and while learning each component, the client will also be taught the correct sequence in which to perform the parts. Chaining can be accomplished in either a backward or forward sequence.

BACKWARD CHAINING

Backward chaining is generally considered the more effective method of teaching a chain. In this case, the behavior which will be performed last in the chain is trained first, and the first behavior is trained last. For example, when training hand-washing, the first behavior which is trained is hand drying (since it is performed last in the chain). Next, the client is trained to rinse, next to soap, and then to wet his hands. Finally, he is taught to turn on the faucet. Similarly, when teaching an individual to assemble a puzzle by backward chaining, the first behavior taught is putting the last piece in the puzzle (all pieces but one are in place). The last behavior trained is putting a puzzle piece into a totally unassembled puzzle (with all pieces out of the puzzle).

Specifically, the sequence begins with presenting a stimulus which the therapist wants to signal occurrence of the last behavior in the chain. For instance, if he wants the sight and feel of wet hands to serve as an S^D for hand drying, he wets the child's hands, then he employs one of the procedures for increasing the response in the presence of this cue. He either waits for the response to occur, and when it does, reinforces it, or, (if the response occurs very infrequently or not at all) shapes the response in the presence of the stimulus, or uses prompting and fading. All of these procedures have been described previously (Chapters 6 and 9.) If a client has previously learned how to perform the component, e.g. hand drying, it may only be necessary to present the cue (wet his hands), wait for him to respond correctly, and then reinforce him for doing so. If the client needs training on the component, the shaping procedure is useful. The therapist reinforces behaviors which resemble correct performance as closely as possible. For instance, this may initially involve reinforcing a single drying movement or only grasping the towel. After reinforcing some approximation to the target behavior, the therapist presents the cue again (wets his hands), and again reinforces behaviors which are similar to correct responding. As training progresses, he steadily raises the standards for reinforcement, until finally he reinforces the individual only for correct completion of the component. Prompting and fading may also be useful in training a behavioral part. In this case, in addition to presenting the cue which will ultimately signal the occurrence of drying (wet hands), the therapist can prompt correct performance, by, for instance, modeling the behavior (drying his own hands), giving verbal instructions ("Dry your hands"), or manually putting him through the behavior. He reinforces correct responding, then again presents the cue (wet hands) and a smaller prompt, and again reinforces appropriate behavior. He steadily fades the prompt while continuing to reinforce the client for performing the behavior with less and less assistance.

In general, he continues to present the stimulus (and a diminishing prompt, if fading is used) and reinforces the response (or an approximation to it if shaping is used) in the presence of this stimulus, until the behavior is performed immediately, correctly, and independently following presentation of the S^D (wet hands). The client should respond correctly several times (at least five to ten) before the therapist begins to train the next step.

The second step in backward chaining is the therapist's presentation of the stimulus which he wants to signal occurrence of the next-to-the-last behavior in the chain (if the sight and feel of soapy hands is to be the S^D, he soaps the client's hands). Then he uses one of the three procedures for increasing the response in the presence of this cue. This procedure may be different from the one used to train the previous behavior, i.e. the last behavior in the chain. For instance, he may have used prompting and shaping to train drying, but the individual may be more skilled at rinsing, and thus requiring less extensive training on this component.

When a correct response on the second component occurs either independently or with prompting, the therapist should reinforce it, but wait for the last component (drying) to occur. When and if it does, it should be reinforced (usually with conditioned and unconditioned reinforcement). As stressed previously, a stimulus such as the sight and feel of wet hands does two things: It reinforces the behavior which precedes it (rinsing) *and* it serves as an S^D for the behavior which follows it (drying). Thus, learning to rinse correctly may be reinforced by wet hands, and wet hands should also signal the client to dry. Reinforcement is then provided for drying. If after rinsing he does not proceed independently to the last component (drying), i.e. if wet hands is not fully established as an S^D for drying, he should be prompted to do so, for instance, by pointing to the towel. Then, he is reinforced as usual for completing the drying step.

It has been indicated that no extra reinforcers should be necessary to train the second component (rinsing), but that the stimuli which naturally result from that behavior (wet hands with no soap) should reinforce the rinsing behavior. However, with very long chains and/or individuals who show severe behavioral deficits, e.g. the profoundly or severely retarded, presenting extra reinforcers when training a new component can often be very useful (or necessary). For instance, the therapist might praise the student several times (and even give bites of food) as he rinses her hands. Thus, although wet hands will eventually reinforce correct rinsing, during initial training extra reinforcers may also be provided.

The therapist continues this procedure: presenting the S^D for the second behavior (rinsing) by soaping the client's hands, if necessary prompting this second behavior with a steadily decreasing prompt and/or using extra reinforcers to shape closer and closer approximations to correct performance. Then, instead of (or, if necessary, in addition to) directly reinforcing appropriate rinsing, he waits for drying to occur (prompting its occurrence if necessary), and then reinforces the student following satisfactory drying.

As the individual acquires skill in performing the second component (rinsing) and learns to follow rinsing with drying, extra reinforcers and prompting should be removed (usually gradually). For instance, if the therapist has praised the client for rinsing each of several parts of his hands properly, then such reinforcement is gradually omitted until the child is only praised for completing the rinse response. Next, the therapist withholds all reinforcement until the client has rinsed *and* dried. Similarly, if the therapist has had to prompt drying after rinsing occurred, he gradually diminishes the size of the prompt until the client proceeds from rinsing to drying with no such reminders.

When the second behavior (rinsing) is consistently performed correctly following presentation of the S^D (soapy hands), the therapist can begin training the next behavior. As before, the client should respond correctly several times before the therapist proceeds to training the next step.

In the third step in backward chaining, the therapist presents the stimulus which he wants to signal occurrence of the third behavior, e.g. points to or hands the client the soap. Then he uses one of the three procedures for increasing soaping in the presence of this cue. This may be the same or a different procedure than employed in training the other two behaviors. If necessary, he presents extra reinforcers and/or prompting to assure correct performance. When the response (or an approximation to it) occurs, soapy hands should serve as an S^D for the second behavior in the chain (rinsing). If it does not, he prompts the occurrence of rinsing ("Rinse"). This should in turn signal drying (if necessary with a small reminder). After the individual dries his hands, he is given a reinforcer. This is continued until he or she consistently soaps properly (and hopefully requires no extra reinforcement or prompting to complete the chain).

The therapist continues the same procedure for training all steps in the chain, e.g. wetting hands and finally turning on the water. The stimulus established as the S^D for the last response trained (the first behavior in the chain) should be the one which is the S^D signaling occurrence of the entire chain. For instance, the verbal cue "Wash your hands" or dirty hands would be a suitable S^D for the entire handwashing skill, and thus may be trained as the S^D for turning the water on, the first behavior in the chain.

In most cases (see examples at the end of the chapter), the objective is to teach the client to perform the chain as independently as possible, i.e. without continued prompting or reinforcement other than that delivered at the end of the chain. Thus, as separate components are taught and these are chained together in the proper sequence, every effort should be made to reduce prompts and extra reinforcers, such as praise for completing individual steps of the chain. However, if training is being completed on the last step of the chain, and the therapist has continued to employ extra prompts or reinforcers, these must now be eliminated. This may be done by presenting the first S^D ("Wash your hands") and after the appropriate behavior occurs, *waiting* to see if that behavior (turning on the faucet) will be an effective S^D for the occurrence of the next behavior, *without* presenting a prompt or extra reinforcer ("Good, now go on"). If the next behavior (wetting the hands) does occur, it probably should be reinforced with an extra reinforcer. If it does not, after allowing enough time for it to be performed, the therapist presents the prompt for that behavior in *a diminished form*. For instance, he presents a verbal stimulus in a softer (quieter) voice or in a partial fashion. In other words, if one cannot remove the prompt abruptly, he fades it out gradually.

After the correct behavior occurs following either the preceding behavior or the slightly reduced prompt, the therapist delivers an extra reinforcer, if necessary. Then he waits for the next behavior to occur. If it does, he may want to deliver an extra reinforcer, and then again wait for the next behavior in the chain to be performed. If the response does not occur, he prompts it with the smallest prompt that will be effective in getting the target response to occur. Then, when that appropriate behavior is emitted, he waits for the next behavior to occur, etc. Of course, at the end of the chain, the client is given a reinforcer! He continues having the client perform the entire chain, and if unable to eliminate a prompt abruptly, he fades it out until he performs each step in sequence without any extra help. If he had to use extra reinforcers during the time that the prompts were being faded out, these reinforcers must also be eliminated, either abruptly or by fading. Obviously, it is best to use as few extra prompts and reinforcers as possible to establish the chain, since much time and energy can be involved in eliminating these. When training is complete, the therapist should be able to present one S^D ("Wash your hands") which signals occurrence of the entire chain, and then deliver a reinforcer after its completion.

FORWARD CHAINING

Forward chaining is a second method of teaching a chain. In this case, the behavior which will be performed first in the chain is trained first, and the last component is trained last. For example, when using forward chaining to teach handwashing, the therapist first teaches the student to turn on the faucet, next to wet his hands, next to soap, and so on. Drying is then the final component trained. Similarly, when teaching recitation of the alphabet, he first teaches the student to say "A," next "A — B," next "A — B — C," etc.

The procedures used to train each component of a forward chain are identical to those employed in backward chaining. For instance, the therapist begins training handwashing by teaching the student to turn on the faucet in the presence of the stimulus "Wash your hands." To do this, he uses one of the three methods described previously: waits for the response to occur in the presence of the stimulus and reinforces it, or uses shaping and/or prompting and fading.

234   *The Power of Positive Reinforcement*

After the behavior is performed consistently and independently, he is ready to teach the second component in the chain.

As usual, he presents the S^D for the first component ("Wash your hands"), and after the individual performs that behavior (turns on the faucet), he does not reinforce him, but signals that the second component (wetting the hands) should now be performed. It may be that the sight of running water is already an S^D for the next behavior, wetting the hands. If he proceeds to wet his hands (or approximates this behavior), he is reinforced. If he does not, the therapist prompts the behavior (gestures toward the water, moves his hands under it or models it). Next, he reinforces this prompted response. Thus, (as with backward chaining) the client is now learning two things simultaneously: to wet his hands, and to perform the first two chain components in the proper sequence. The therapist continues this procedure: He presents the S^D for the first component; following completion of that behavior, he requires the client to proceed to the next component (or prompts it, if necessary, with a steadily diminishing prompt), and then reinforces him for performance of both components (or an approximation to the second behavior). After the second component is performed correctly and consistently, he next withholds reinforcement until he performs the third component (soaping) even if initially this behavior must be prompted, and only approximations to soaping can be reinforced. In a similar fashion, he continues to train each chain component and the proper sequence in which to perform the separate behaviors.

As mentioned under backward chaining, sometimes extra reinforcers (such as praise following one or more individual components) and continued prompting are necessary to assure that the individual will continue to perform previously learned components. For example, while soaping is being trained, it may be essential to at least praise the student for performing the other components correctly (turning on the faucet and wetting hands). These extra reinforcers, as well as prompts such as "Now wet your hands," must be eliminated either during training or after all components are trained. If the student is to perform the chain independently (which is usually most desirable), the therapist should only have to present one S^D to "get the chain started"; then the performance of one behavior should signal the occurrence of the next until the last component is performed. The therapist should then present a reinforcer for completion of the entire chain.

The resulting performance of a chain (either trained in a backward or forward sequence) can be outlined in the following example:

S	Response	S for next behavior, and Reinforcement for preceding behavior	Reinforcement
1. "Wash your hands	2. Turning on water	3. Sight of running water	
	4. Wetting hands	5. Sight and feel of wet hands	
	6. Soaping	7. Sight and feel of soapy hands	
	8. Rinsing	9. Sight and feel of wet, nonsoapy hands	
	10. Drying		11. Food and praise

FACTORS INFLUENCING THE EFFECTIVENESS OF TRAINING A CHAIN

The Size of Each Step

If the therapist is having difficulty teaching a step, it may help to break the step down into two or more smaller behaviors and train each separately. For instance, soaping in the shower may more easily be trained if it is divided into parts (soaping one arm, soaping the chest, soaping the other arm, etc.). In this case, the overall chain would have more steps, each composed of a smaller behavior.

The Procedure Used To Train Each Step and Bring It Under Proper Stimulus Control

In some cases, the therapist will need to both train the behavioral step and establish a stimulus as an S^D signaling its occurrence. In other instances, the step may have been learned previously, but must be taught to occur in the correct sequence in the chain, i.e. brought under the proper stimulus control. In either case, chaining will not be successful unless the proper training method is employed. Three procedures are available to train the response to occur in the presence of the S^D: (1) presenting the stimulus, waiting for the response to occur and if it does, reinforcing it, (2) shaping or (3) prompting and fading. Each of the procedures is appropriate in specific cases. For instance, if the response almost never occurs, then shaping or prompting and fading will be required. If one procedure is not effective, another should be tried. Of course, no procedure will work unless it is conducted properly. Before changing the procedure entirely, the therapist should check the list of factors which influence the effectiveness of each procedure (see Chapter 6) and modify the current training method on the basis of these guidelines. For instance, shaping will not be effective if the standards for reinforcement are raised too fast; prompting and fading will not work if an improper prompt is used initially.

Reinforcer Effectiveness

Of course, no procedure employing positive reinforcement will be successful if the reinforcer is not effective. Such factors as immediacy of reinforcement and extent of deprivation should always be checked if chaining is not proceeding smoothly.

Adequate Training of Each Step

It is very important to thoroughly train one behavioral step and bring it under good discriminative control before proceeding to train the next step in the chain. If this is not done, the previously learned behavior may decrease while the second behavior is being trained. The student should thus demonstrate each behavior consistently, e.g. following each of at least five to ten presentations of the S^D before training begins on the next chain component.

EXAMPLES OF CHAINS

The training of self-help skills has been used exclusively in the previous description of chaining, and indeed it is a very common application of the chaining procedure with the retarded. However, there are numerous other examples of chains, including:

1. Reciting the alphabet
2. Counting
3. Home living routines, such as getting up in the morning, dressing, eating, brushing teeth, combing hair and traveling to work or school. In addition, each of these components consists of a chain. For instance, dressing involves putting on a series of clothing such as underwear, pants, shirt, socks, and shoes.
4. Housekeeping chores, such as cleaning a bathroom which includes cleaning the toilet, sink, mirror, tub, and floor. (Each of these components also comprises a chain.)
5. Vocational tasks, such as assembling a bicycle brake.
6. Social skills such as greeting people, which entails smiling, saying hello and shaking hands.

Skills such as these are trained in an identical manner to the self-help skills described previously. For instance, when teaching an individual to clean a sink (and then ultimately to clean an entire bathroom), the therapist might employ backward chaining. First the individual is taught to rinse cleanser off each area of the sink, then to scrub the sink (in the presence of the usual stimulus of cleanser all over the sink), next to apply the cleanser, next to find the cleanser in the cabinet, etc. If counting is to be trained (usually by forward chaining) first the therapist teachers "1," then "1-2," then "1 — 2 — 3," and so on.

Chapter 11

MAINTENANCE OF
BEHAVIORAL IMPROVEMENT

CLEARLY, the objective of any treatment program should not only be to increase or decrease a target behavior(s), but to *maintain* the improvement in the individual's normal routine without extensive, continued intervention by staff. Practical as well as humanitarian considerations dictate that an individual be phased as quickly as possible into a relatively normal situation. Of course, if this normal routine promotes inappropriate behavior, e.g. by reinforcing it, and does not support desirable behavior, e.g. by *not* reinforcing it, improvement will not continue. Thus, the maintenance environment must be designed to promote the continuation of the behavioral gains made during treatment. It is often possible to arrange such an environment without the intensive amounts of teacher time and effort that may have been necessary to produce the behavioral change in the first place. Procedures which can facilitate maintenance of improvement are discussed below. (Most of these techniques have been described previously and therefore are only summarized in this chapter.)

If an "artificial" reinforcer was used to teach a response, the reinforcer should be changed to one that is "naturally" available in the usual environment. For instance, in some cases bites of a meal may have to be used as reinforcers to train a self-help skill such as dressing. After the individual has been taught to dress, and performs this behavior consistently, the therapist can simply allow the client to have his meal, e.g. breakfast, in the dining room after he dresses. This is not only more convenient for trainers, but most importantly, it is a more natural routine, one that is likely to exist in whatever setting the resident will live in in the future.

In addition to events like meals,* other natural reinforcers can and should be used in a maintenance program. For instance, social approval is a very common reinforcer in normal situations and thus every effort should be made to establish praise as a reinforcer and employ it during training and maintenance. Similarly, activities and privileges are often natural reinforcers. In public school classrooms, for instance, it is a common practice to reinforce appropriate behavior with privileges such as helping the teacher, wearing a star on one's forehead, and being first in line. Therefore, activities and privileges can and should be used in maintenance programs. Indeed, since many activities and privileges cannot easily be used as reinforcers when a response is initially being trained, activities such as bus rides are often more convenient reinforcers in a maintenance program than in the early stages of training. (Unless an activity or privilege is used in a token program, in which case each correct response, or approximation to it, is reinforced with a token, and when a sufficient number have been earned, these are traded for the activity or privilege.) Finally, if a token system has been employed, a maintenance program should usually use tokens which resemble money as closely as possible. For instance, if poker chips have been used as tokens, money can be paired with these chips so that money becomes a conditioned reinforcer, and then poker chips are phased out altogether, allowing individuals to earn and spend money directly for items and activities.

It is simplest to initially train a response with whatever reinforcer will be used to maintain the behavior in the individual's natural routine. If this cannot be done (for instance, if the therapist intends to maintain the behavior with social reinforcement and socials are not yet effective as a reinforcer), then he makes the event into a reinforcer while training the response. Similarly, if he intends to maintain the response with an event which is not convenient to use in training, he simply changes the reinforcer after the response has been established. In either case, he gradually substitutes the natural reinforcer for

---

*The use of meals as reinforcers usually requires special permission.

the artificial reinforcer used in training.

After an appropriate response has been increased with continuous reinforcement, it should be maintained by intermittent reinforcement. Not only is intermittent reinforcement more convenient for teachers, but most importantly it resembles the reinforcement schedule which exists in much of the real world. No one lives in an environment in which each appropriate response is reinforced. A maintenance program featuring intermittent reinforcement will prepare the individual for these settings by making his behavior resistant to extinction.

It is sometimes noted that behavior which has been reinforced by someone or something, i.e. "extrinsically" reinforced, will be maintained even though all or most extrinsic reinforcement is no longer presented. For instance, after a nonambulatory individual has been reinforced (for instance, by praise and a favorite food) for walking, eventually that behavior may persist at an appropriate level even though it is no longer reinforced by a trainer. Similarly, an individual who has been taught to read, and has consistently been reinforced for doing so, may continue to read after all extrinsic reinforcement is discontinued. In such cases, it is often assumed that the behavior itself, e.g. walking or reading, becomes "intrinsically" reinforcing. That is, the individual no longer requires reinforcement from a trainer, but will continue to display the behavior because something about engaging in it is self-reinforcing. In short, some behaviors appear to serve as their own rewards. Intrinsic reinforcement is perhaps most likely with behaviors such as playing with toys, participating in games, and walking. For instance, after teaching an individual to play on a swing set, reinforcement may be easily removed and the individual will probably continue to play appropriately. Playing appears to be intrinsically reinforcing to many "normal" individuals and may certainly become so for retarded individuals. Other behaviors such as toothbrushing, studying, making a bed, and being punctual may or may not become intrinsically reinforcing. That is, these *may* require continued extrinsic reinforcement if they are to be maintained.

Whether or not a behavior will become intrinsically reinforcing cannot be predicted in advance. While artificial reinforcers are being changed to natural reinforcers, and reinforcement is being scheduled more intermittently, the therapist may occasionally omit reinforcement for a time and note whether the behavior persists. If it does, he extends the period of nonreinforcement and again observes if the individual continues to engage in the appropriate behavior. If he does, the time between extrinsic reinforcements can be extended gradually until it is no longer delivered. If at any point appropriate responding begins to decrease, the therapist returns to reinforcing the individual with praise and/or tangible reinforcement. After responding has been reestablished, if possible he begins again to reduce extrinsic reinforcement. Thus, changes to natural reinforcement, intermittent reinforcement, and (if possible) intrinsic reinforcement may all be accomplished simultaneously.

After an appropriate behavior has been increased with immediate reinforcement, it may be possible to gradually introduce a delay between the correct response and its reinforcement. For instance, the therapist can gradually delay payment of money for housekeeping chores from immediate payment following completion of a task to payment at the end of each week. Similarly, instead of allowing a student access to the playground immediately following correct completion of his arithmetic assignment, he might gradually introduce a delay between the behavior and reinforcer. Eventually, although the arithmetic period might be scheduled several hours before recess, correct arithmetic performance may be maintained by that reinforcer. It also may be possible to gradually delay a consequence such as time-out or response cost. For instance, removing a student's TV privilege for an evening after he fails a test at school earlier in the day may be effective in maintaining improvement in exam scores.

Whether behavioral improvement can be maintained with delayed reinforcement (or other procedures) depends on the following factors.

A signal, e.g. a conditioned reinforcer or conditioned punisher, should be presented immediately following the response, to indicate that the consequence will occur sometime in the future. For instance, after a student finishes his arithmetic problems, the teacher might say, "Johnny, you have failed the test. I am going to have to call your parents and ask that you not be allowed to watch TV tonight." Of course, tokens are most helpful in bridging a delay between a response and back-up reinforcement. With a token system, an individual can receive tokens immediately following appropriate behaviors and then trade these for back-up reinforcers at a later time.

Delayed consequences are probably most useful with individuals who can understand some verbal instructions. For instance, it may be difficult to use delayed reinforcement with some profoundly retarded individuals.

Delayed consequences are probably more effective with responses which leave products (see Chapter 3 for a more complete description). For instance, it may be possible to keep toileting accidents at a low rate by having the child practice correct use of the toilet *whenever* the accident is discovered, even though the child wet himself some time earlier.

In any case, the therapist must *try* delayed consequences before concluding that they will or will not maintain behavioral improvement. If an appropriate response begins to decrease or an inappropriate behavior begins to increase in frequency, the delay may have been increased too rapidly or it may be too long. The therapist backs up to a shorter delay and, after desirable responding is reestablished, he *may* be able to increase the delay more gradually. If this is not successful, he simply uses the consequences more immediately.

After an inappropriate behavior has been reduced, the procedure which produced the decrease must continue to be available if the behavior should appear again. It is not uncommon to observe a period in which the individual does not perform the undesirable response, and then unexpectedly displays it again.

If an inappropriate behavior was decreased by, for instance, extinction, attending to the victim of aggression, time-out, or punishment, that procedure should continue to be used *each time* the inappropriate behavior occurs. In short, these techniques are *not* to be used intermittently but instead should follow *each* occurrence of an undesirable response. On the other hand, if an inappropriate behavior has been reduced by the DRI or DRO procedures, which provide for reinforcement of other behavior, or if a DRL procedure has been used to maintain the behavior at a low rate, reinforcement may be scheduled less and less often (that is, more intermittently). For instance, when using a DRI technique, appropriate incompatible behavior may be reinforced every other time it occurs, then every third time, etc. Similarly, DRO reinforcement may be presented after longer and longer periods of time in which the inappropriate behavior has not occurred. Further, DRL reinforcement may be scheduled less and less frequently.

Contingent education is typically not employed in a maintenance program. It is primarily designed for use early in treatment to reduce an undesirable response by teaching appropriate alternative behavior. However, occasional reminders, feedback, practice of desirable behavior, or other components of the contingent education procedure may be helpful in keeping appropriate behavior at a decreased level.

Just as a consequence for desirable behavior should be changed from an artificial to a natural reinforcer, consequences for inappropriate behavior may also be altered to render them more natural and less severe. For instance, a verbal reprimand such as "No, Susan, do not draw on the walls," is an event which is easily presented immediately following an inappropriate behavior, is likely to be used by others in normal situations, and is generally considered a less severe procedure than, for instance time-out or a spanking. If a consequence such as a verbal reprimand is not initially effective in decreasing an undesirable response, it can be established as a conditioned punisher by pairing it with an already effective punisher. This can be done during the time in which the response is initially decreased by the already effective punisher. For instance, the reprimand can be paired with response cost, e.g. a token fine, during initial treatment. As the behavior is decreased, the reprimand (conditioned punisher) can maintain improvement, i.e. keep the behavior at a low or zero level (as well as reduce other inappropriate behaviors if used properly.) Thus, instead of fining the client following each inappropriate response, the therapist can reprimand him and maintain the reduction of inappropriate behavior, with only occasional re-pairing of the reprimand and fine. Reprimands may be similarly paired with, for instance, time-out, overcorrection, and spanking (if allowed), and eventually may be established as an effective consequence to decrease behavior and maintain the behavioral improvement.

In addition, it *may* be possible to substitute more natural and less severe procedures without pairing. For instance, if it was necessary to decrease aggression by a time-out procedure in which the individual was locked in his room, it may be possible to maintain improvement by simply placing him or her in a chair if the behavior re-occurs. Similarly, a reduced level of toileting accidents may be maintained by five minutes of positive practice following each accident, rather than the twenty minutes of restitutional overcorrection which may have been necessary to decrease the behavior in the first place. In general, an attempt should be made to maintain improvement with natural and mild procedures, if indeed more artificial and severe methods were necessary in the first place. If the behavior does not remain at a low or zero level, a return to the use of more severe procedures may be required.

If proper stimulus control has not been established during the initial modification of the target response, it should be done after the behavior has increased or decreased. In general, the response should occur at the proper time and place, and in the presence of all appropriate staff, relatives, and peers with whom the individual now has contact (or will in the future). For instance, if a child has been trained to brush his teeth, he should probably perform the skill when any adult tells him to and after all meals. In other words, he must be taught the proper discriminations and generalizations so that he responds in the presence of all S^D's for reinforcement.

During a maintenance program, it is also desirable to change from "artificial" cues to ones that may naturally precede the target behavior in the individual's normal environment. For instance, it may be most convenient during initial training to teach the client to wash his hands when he is told to. However, during maintenance every effort should be made to change this S^D to a natural one, in this case, to dirt on the individual's hands.

A maintenance program may also include a transition from staff control of consequences, e.g. positive reinforcement and punishment, to client control. When clients regulate their own treatment procedures, they are engaging in self-control. Self-control involves manipulating environmental events which influence one's own behavior, for the purpose of changing that behavior. For instance, if a student is distracted in the library, and therefore isolates himself in his room to study, he is engaging in self-control. He is presenting a situation which is an S^D for studying and thereby increasing the chances that such behavior will occur and can be reinforced. It is of obvious benefit to teach an individual to control himself, rather than continuing to rely on extrinsic agents, e.g. staff, employers, parents, or peers, to modify his behavior.

Self-control can involve any or all of the following dimensions:

1. Self-assessment, in which the individual identifies his own appropriate and inappropriate behavior.
2. Self-measurement, in which the person objectively records his own behavior.
3. Self-determination, in which an individual decides the type and amount of reinforcement he will receive for specific behaviors.
4. Self-administration of reinforcement, in which the person delivers his own reinforcement contingent upon his own performance.

These basic dimensions of self-management may be extended to various forms of a self-government program. For instance, systems have been developed for delinquents in which the youths participate in designing and running their token economy. Boys in an Achievement Place group home (Fixen, Phillips, and Wolf, 1973) successfully established many rules of conduct, monitored each other's behavior, and participated in

group "court sessions" in which a rule violator's guilt or inno-
cence, as well as the consequences for violations, were determined.

The transition to any form of self-control is usually made
after a period of time in which measurement and reinforcement
have been regulated by another. After a self-management program is begun, continued monitoring by others, e.g. staff or
peers, is probably necessary to insure that behavioral improvements are maintained. For instance, individuals may become
very lenient and give themselves large amounts of reinforcers
for inadequate performance.

Finally, it must be cautioned that although self-management
programs hold promise for retarded persons, they have not been
extensively and formally tried with this population. Their use
has been almost entirely restricted to "normal" individuals, e.g.
students in public school classrooms and in a small number of
cases with disruptive or delinquent adolescents. Further, even
with these populations, self-control programs have been evaluated over relatively brief periods of time, and some of the results
have not been entirely positive. Nevertheless, self-control is an
important objective, and should, when possible, be explored.

In general, a maintenance program should consist of a
gradual change to as natural a situation as possible. For
example, the therapist may move from a structured, intense
training program to the client's present normal routine or
eventual placement, such as in the community. Specifically, if
it is necessary to start training in a special class with only the
teacher and student present, as the behavior improves in that
situation, gradually more students and other distractions may
be added until the improvement is maintained in a regular
class. Token systems, too, can be made more natural. An individual can begin on a highly structured level, where he earns
frequent reinforcement for small bits of behavior. As he improves, he can be gradually moved to an honor system, in
which privileges such as TV are provided noncontingently (just
as they often are in the real world), and no artificial reinforcers
are given for behavior which normally would not receive such
reinforcement. The individual may remain on the honor system

as long as he continues to respond appropriately. In general, such transitions include many of the separate points described above, for instance, changes to natural, intermittent, and delayed reinforcement.

During maintenance, if improvement begins to slip, e.g. if the client ceases to perform an appropriate response, or if an inappropriate behavior begins to increase, then two steps are generally taken: the therapist returns to using the treatment procedure(s) to re-establish the improvement, and/or then designs a more effective maintenance program on the basis of the guidelines presented previously (for instance, reinforces the behavior more frequently on an intermittent schedule).

REFERENCES

Fixsen, D. L., Phillips, E. L., and Wolf, M. M.: Achievement place: Experiments in self-government with pre-delinquents. *Journal of Applied Behavior Analysis, 6*:31-47, 1973.

DOCUMENTING THE EFFECTS OF
TREATMENT: EXPERIMENTAL DESIGNS

T HE preceding chapters have described a variety of procedures for changing behavior, and an array of measurement methods designed to evaluate the effects of those treatment techniques. However, measuring the target behavior is only part of the way that the effects of a treatment procedure are documented. Measurement allows a comparison of the behavior before treatment ("baseline") to a measure recorded after a treatment procedure is introduced. Such a comparison can show if a behavior is changing during treatment, and if so, how much. For instance, the following graph shows that food snatching has decreased from between eight and ten responses per day during baseline to zero after treatment was introduced.

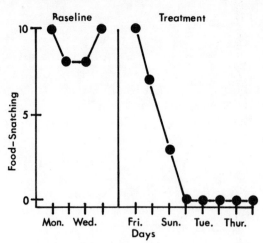

However, measurement *alone* cannot show if the treatment

caused the observed change in behavior. For instance, in the previous graph, food snatching clearly did decrease after the treatment procedure was introduced. However, treatment may not have actually been responsible for this improvement. Perhaps the behavior was about to decline anyway and treatment was by chance started just before the improvement began. Behavior often increases or decreases in the absence of a formal program to change it. Thus, if a behavior changes following the introduction of a procedure, it is possible that the improvement was going to happen without treatment. Further, clients live in environments in which many things happen at the same time. For instance, at approximately the time that a treatment program was begun for food snatching, the individual's appetite may have diminished because of illness. Thus, the decrease in stealing food may have been due to diminished hunger. Alternatively, perhaps a new cook began work, and the food was no longer as tasty. If these or other changes in the client's environment occurred around the beginning of the treatment program, it would be impossible to conclude which was responsible for the improvement in food snatching.

It is very important to discover the precise cause of improvement. Implementing a treatment program takes a great deal of time and effort. Further, the behavioral problems and deficits which require therapy are generally in need of immediate and certain remediation. The use of ineffective treatment procedures is wasteful of both therapist's and client's time and neglects the individual's right to adequate treatment. Thus, ineffective techniques must be identified and discarded.

On the other hand, if an individual's problem is improved following the introduction of therapy, it *may* be due to the treatment procedure. In this case, it is important to determine if this is so, i.e. if treatment *caused* improvement. The major purpose of the science of human behavior is not only to remediate one individual's problem, but to accumulate a group of effective therapeutic techniques. If a procedure is demonstrated successful with one individual, it provides justification to try that technique with other individuals, other behaviors, and in other situations. If the treatment procedure continues to be found effective in a variety of cases, it may eventually become part of the formal technology of behavior modification. That is, if research consistently proves that the technique is effective (and within what limits it is effective), teachers and therapists may consider using that procedure with their own clients. Only experimental research can document that a procedure actually *causes* improvement in each case, and thus only through experimentation can truly effective therapeutic techniques be developed and retained and ineffective procedures be discarded.

Of course, just because a treatment procedure has been thoroughly researched and shown to be effective in many cases, it is not guaranteed to work with each individual, behavior, and in each situation in which it is applied. All procedures have limits within which they are effective. For instance, some procedures only work (or are more effective) with certain types of behavior problems or learning deficits, and some only work (or work best) with particular types of individuals, e.g. "normal" individuals. In addition, every treatment procedure has proper ways of being conducted, which can influence whether it will be effective, and if so how successful it will be when applied to new cases. Research can determine limits such as these and aid therapists in both selecting procedures which are appropriate to the specific needs of their clients and using these procedures correctly.

Thus, research is the key to the accumulation of effective therapies. Although some readers will not participate in research, all should be aware that only through experimentation have the behavior modification procedures described in this book been developed and can be recommended for use.

There are several ways of demonstrating whether or not a procedure is responsible for (causes) improvement in a target behavior. Each of these methods is called an *experimental design*.

GROUP DESIGNS

One method is a *group design*. In its simplest form, individuals are first randomly assigned to one of two groups. For instance, each individual's name is placed on a slip of paper; their names are then drawn "blindly" and every other name that is drawn is placed in one group, while alternating names are placed in the other group. A pretest measure of the target behavior is then obtained, for instance, of the number of words that individuals in each group can read. Next, a treatment procedure is applied to each member of one group (the experimental group). The treatment is not given to members of the other group (the control group). The behavior of the two groups is measured again by a posttest, and the scores are compared. If the group receiving treatment shows significant improvement in comparison to the control group, it is verified that the treatment caused the improvement. That is, only the treated group improved, whereas the performance of a similar group of individuals who did not receive treatment did not change. Thus, it is unlikely that improvement occurred by chance, or was caused by unknown environmental factors which were not a part of the treatment procedure. If such extraneous factors were responsible for the behavior change, it is likely that the control group's behavior would *also* have improved despite the fact that they were not exposed to treatment.

Arranging a group design and analyzing the data from it requires a great deal of training. Thus, it may not be practical for use by many teachers and therapists. Further, many behavior modifiers are critical of group designs for a variety of reasons, primarily because they do not provide a clear picture of the exact effects of a treatment procedure on an individual. That is, usually scores of individuals are averaged or otherwise grouped and thus although the group as a whole might improve (or change in some other way) the behavior of individuals within that group might not (or might change in some way other than the average). Thus, group scores may not reflect the behavior of individuals who comprise that group and therefore group designs may not be useful in identifying treatment procedures which work with individuals. Most behavior modification programs are aimed at changing *each* individual's behavior (even if the individual belongs to a group).

SINGLE SUBJECT DESIGNS

Behavior modifiers typically prefer *single subject designs* in which the primary focus is on the effects of a treatment procedure on an individual. With single subject designs, an individual is exposed to *both* treatment and nontreatment conditions, and his behavior is compared under the two. There are several such experimental designs.

The *reversal design* involves first obtaining a baseline, i.e. measuring the target behavior on several occasions before treatment is introduced. Next, while recording continues, treatment is started. The behavior before and during treatment is then compared to see if it has changed. If improvement is observed, the treatment procedure is discontinued temporarily and the conditions which existed before treatment (during baseline) are reinstated. If the behavior returns to the level seen in baseline, it is likely that the treatment was responsible for the improvement seen. The behavior changed when that procedure was introduced, but returned to its previous level when the treatment was discontinued. Next, the treatment is reintroduced. If the behavior again improves, it is more strongly confirmed that the treatment does cause the behavioral improvement. It is unlikely that the behavior was going to change anyway because it returns to baseline levels ("reverses") when treatment is stopped. It is also unlikely that the improvement was due to factors other than treatment (such as illness), since such factors are unlikely to occur each time treatment is reintroduced, and the behavior only changes during treatment. Confidence in the effectiveness of treatment increases with each "replication." That is, each time behavioral improvement accompanies treatment and reverses after treatment is discontinued, it becomes more likely that the behavioral change is caused by the therapeutic procedure.

The "reversal design" is also called an "ABAB" design because baseline conditions (labeled A) are alternated with treatment conditions (labeled B).

The following graph shows a completed ABAB design in which a treatment procedure is demonstrated to be the cause of a decrease in food snatching.

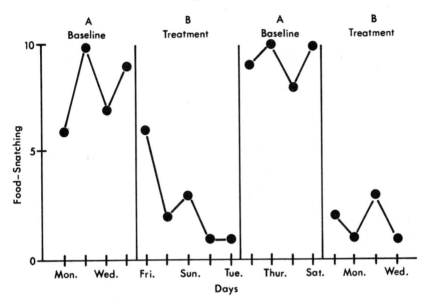

A second type of single-subject design is called a *multi-element design* (also called a *multiple-schedule design*). In this case, baseline and treatment are alternated as with a reversal design, but they are alternated frequently and each condition is usually run for a brief period of time. For instance, if the effects of a time-out program on self-injury are to be evaluated, every day the client might be exposed to several sessions, some of which consist of a baseline condition (no time-out), and some of which include a time-out procedure. Specifically, the client might receive three half-hour sessions of time-out and three half-hour baseline sessions daily. It is considered best if the two types of conditions are alternated irregularly. For instance, the individual might be exposed to the following sequence of conditions:

> Monday:
> 1st session: Treatment, e.g. time-out
> 2nd session: Baseline
> 3rd session: Baseline

4th session:	Treatment
5th session:	Baseline
6th session:	Treatment

Tuesday

1st session:	Baseline
2nd session:	Treatment
3rd session:	Baseline
4th session:	Treatment
5th session:	Treatment
6th session:	Baseline

Similarly, if one baseline and one treatment condition are run each day, sometimes the therapist conducts baseline first, and on some days he imposes treatment first. Finally, if one condition is to be employed each day, he varies on the day on which each condition is conducted. For instance,

Monday:	Baseline
Tuesday:	Treatment
Wednesday:	Baseline
Thursday:	Treatment
Friday:	Baseline
Monday:	Treatment
Tuesday:	Baseline
Wednesday:	Treatment
Thursday:	Baseline
Friday:	Treatment

Note, in the above example, that during one week treatment was conducted on Tuesday and Thursday; the next week it was employed on Monday, Wednesday and Friday. Instead of this arrangement, the order of conditions might have been alternated in a more "random" manner. For instance:

Monday:	Treatment
Tuesday:	Treatment
Wednesday:	Baseline
Thursday:	Treatment
Friday:	Baseline
Monday:	Baseline
Tuesday:	Treatment
Wednesday:	Baseline

Thursday: Treatment
Friday: Baseline

In short, the order of conditions is varied so that baseline and treatment are each conducted at varying times of the day or week (and thus in varying situations). This random sequencing is done to avoid accidentally associating one condition with a natural cycle of increases or decreases in a target behavior. For instance, if a time-out procedure is always employed in the afternoon, and baseline (no time-out) is always assessed in the morning, decreases in behavior during the time-out program may be due to the client's fatigue or other factors which exist in the afternoon (but not the morning). Varying the time (the hour or day) that each condition is employed is important not only because some behavioral changes (such as fatigue) occur as a result of the passage of time, but *also* because many environmental factors are often associated with different times. For instance, in many classrooms more difficult academic subjects may be taught in the morning (when the students are "alert"). An individual's behavior may consistently be either better or worse under this challenging regime, and thus the effects of both baseline and treatment should be assessed at this time. Similarly, it is best not to always conduct a treatment condition on Friday, since the student's behavior may improve *anyway* on this day each week, as he looks forward to being at home on the weekend, or because special recreational programs may be conducted on Fridays

The following graph shows a completed multi-element design. In this example, time-out was documented to cause a decrease in self-injury. Self-injury declined when time-out was employed and increased again each time it was discontinued, i.e. when a baseline condition was scheduled. Thus, it is unlikely that the behavioral change would have occurred anyway or was due to the coincidental occurrence of environmental factors other than time-out.

Since a multi-element design dictates that conditions be varied frequently and that each condition be employed for a brief period of time, this experimental method is best used in

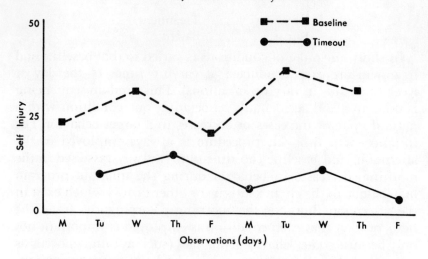

certain cases (and is inappropriate in others). Experience with research and behavior modification is required to gain an understanding of when the behavior and treatment being investigated is suited to a multi-element design. However, several guidelines may be helpful.

1. Use a multi-element design when the presence of treatment is very discriminable, i.e. when individuals can clearly perceive when treatment is imposed and when baseline is in effect.

2. The treatment procedure usually takes effect rapidly when introduced and loses its effect quickly when it is removed. For instance, response cost may decrease a behavior rapidly and the improvement may reverse quickly when the procedure is withdrawn. Therefore, a multi-element design may be a suitable method for evaluating if response cost causes improvement. On the other hand, intense punishment has rapid and dramatic effects, *but* this decrease in behavior usually persists for some time after punishment is discontinued. Thus, a multi-element design is not appropriate when investigating intense punishment. Similarly, since shaping often takes many hours, days, or weeks to take effect, it may not lend itself to analysis with a multi-element design.

3. The behavior can change (improve and reverse) rapidly.

Many appropriate and inappropriate responses which occur with some frequency can be modified *relatively* quickly. On the other hand, if an appropriate behavior does not occur at all and thus the goal is to teach the skill, acquisition may be a lengthy process. Since a multi-element design involves frequent return to baseline, training conditions would be frequently interrupted; thus, it is unlikely that much progress would be shown in each brief treatment phase. This is particularly true with complex behaviors such as self-help and academic skills. It is best not to employ a multi-element design when investigating the acquisition of new behaviors.

All previous examples of both multi-element and reversal (ABAB) designs have illustrated the use of these to compare the effects of one therapeutic technique to the effects of a baseline (no treatment) condition. In addition, both experimental methods can also be used to compare the effectiveness of two (or more) treatment procedures. For instance, if one is interested in determining whether DRO or overcorrection is more effective in reducing self-injury, these two procedures can be compared by either a reversal or multi-element design. In short, simply alternate between treatment techniques. For instance, if a reversal design is used, begin with several sessions of DRO, then change to an overcorrection procedure. Next, "reverse" back to a series of DRO sessions, and finally, reintroduce overcorrection. In this way, two (or more) treatments can be compared, and it can be determined which causes the greater improvement. (It is usually desirable to *also* conduct a baseline at the beginning of the study and at least once or twice between the treatment conditions. In this way, the treatments can be compared to each other and each can be compared to baseline, i.e. no treatment.)

Both reversal (ABAB) and multi-element designs require that the target behavior repeatedly reverse back to baseline levels to document the causal role of treatment. However, in some cases reversals are not advisable and thus these types of experimental designs cannot be employed. For instance, in some instances the behavioral change cannot be reversed. As discussed previously, some improvements persist "naturally" even after treatment is discontinued. Further, it may be unwise to attempt to reverse certain behaviors, such as severe aggression. The therapist must assess the danger, disruption, and demoralization to staff, parents, peers, and the client if treatment is deliberately discontinued to demonstrate its effects.

A *multiple baseline design* is frequently employed in cases where a reversal is impossible or undesirable. In this case, two or more behaviors of an individual are simultaneously measured during baseline. These behaviors should be ones that are similar to one another, e.g. types of aggression (biting, kicking, and scratching), or self-help skills (putting on pants, putting on a shirt, and putting on a coat). A treatment procedure is then applied to one of the behaviors. For instance, treatment may be arranged for biting only. The level of this behavior is compared during baseline and treatment to determine if a change has occurred. If only the treated behavior changes during treatment and the other behaviors do not increase or decrease substantially during this time, then the notion is supported that treatment caused the improvement in the treated behavior. The procedure is next applied to a second behavior. If it changes, but the third, untreated behavior remains unchanged, that provides an even stronger verification that the procedure caused the behavioral change. The third (and final) behavior is then treated. If some factor other than treatment was responsible for improvement in each treated behavior, then one would expect it also to change the other, similar behaviors which had not yet been treated. That is why the behaviors must be similar; they must be sensitive to the same environmental events.

Multiple baseline designs can be employed with similar behaviors in the same individual as described above. Alternatively, the same behavior of a particular individual can be simultaneously measured in two or more different situations. For instance, a student's tantrums might be measured in the classroom, on the playground, and in his home. Then instead of applying the treatment to three different behaviors in sequence, one might apply the treatment to the same behavior but sequentially in three different settings.

Multiple baseline designs can also employ the same behavior

of different individuals, simultaneously measured in the same situation. For instance, tantruming by John, Susan, and Peter can each be measured in the classroom; then a procedure is applied to the tantrums of one student at a time.

The following graph shows a completed multiple-baseline design in which a training procedure is demonstrated to cause an improvement in handwashing by each of three individuals.

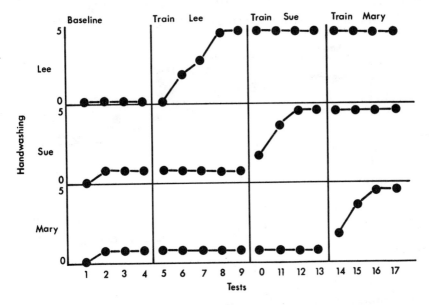

A fourth type of single-subject experimental design which is sometimes employed is called a *changing criterion design*. In this case, [the criterion (standard) for consequation, e.g. reinforcement or punishment, is successively changed from baseline to a desired target level.] For instance, if baseline data indicates that the student presently reads less than three words correctly during reading period, first the criterion for reinforcement might be established at four words, next five words, next seven and finally ten correct words per assignment. Thus, [the criterion for consequation (reinforcement) is successively changed from baseline (three words read correctly) to a desired target level (ten correct words). With a changing criterion design, if the target behavior successively changes at or close to each criterion level, it is likely that the treatment procedure caused the change in the target behavior. In the example above, if each time the criterion for reinforcement is raised correct reading behavior increases to meet that criterion, it is considered likely that reinforcement is causing the improvement in reading. If correct reading increases a great deal more or less than each criterion, it would not be possible to conclude that the reinforcement is responsible for the behavioral change.

A completed changing criterion design is shown below:

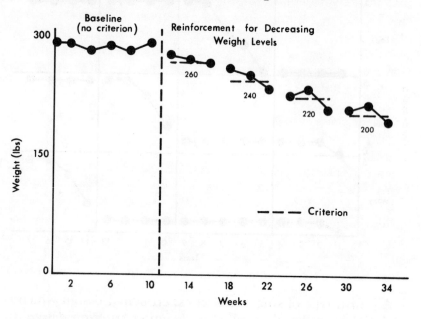

In this example, after baseline data were obtained on the individual's weight, a series of criteria was established. The client earned reinforcement each time his weight met the criterion in effect. First, reinforcement was delivered for meeting a 260 pound criterion. Next, a weight reduction to 240 pounds was reinforced. The criterion was successively changed until the desired target weight (200 lbs) was reached and reinforced. In each case, the individual's weight decreased to the criterion level (no more, no less) and thus it was documented that reinforcement of weight loss caused the measured reduction.

The use of these single-subject experimental designs has resulted in a collection of truly effective procedures, i.e. ones which consistently change behavior in very predictable directions. It has been previously stressed that these experimental designs should be used in conjunction with all therapeutic attempts in order to evaluate the effects of any procedure to change behavior. On the other hand, it should be mentioned that an experimental analysis does have disadvantages. First, employing an experimental design requires time to plan and implement. It also often requires consultation with a professional researcher. Many situations in which behavior modification is employed, e.g. homes and institutions for the retarded, simply do not have enough of either. Second, an experimental analysis requires that a treatment procedure be deliberately withheld for a time from an individual, a particular behavior or in particular situations. In some cases, e.g. with severe aggression, those responsible for that individual (and others around him) simply cannot accept the postponement of treatment, even temporarily.

In training situations with limited resources and serious behavior problems, obviously a treatment procedure must be applied even if an experimental analysis cannot be conducted. In cases such as these, simply measuring the behavior before, during, and after treatment will have to suffice. This will reveal if treatment is not working, and thus indicate if some other procedure should be tried or the present treatment modified. If measurement shows that the behavior has improved, at least the client's problem has been remedied (although not necessarily by the treatment employed). In situations where an experimental analysis is not attempted, only extremely well-known behavior modification procedures should be used. Any "new" technique, or substantial modification of a well-known procedure should *always* be employed with an experimental design.

INDEX